Contemporary Theories of Liberalism

Sage Politics Texts

Series Editor
IAN HOLLIDAY
City University of Hong Kong

SAGE Politics Texts offer authoritative and accessible analyses of core issues in contemporary political science and international relations. Each text combines a comprehensive overview of key debates and concepts with fresh and original insights. By extending across all main areas of the discipline, SAGE Politics Texts constitute a comprehensive body of contemporary analysis. They are ideal for use on advanced courses and in research.

Published titles:

The Politics of Central Europe
Attila Ágh

The New Politics of Welfare
Bill Jordan

Rethinking Green Politics
John Barry

Democracy and Democratization
John Nagle and Alison Mahr

International Political Theory
Kimberly Hutchings

Politics and Society in South Africa
Daryl Glaser

Theorizing European Integration
Dimitris N. Chryssochoou

Transforming the European Nation-State
Kjell Goldmann

Local Governance in Western Europe
Peter John

The Politics of Migration and Immigration in Europe
Andrew Geddes

Contemporary Theories of Liberalism

Public Reason as a Post-Enlightenment Project

Gerald F. Gaus

SAGE Publications
London • Thousand Oaks • New Delhi

First published 2003

SAGE Publications Ltd
6 Bonhill Street
London EC2A 4PU

SAGE Publications Inc.
2455 Teller Road
Thousand Oaks, California 91320

SAGE Publications India Pvt Ltd
B-42, Panchsheel Enclave
Post Box 4109
New Delhi 110 017

British Library Cataloguing in Publication data

A catalogue record for this book is available
from the British Library

ISBN 0 7619 6138 0
ISBN 0 7619 6139 9 (pbk)

Library of Congress Control Number 2002112354

Typeset by C&M Digitals (P) Ltd., Chennai, India
Printed in Great Britain by Athenaeum Press, Gateshead

Summary of Contents

Contents

List of Figures

Preface

Liberalism is commonly criticized today on the grounds that it is inherently a part of the Enlightenment. As an Enlightenment doctrine, it is said, liberalism is irremediably based on the faith that progress in the moral and political sciences will bring about increased convergence among all rational people on the moral and political truth. However, it is added, this Enlightenment faith is no longer plausible; the modern condition is one of permanent diversity and rational disagreement. Liberalism, it is said, lives in the past. Like most distortions that gain wide currency this one is based on a truth, which I shall explore in the first chapter. Overall, though, this popular view gets things almost exactly wrong. The main current of contemporary liberal political theory seeks to develop a post-Enlightenment account of politics. The question driving contemporary liberalism, and the analysis of this book, is whether ordered political life based on mutual respect, with a politics that aims at justice, is possible in the modern world of deep disagreement about values, justice and what is reasonable. We shall see that contemporary liberals have advanced thoughtful and sophisticated answers to this query, at the heart of which are their accounts of public reason.

These contemporary liberal theories of public reason are, I think, the most philosophically interesting and innovative developments in contemporary political theory. Although they do not start from scratch – their debts to Hobbes, Locke, Rousseau and Kant will become clear – they constitute a fresh approach to political philosophy, raising new issues and, to some extent at least, putting older ones to the side. Thus some of the most familiar debates in political theory, such as the market versus the welfare state, property rights versus distributive justice, and equality versus liberty do not loom large here. Instead, our focus will be on the nature of value comparisons, rational disagreement, coordination games, moral reasoning, justification, consensus, preference aggregation and the idea of the political, as well as, to be sure, more familiar issues such as the nature of democracy, political authority and the extent of political obligation. As Michael Freeden has observed in his *Ideologies and Political Theory* (Oxford: Clarendon Press, 1996), this is a distinctively philosophical understanding of liberal theory. Providing an overview and analysis will thus lead us to a range of philosophical problems. I have endeavored to introduce and analyze the philosophical issues in ways that will be accessible to advanced undergraduates and postgraduate students, while also engaging other scholars.

I would like to thank Ian Holliday, for encouraging me to write this book for the Sage Political Texts series, and Lucy Robinson, the politics editor at Sage (UK) for her patience and support as deadlines came and went with breathtaking speed. My thanks to my good friend Fred D'Agostino for reading an entire draft. I am also grateful to two anonymous readers for their extremely useful comments and criticisms. I have learned a lot from my discussions with two graduate students at Tulane. Shane Courtland led me to revise my thoughts on Hobbesian public reason; Andrea Houchard pushed me to think harder about problems of incommensurability. My thanks to both.

Parts of some chapters are based on papers I have previously published, though in all cases the papers have been extensively revised and ruthlessly edited for this book. I especially draw on 'Reasonable Pluralism and the Domain of the Political', *Inquiry*, vol. 42 (June 1999): 229–258; 'Reason, Justification and Consensus: Why Democracy Can't Have it All' in James Bohman and William Rehg, eds, *Deliberative Democracy* (Cambridge, MA: MIT Press, 1997), pp. 207–242; 'Looking for the Best and Finding None Better: The Epistemic Case for Democracy', *The Modern Schoolman*, vol. 74 (May 1997), pp. 277–284; and 'Does Democracy Reveal the Will of the People?', *Australasian Journal of Philosophy*, vol. 75 (June 1997): 141–162; 'The Legal coordination Game', *APA Newsletter on Law*, vol. 1 (Spring 2002): 122–128; 'Backwards into the Future: Neo-Republicanism as a Post-Socialist Critique of Market Society', *Social Philosophy & Policy*, vol. 20 (Winter 2003): 59–91; 'Public Reason', *International Encyclopedia of the Social and Behavioral Sciences* (Oxford: Elsevier Scientific Publishers, 2002), pp. 12572–12578.

1

Liberalism and Reason

1.1 Freedom, reason and the 'Enlightenment View'

Freedom and truth

The liberal tradition in politics is, first and foremost, about individual liberty. Although its roots go far back in the history of political thought, liberalism emerged as a distinct political theory as a call for freedom of speech and of thought. As one eminent political theorist observed, freedom of thought 'is an idea which emerges slowly in the West in the course of the sixteenth and seventeenth centuries; and yet today, in the eyes of the liberal, it is this liberty which is most precious of all'.[2] Right from the outset, the liberal case for freedom of conscience has derived from devotion to human reason.[3] In *Areopagitica: A Speech for the Liberty on Unlicensed Printing* (1644), John Milton argued for freedom of conscience and of the press by appealing to reason and truth. 'Truth', Milton argued, is 'our richest Merchandise'.[4] 'Let her [i.e., truth] and Falsehood grapple; who ever knew truth put to worse, in a free and open encounter?'[5] Given freedom of speech and thought, truth will win out because, unlike superstition and error, which varies from group to group and time to time, truth appeals to our universal, shared, reason. Hence, proclaimed Milton, 'Give me the liberty to know, to utter, and to argue freely according to conscience, above all liberties'.[6] Over two hundred years later (1859), John Stuart Mill again appealed to truth and reason in his case for freedom of thought and speech:

> The beliefs which we have most warrant for, have no safeguard to rest on, but a standing invitation to the whole world to prove them unfounded. If the challenge is not accepted, or is accepted and the attempt fails, we are far enough from certainty still; but we have done the best that the existing state of human reason admits of; we have neglected nothing that could give the truth a chance of reaching us: if the lists are kept open, we may hope that if there be a better truth, it will be found when the human mind is capable of receiving it; and in the meantime we may rely on having attained such approach to truth, as is possible in our own day. This is the amount of certainty attainable by a fallible being, and this the sole way of attaining it.[7]

Mill is struck by our fallibility: no matter how much we have thought an issue through, we can never be certain that we are correct – it is always possible we have fallen into error. Such fallible creatures, Mill insists, can only suppose their beliefs approach the truth if those beliefs are subject to criticism in free debate. Like Milton, Mill believes that true opinions are more likely to be embraced in free discussion because they appeal to our reason.

Milton and Mill advance classic statements of a basic liberal theme: given freedom of thought, speech and inquiry, our common human reason leads us toward increasing agreement on truths and rejection of falsehoods. Sometimes this is put in terms of the 'free marketplace of ideas': in a free competition of ideas, the truth will eventually win out, and the longer the competition goes on, the more truths will be uncovered. Underlying this is the conviction that while we are all subject to various sorts of biases, superstitions, and errors, these differ from one person (or group) to another. My biases and superstitions may appeal to me and some like-minded bigots, but they are unlikely to gain universal acceptance because not everyone shares my biases and superstitions. But, the liberal insists, the powers of reason are shared and universal. Reason is what unites us. In the words of a twentieth-century liberal, '[a]ll that man is and all that raises him above animals he owes to his reason'.[8] Overall reason selects the case for what is true rather than what is false. The exercise of our reason, then, leads us to agree. Mill – and here he speaks for much of the liberal tradition – was thus convinced that one aspect of social progress was convergence on an increasing body of truths.

Science and truth

According to this traditional liberal view, when we employ our reason we can achieve *objectivity*: we can see the world as it truly or really is – that is what is meant by saying that we discover *the truth*. Although Mill and his followers are always cautious about claiming that they have fully grasped the truth – remember, Mill stresses our fallibility – there is no doubt that Mill believes that on a wide variety of issues there is indeed a truth to the matter that can be uncovered through free, rational, inquiry. For liberals science is the ideal or model of a truth-centered inquiry that produces consensus under conditions of free inquiry. The aim of science is the pursuit of truth. According to what has been called the 'realist' presupposition of science, the world investigated by science is real and independent of people's theories about it, and can be known.[9] Scientific hypotheses seek to describe and explain this world: they are true when they do so – when they accurately describe the world as it really is. Debate among scientists is thus debate about what is true. On some views, the scientific method – e.g., the formulation of testable hypotheses, reliance on observations and recordable data to test these hypotheses – is justified because it is the best way to discover the truth. The progress of science is the progress in the discovery of truths about the world. Thus, according to liberal proponents of this conception of the scientific endeavor, the free inquiry of scientists structured by the norms of scientific inquiry leads to the discovery of truth – knowledge of the way the world really is. Consequently, free inquiry relying on the norms of science produces convergence of scientific opinion – convergence on the truth about the world.

According to this conception of reason, which dominated the European Enlightenment of the seventeenth and eighteenth centuries, the free inquiry of scientists produces agreement because (1) the truth is the same for everyone, (2) reason is a shared capacity of all human beings, and (3) the norms of good reasoning are universal. Thus, people reasoning correctly about the world will arrive at the same answer. Any premise p that is true for one person is necessarily true for all others; if the inferential rule '$(p \ \& \ [p{\rightarrow}q]){\rightarrow}q$' is valid for one person, it is necessarily valid for all. The true and valid results of one person's reasoning are thus necessarily true and valid for all. Moreover, as John Passmore, a historian of philosophy notes, 'Enlightenment philosophers' were convinced that 'mankind had in the seventeenth century lit upon a method of discovery [the scientific method], a method which would guarantee future progress'.[10]

Though science has been the paradigm of free, rational inquiry, the liberal's devotion to the pursuit of truth through the exercise of reason is by no means limited to natural science. The application of human reason, liberals have insisted, will lead to advances in social science, political philosophy and social policy. According to Ludwig von Mises, a great twentieth-century liberal,

[T]he essence of liberalism is just this, that it wants to have conceded to reason in the sphere of social policy the acceptance that is conceded to it without dispute in all other spheres of human action.... Problems of social policy are problems of social technology, and their solution must be sought in the same ways and by the same means that are at our disposal in the solution of other technical problems: by rational reflection.[11]

Even regarding personal lifestyles convergence of opinion may be expected. Mill is famous for endorsing the pursuit of individuality, and the freedom of each to choose a life that suits her, so long as she does not harm others.[12] But here too Mill suggests that reason may eventually lead to some convergence:

> As it is useful that while mankind are imperfect there should be different opinions, so is it that there should be different experiments of living; that free scope should be given to varieties of character, short of injury to others; and that the worth of different modes of life should be proved practically, when any one thinks fit to try them.[13]

To Mill, then, individual lifestyles are 'experiments': some types of living will be 'proved practically' while in other cases the experiment will fail, and so rational people will come to reject it. The language of 'experiments' indicates that even the choice of lifestyles can be understood on the model of science, where we can expect that the free use of human reason will produce convergence of opinion.

Universal reason and morality ⟵ rationality

Liberals influenced by this view of reason believed that free exercise of human reason produces convergence of moral and political views. Morality, many liberals have believed, can be derived from rationality. That is, liberals have sought to show that reason itself tells us all what moral beliefs are justified; since, as we have seen, good reasoning is the same for everyone, this seems to imply that rationally justified moral beliefs will be the same for all. The most famous attempt to derive universal morality from reason is that of Immanuel Kant. For Kant, it is 'a necessary law for all rational beings that they should always judge their actions by such maxims as they themselves could will to serve as universal laws'.[14] This principle of morality arises from 'pure reason' and tells us that morality is inherently universal.[15] An act is moral, says Kant, only if the principle or 'maxim' on which it is based could serve as a universal law for all rational beings. Thus theft and murder are immoral because the maxims 'steal when you want something' and 'murder those you do not like' could not be willed as laws for all rational beings; we cannot accept a society in which everyone acted on these principles. With Kant, then, we see the quintessential attempt to derive morality from rationality, and by so doing show that all rational creatures would converge on the same, universalizable, moral code.

Of course Kant and other Enlightenment liberals recognized that people often disagree on matters of science or ethics. But such disagreement must have its roots in mistaken beliefs or irrationality: some have arrived at the wrong answer. The process of enlightenment was the only remedy for this – the increasingly better use of reason to uncover truths about the natural, social and moral realms. The ideal model was Newtonian physics: just as our common reason had uncovered the laws of matter and motion, so too could it be expected to uncover the laws of human nature, society, morals and politics. Each field was awaiting its Newton: 'in the eighteenth century there was a fairly wide consensus that what Newton had achieved in the region of physics could surely also be applied to the regions of ethics and politics'.[16] As a contemporary philosopher observes:

> It was a central aspiration of the Enlightenment, an aspiration the formulation of which was its great achievement, to provide for debate in the public realm standards and methods of rational justification by which courses of action in every sphere of life could be adjudged just or unjust, rational or irrational, enlightened or unenlightened. So, it was hoped, reason would replace authority and tradition. Rational justification was to appeal to principles undeniable by any rational person and therefore independent of all those social and cultural peculiarities which the Enlightenment thinkers took to be mere accidental clothing of reason in particular times and places.[17]

1.2 Free reasoning and diversity of beliefs: challenges to the Enlightenment View

The 'Enlightenment View' of reason

I have identified a view of human reason that stresses its universality, that properly applied it yields the same result for everyone, and that human reason thus tends to converge on the truth in morals and politics as well as science. This view, I have argued, is associated with the European Enlightenment. Scholars point out that the Enlightenment was not a single movement: the Scottish, French and German enlightenments significantly differed, and views about reason and truth differed even among manifestly Enlightenment thinkers. It always runs the risk of distortion to talk about '*the* Enlightenment' view of reason (or anything else), as it is risky to talk about '*the* Protestant' view of salvation, or of sin. Still, Enlightenment thinking does demonstrate dominant concerns or themes,[18] as does Protestantism. Just as we run the risk of oversimplification by too easily identifying '*the* Enlightenment' view, or thinking that all Enlightenment thinkers advocate this view, so too do we run the risk of failing to appreciate themes and overriding concerns if refused to allow such general descriptions. Let us, then, use the label the 'Enlightenment View' to describe this view of human reason, while being aware that some Enlightenment thinkers had real doubts about it, and even those who share it offered different interpretations of it. Less important than what we call it is that, while this general understanding of reason and truth has been attractive to many thinkers, and many have based liberal freedom on it, the view has been subject to a number of challenges, according to which the free exercise of human reason tends not to agreement but to disagreement and diversity of beliefs and opinions. Reason, rather than being our common faculty that produces human convergence, has been seen as the source of our differences and disagreements.

Challenges from the social sciences

One challenge to the Enlightenment View arose from the European voyages of exploration, and discovery of radically different cultures. A striking case was the first contact of Europeans with the Eskimo culture. Kund Rasmussen, one of the first explorers, encountered practices that shocked Europeans. He reported that one Eskimo woman he met had borne twenty children, ten of whom she killed at birth.[19] Female babies were especially apt to be killed by their parents, with no condemnation by other members of the community. He also encountered the Eskimo practice of leaving old, ill people on the snow to die. Europeans were also shocked by the sexual practices of the Eskimos: men would share their wives with guests, and high status males often received sexual access to the wives of others. More generally, European explorers and, later, anthropologists, continually brought back tales of radically different sexual practices in other lands, and, to many, sexual norms were the heart of morality.

These revelations led to several different reactions. Perhaps the first – consistent with the Enlightenment View – was simply to condemn these practices as wrong or barbaric. After all, if morality is based on reason, and reason is the same for everyone, then such radical differences in moral views must show that at least one of the cultures is simply wrong. To be sure, it might have been the case that the sexual and other rules of these alien cultures were right and the European views mistaken, but, not too surprisingly, only a few Europeans believed that. Confronted by these shocking practices, the typical response was to conclude that these other cultures were morally primitive. This helped justify a liberal imperialism. If reason revealed universal moral truths, then it seems plausible to conclude that liberals are under an obligation to enforce proper moral behavior and individual rights. Thus, when confronted by the practice of some Indian communities of throwing wives onto the funeral pyre of their husbands, the British prohibited the practice as immoral and wrong.

Another response consistent with the Enlightenment View, advocated by Montesquieu, the eighteenth-century French philosopher, was to show that these differences in specific practices were simply local adjustments to different conditions and/or beliefs, and did not show any radical differences in basic moral principles.[20] Writes one contemporary philosopher:

> Consider the Eskimos again. They often kill perfectly normal infants, especially girls. We do not approve of this at all; a parent who did this in our society would be locked up. Thus there appears to be great difference in the values of the two cultures. But suppose we ask *why* the Eskimos do this. The explanation is not that they have less affection for their children or less respect for human life. An Eskimo family will always protect its babies if conditions permit. But they live in a harsh environment, where food is often in short supply. A fundamental postulate of Eskimo thought is: 'Life is hard, and the margin of safety is small'. A family may want to nourish its babies but be unable to do so....
>
> Infant girls are more readily disposed of because, first, in this society males are the primary food providers – they are the hunters, according to the traditional division of labor – and it is obviously important to maintain a sufficient number of food gatherers. But there is an important second reason as well. Because the hunters suffer a high casuality rate, the adult men who die prematurely far outnumber the women who die early. Thus if male and female infants survived in equal numbers, the female adult population would greatly outnumber the male adult population.[21]

The claim, then, is that underlying the diversity of specific practices are common principles and reasons – the importance of arranging social practices so that as many people as possible survive, or that the overall welfare of society is promoted.

Although many philosophers have insisted that the basic moral differences between cultures are small, anthropologists and other social scientists – as well as the typical educated person – tend to draw a more radical conclusion that challenges the Enlightenment View. For them, the acquaintance with other cultures shows that morality is relative to culture: different cultures adopt basically different moral codes, and there is no right and wrong to the matter. Thus, in the 1930s, when confronted with the very different customs and mores of the Zuñi and Kwakiutl Indians and Dobu Islanders of Papua New Guinea, the famous anthropologist Ruth Benedict endorsed cultural relativism; their basically different rules and norms were justified for them, just as western norms were for Europeans.[22] And there is evidence to suggest that many well-educated moral reasoners adopt a similar view.[23] If so, then the exercise of human reason on matters of morality and social rules leads to fundamentally divergent results. Many have held that an appreciation of the diversity of good reasoning about morals endorses toleration of the morality of other cultures. Indeed, at one point the executive committee of the

American Anthropological Association concluded that the absence of any scientific method for 'qualitatively evaluating cultures' validates an attitude of 'respect for the differences between cultures'.[24]

As anthropologists began to study non-European cultures in more depth, and became increasingly more sophisticated and self-reflective in their techniques, disputes arose about the proper method for interpreting the belief systems of other cultures. For example, was a belief in magic or a deity to be understood as simply a false belief on which the 'natives' relied? Mill believed that an investigator could best understand the magical beliefs of other cultures by attributing to them erroneous beliefs and invalid inferential rules.[25] On this view, assuming (1) realism (see section 1.1) and (2) that valid reasoning is the same for all, and thus (3) reason leads to convergent conclusions about the world, then (4) in the face of drastically different beliefs of other cultures (for example, a belief in magic), we can best explain these beliefs in the other culture by supposing that they are irrational. To hold that they and we are both correct in our divergent beliefs would be to reject one of the assumptions of the Enlightenment View. Others, adopting a *principle of charity*, have insisted that the best interpretation of a culture minimizes the number of false beliefs attributed to its members.[26] On this view, the best *interpretation* – which makes sense of the 'native's' metaphysical theories, religious convictions and their beliefs about nature – might seek to show that a belief in spirits is, after all, rational given their worldview. Thus the second step in the relativist attack on the Enlightenment's ideal of reason was to endorse *relativism concerning what beliefs are rational* in different cultures. The belief in spirits may be a rational belief in some cultures and not in others.

The point may be applied within our own culture. Some Fundamentalist Christians have argued that the belief that the earth is less than 5,000 years old is rational within the Christian outlook, which takes the Bible as a definitive source of knowledge, though it is not rational within the outlook sometimes called 'scientific humanism'. What is rational, we are told, depends on the perspective one is assuming. Note that this undermines the objectivity of reason. Whereas the Enlightenment View maintains that reason allows us to see things as they really are – it provides an objective viewpoint for knowing the world – this conception of reason denies there is such an objective point of view. Everybody sees things from a certain perspective, and thus how they reason depends on the perspective from which they begin. If so, then the free exercise of human reason will not produce convergent beliefs about the world.

The last step in the relativistic challenge to the Enlightenment View is to apply tolerance to the idea of reason itself. Can western anthropologists properly interpret other cultures if they apply their western conception of reason in their interpretation? Some have held that the very idea of reason is itself culturally relative, or relative to traditions of inquiry. Alasdair MacIntyre, a relentless critic of the Enlightenment View, insists that it has 'made us blind to … a conception of rational inquiry as embodied in a tradition, a conception according to which standards of rational justification themselves emerge from and are a part of a history … of that … tradition'.[27] MacIntyre, though, actually endorses a core element to all rationality; the laws of logic – such as the 'law of the excluded middle' that a statement (*p*) and its contradictory (not-*p*) cannot both be true – are in his view elements of all rational inquiry, which different traditions expand on in different ways.[28] However, even more radical views have been advanced. Consider, for example, the Roman Catholic belief in the Trinity of God, according to which God is simultaneously both one and three. Now this violates fundamental canons of standard logic. Since one is not three, the claim is that God both 'is one' and 'is not one'. But according to the law of the excluded middle, contradictory statements cannot be both true; it cannot be the case that the statement *p* and the statement not-*p* are both true. Thus given standard logic, the belief in the Trinity is irrational. Some, however, have maintained that within the Catholic tradition, the belief in the Trinity is indeed rational; interestingly, this has been supported by the development of alternative logical systems that deny the law of excluded middle.[29] Thus the law of the excluded middle, which many have taken as the very bedrock of reason, is denied by some modes of inquiry.

Independently, psychological studies of human reasoning have led to doubts about whether everyone shares the same norms of reasoning. The work of, among others, Richard Nisbett, Lee Ross, Paul Slovic and Amos Tversky showed that normal adults often do not employ the norms of reasoning long-advocated as correct by philosophers.[30] For example, many normal adults adhere to the 'gambler's fallacy'. According to standard probability theory, the odds of an independent event occurring do not depend on whether that kind of event has occurred in the past: if the odds of a 'six' being rolled by a fair dice is one-in-six, this probability in no way depends on whether no sixes have been rolled or all sixes have been rolled in the past. Yet many normal reasoners believe that, after a long run of sixes, the odds of another six are less than one-in-six, or if none recently have been rolled, many are convinced that a six is 'due'. Based on a variety of studies of such ordinary reasoners some philosophers advocate 'normative cognitive pluralism'. According to Stephen Stich, '*Normative cognitive pluralism* is not a claim about the cognitive processes people do use; rather it is a claim about *good processes* – the cognitive processes that people ought to use. What it asserts is that there is no unique system of cognitive processes that people should use, because various systems of cognitive processes that are very different from each other are equally good'.[31] Again we witness a challenge from social science to the Enlightenment View: if the norms of good reasoning differ from person to person, the free exercise of human reason will not, as Milton and Mill supposed, necessarily lead to a convergence of belief.

Challenges from the philosophy of science

Social science thus provided one source of the 'fragmentation of reason'. Of course there was, and still is, lively debate within social scientific and philosophical circles about whether any such relativistic view of reasoning is justified, and if so to what extent individuals employ different, but equally good, norms of reasoning. Nevertheless, some form of relativism about rationality and/or morality is widely accepted. Concurrently, developments in the philosophy of science were challenging the very citadel of the Enlightenment View – science itself. It may seem that whatever doubts can be entertained about the application of western reason to other cultures, or departures from expert norms by ordinary reasoners, the defenders of the Enlightenment View surely can claim that science is the model of rational discourse tending to convergence of opinion leading to the truth. As we have seen, according to the Enlightenment View scientific inquiry is the model of free exercise of human reason in the pursuit of truth. Free speech and thought, guided by reason, appear to produce an ever-increasing body of knowledge – a progressive uncovering of truths.

Some philosophers who have reflected on the scientific enterprise – known as philosophers of science – have come to doubt this simple picture. The simple picture of science tells us that the rules of science are justified because they maximize the discovery of truth. But how could we know that? Most obviously, how could we possibly know what rules would maximize the discovery of truth; we would have to know the alternative rules and the truths that their use would have uncovered that are not presently known to us. But how could we know that? More insidiously for the Enlightenment View, it is not entirely clear how we can identify truths independently of our scientific theories. Many claims of science are theory-dependent; they make claims about the world in terms of entities or concepts that are internal to the theory. For example, 'gravity' is a concept within Newtonian physics, whereas *'telos'* (or end) is a concept in Aristotelian science. Whereas in Newtonian physics an apple falls to the ground because of the force of gravity, in the Aristotelian account it is seeking its natural end or *telos*, at which it will rest. Both theories accurately predict that an apple falls when it is no longer attached to the tree. How do we know that the Newtonian theory reveals more truths about the world? Perhaps, one might say, the additional truths about the operation of gravity show why Newtonian physics is a scientific advance on Aristotelian science. But 'gravity' is a theoretical term within Newtonian physics; to talk in terms of gravity is already to presuppose the truth of (at least parts of) the Newtonian view. Nor can we say that Newtonian theory is a progress in the discovery of truths simply because it allows us to say *more* – it allows us to make all these statements about gravity, and so there is more we can say about the world – for Newtonian theory also *precludes* us from saying things about the world that Aristotelian theory could say, such as 'the falling apple was seeking its *telos*'. To simplify, the crux of the problem is this: to the extent that the truths revealed by a scientific theory presuppose concepts and entities that are themselves part of that theory, we only know that they are truths after we have embraced the theory as the correct one, but then their status as truths cannot be the reason why we embrace the theory as correct.

As Thomas Kuhn, an influential philosopher of science has put it, 'Unless … we simply define the approach to truth as the result of what scientists do, we cannot recognize progress toward that goal'.[32] Kuhn distinguishes periods of 'normal' science and 'revolutionary' science. During periods of normal science, Kuhn argues, scientists work within an accepted world view or 'paradigm'. Their goal is to develop this paradigm, and discover more truths about the world *in terms of it*. Challenges to this paradigm are resisted and, at least at first, dismissed. For example, a claim of Aristotelian science is that the heavenly bodies are perfect spheres.[33] When Galileo developed the telescope, he observed that the moon was not a perfect sphere, but marked by craters. This would seem to be a case where an observation disproves or falsifies a theory. But defenders of Aristotle, including the Roman Catholic Church, concluded either that the telescope was faulty, that the appearance was deceptive and the moon really was spherical, or that the object viewed was not really the moon. The important point here was that for those operating within the Aristotelian paradigm, something *must* be wrong with Galileo's apparent observation, for it contradicted *known truths*, namely, those of Aristotelian science.

Kuhn contrasts such normal science to revolutionary science, when two different paradigms are competing for scientists' allegiance. Consider again the case of Aristotelian science: as telescopes developed, an increasing number of celestial observations had to be dismissed as somehow wrong or anomalous, since they did not conform to what Aristotelian science predicted. Some scientists – call them the rebels – began to be attracted to an alternative account, which made more sense of these anomalous observations. Thus the rebels began to switch allegiance to the new paradigm. This might appear a clear case of an increase in truth through the progress of science; rebel scientists reject the old paradigm for a newer, truer, one. But, Kuhn insists, the grounds on which scientists switch allegiance to the rebels are complex, and include considerations beyond simple descriptive and predictive accuracy, for mere predictive and descriptive accuracy is not enough to dictate a clear choice between the two competing paradigms. In addition to being able to explain observations, scientists seek a simple rather than a complex theory, a plausible instead of an implausible theory, and a consistent over an inconsistent one. Thus, for example, the claim that earth is the center of the solar system could have been reconciled with observations of planetary movements, but only at the cost of postulating exceedingly complex orbits, and all the complexities which that, in turn, involved. Modern scientists do not seek to develop Aristotelian theory in a way that conforms to accepted observations because, whether or not it could be accomplished, it would lead to a cumbersome and implausible account.[34] The crucial, point, then, is that on Kuhn's analysis the allegiance of scientists to their theories is determined by a set of scientific values, and while almost all scientists give some allegiance to all of them, they differ on the weight they give to each. According to Kuhn:

> To a greater extent than other sorts of components of the disciplinary matrix, values may be shared by men who differ in their application. Judgments of accuracy are relatively, though not entirely, stable from one time to another and from one member to another in a particular group. But judgments of simplicity, consistency, plausibility, and so on often vary greatly from individual to individual.... Even more important, in those situations where values must be applied, different values, taken alone, would often dictate different choices. One theory may be more accurate but less consistent or plausible than another.[35]

The crucial claim is that there is no uniquely rational way to order these various desiderata – simplicity, consistency, plausibility – and different orderings endorse different scientific theories upholding competing truth claims. Equally well-informed scientists employing their reasoning in perfectly legitimate ways can arrive at different judgments about what is the preferred theory, and so about what is true. These developments in the philosophy of science have thus systematically challenged the very heart of the Enlightenment View – the link between reason and truth as exemplified by scientific inquiry.

The challenge of pluralism

Kuhn's analyses of the 'value choice' involved in the decisions of scientists can be generalized to a wide range of choices, including those concerning morality and politics.[36] For any decision, when there exists both a plurality of criteria and no impartial way to order the criteria, the criteria are apt to be inconclusive or indeterminate in their application. That is, suppose that we all agree that values V_1, V_2, and V_3 are relevant to a decision. In the case of a scientist, these may be the simplicity, plausibility and consistency of two rival theories; in the case of a political decision whether to endorse a certain regime, these may be the values of liberty, equality and fraternity. Now Kuhn's analysis indicates that even if we agree on the relevant values at stake, we may still disagree about the proper decision because we rank or order the values differently.

Different orderings produce different outcomes. Socialists and liberals may agree that liberty, equality and fraternity are core political values, but whereas the liberal may rank liberty above equality, and equality above fraternity, the socialist may order them, say, equality, fraternity, liberty. Thus a different ordering of the same values may lead to radically different decisions and beliefs. If the free exercise of human reason is to lead to convergence of belief, reason must not only tell us what is important, but it must tell us how to rank values.

According to *pluralists* there are a plurality of values for which the free exercise of human reason cannot discover a single correct ordering. We can usefully distinguish two varieties of pluralism. According to *radical pluralism*, because of the inherent plurality of relevant considerations there is no single rational, or correct, ranking of important personal, social, political and scientific values. Reason does not determine choice between various theories and moral/political perspectives. According to the radical pluralist there simply is no rational, right way to order values: any ordering is a matter of choice rather than reason. The most famous radical pluralist is Isaiah Berlin (see Chapter 2), who stresses the way in which different values compete with each other, and so we must choose to what values we will devote ourselves. Writes Berlin:

> It is a commonplace that neither political equality nor efficient organization nor social justice is compatible with more than a modicum of individual liberty, and certainly not with unrestricted *laissez-faire*; that justice and generosity, public and private loyalties, the demands of genius and the claims of society can violently conflict with each other. And it is no great way from that to the generalization that not all good things are compatible, still less all the ideals of mankind.... The world that we encounter in ordinary experience is one in which we are faced with choices between ends equally ultimate, and claims equally absolute, the realization of some which must inevitably involve the sacrifice of others. ... If, as I believe the ends of men are many, and not all of them are in principle compatible with each other, then the possibility of conflict – and tragedy – can never wholly be eliminated from human life, either personal or social. The necessity of choosing between absolute claims is then an inescapable characteristic of the human condition.[37]

Many advocates of such radical pluralism insist that, with regard to decisions between such ideals, 'there are truths incompatible with each other'.[38] The 'truth' you see about the proper way to choose among the values is different from, and conflicts with, the 'truth' that I see. Note the radical challenge to the Enlightenment View posed by this version of pluralism. Fundamental to the Enlightenment View is that, on any issue, there is only one truth. The Enlightenment View adamantly denies that it can ever be the case that both p and not-p are true. To be 'true' is to in some way correspond to the way things really are, and, according to the realism assumption, the world is real, and the same for everyone. The idea of 'competing truths' is thus totally alien to the Enlightenment View; if there are competing truths, p may be true for you and not-p for me. The free exercise of human reason would thus not tend toward convergence of belief.

A less radical view is *reasonable pluralism*, according to which our powers of reasoning are inconclusive on many complex matters of science, morality and politics. Roughly speaking, a decision is characterized by reasonable pluralism if perfectly reasonable agents, exercising their powers of reasoning without obvious errors and in good faith, reach conflicting conclusions. For a controversy to be characterized by reasonable pluralism it is not simply the case that people actually disagree on some issue; the claim is a stronger one – that it is reasonable for one person to believe *p* and another not-*p*. Unlike radical pluralism, the reasonable pluralist does not maintain that the question '*p* or not-*p*?' is inherently *indeterminate* (there is more than one 'true' answer to the question), but only that present beliefs about *p* and not-*p* are *inconclusively* justified.

John Rawls (see Chapter 7) insists that our disputes about values are subject to reasonable disagreement because our understanding of what is good and valuable is especially subject to what he has called the 'burdens of judgment'. According to Rawls, reasonable judgments so often are at odds because:

1   the evidence is often conflicting and difficult to evaluate;
2   (as in Kuhn's example) even when we agree on the relevant considerations, we often weigh them differently;
3   because our concepts are vague, we must rely on interpretations that are often controversial;
4   the manner in which we evaluate evidence and rank considerations seems to some extent the function of our total life experiences, which of course differ;
5   because different sides of an issue rely on different types of normative considerations, it is often hard to assess their relative merits;
6   in conflicts between values, there often seems to be no uniquely correct answer.[39]

Because these matters are so complex and uncertain, different people will reach different, competing, credible or reasonable conclusions. Rawls believes that this type of pluralism is 'the natural outcome of the activities of human reason under free enduring institutions'.[40] This is not to deny that there is a true answer to these complex questions. The point, rather, is that because of the complexity and difficulty of these value choices, we cannot expect rational people to converge on common beliefs. Thus, whereas the Enlightenment View believed that free inquiry and debate about religious matters would move us closer to the religious truths, the advocate of reasonable pluralism sees diversity of religious opinion as a permanent feature of societies characterized by freedom of religion and thought.

1.3 Liberalism and public reason

The Enlightenment View and liberalism

John Gray has repeatedly insisted that the traditional liberal project presupposed the Enlightenment View of reason; it supposed that the application of reason would lead to a set of principles with universal, rational, authority. As I have emphasized, the Enlightenment View maintains that rational agents will tend to converge on the same conclusions, producing a universal consensus on liberal values and principles. According to what we might call 'Enlightenment Liberalism', the application of human reason leads to the progressive uncovering of moral and scientific truths. Thus freedom of conscience and thought are the most basic freedoms, for they are necessary for the use of reason. And under conditions of freedom, humans will tend to agree about the truths of moral and political life. Freedom, especially freedom of thought, does not lead to disagreement and strife, but to an ever-increasing shared body of truths. Moreover, this idea of scientific progress was often linked to a belief that humans themselves would be perfected. Speaking in 1750, Anne Robert Turgot, a French liberal, proclaimed:

> Manners are gradually softened, the human mind is enlightened, separate nations draw nearer to each other, commerce and policy connect at last every part of the globe, and the total mass of the human race, by altering between calm and agitation, good and bad, marches always, however slowly, towards greater perfection.[41]

Reason, leading to scientific progress and convergence on true belief, would produce moral progress, for 'to a striking degree, Enlighteners accepted the Socratic doctrine that vice is always a form of ignorance'.[42]

We need, however, to be careful here. Although liberals have often embraced the Enlightenment View of reason, they also have typically recognized that our ability to reason is, at least at this point in history, limited, and so the actual exercise of free human reason, often produces disagreement. Indeed, throughout its history, liberalism has both relied on the idea that the free exercise of human reason produces shared belief on many matters while also recognizing that in important areas of life such enlightenment has not occurred. Recall that the roots of liberalism lie in religious toleration. Now, as John Locke recognized in his classic defense of toleration, for a wide range of religious disagreement, the exercise of reason has not produced agreement – reasonable people thinking the questions through to the best of their ability come to differing conclusions.[43] Only once it was accepted that the free exercise of reason fails to produce shared religious belief did liberalism arise as a political theory. In pre-liberal theory, it was widely expected that all who were decent would arrive at the correct religious beliefs, hence persecution of those corrupt enough to dissent was often seen as justified. In an important sense, then, liberalism has always been a response to the failure of the free exercise of reason to produce agreement on matters of religious belief and ways of living, and indeed even on some issues of justice.

Kant explicitly recognized this. Despite his belief that the free exercise of human reason could reveal universal moral principles (see section 1.1), Kant also believed that on a broad range of moral issues, actual people come to divergent conclusions when they reason about matters of morality and justice (see section 8.3). For Kant, relying on one's own individual judgment characterizes what he called 'the state of nature', a condition without law and government: 'even if men were to be ever so good natured and righteous before a public lawful state of society is established, individual men, nations and states can never be certain they are secure against violence from one another because each will have the right to do what *seems just and good to him*, entirely independently of the opinion of others'.[44] For Kant, reason tells us that, if we are to avoid such conflict, we must submit to a lawful public with authority to adjudicate disputes about justice.

The liberal project begins with recognition that on many matters, the free exercise of human reason leads us to disagree. But the solution to the failure of reason on these matters, Enlightenment Liberalism maintained, is further appeal to reason, and so freedom of thought, speech and religion. Essential to liberalism has been the claim that, though the exercise of human reason sometimes leads to disagreement – especially on matters of religion – we can manage these disagreements because our shared reason leads us to converge on liberal political principles and government. Moreover, freedom of thought and speech are so central because they work to reduce the areas of private disagreement while expanding shared belief.

Challenges to the Enlightenment View as challenges to liberalism

As we saw in section 1.2, modern developments in the social sciences, philosophy of science and ethics, have led to real doubts about the plausibility of the Enlightenment View. Is there such a thing as universal reason and moral truth, or are reason and truth relative to cultures or, perhaps, even to individuals? John Gray concludes that 'in our time' the Enlightenment project is seen as a failure, and so traditional liberalism 'has reached a dead end in which its intellectual credentials are negligible and its political relevance is nil'.[45] While, as is his wont, Gray exaggerates the point, in the face of the accumulated challenges to the Enlightenment View, it is certainly harder to rest assured that the free exercise of human reason will lead to an ever-increasing body of moral and political truth.

The great classic liberals such as Locke, Kant and Mill sought to demonstrate that on some issues the free exercise of human reason leads to divergent results; they never seriously doubted that on many other issues the use of reason led to common recognition of the truth. Liberals such as Kant and Mill were sufficiently close to the Enlightenment View that they never questioned that large areas of life were subject to what Kant called the 'public use of reason'.[46] All of science, of course, was public, as were the basic principles of morality and politics; and in time the free use of reason may even produce some agreement on ways of living. And, of course, they never doubted that the norms of good reasoning themselves were shared and public. Nor did they doubt that public standards of reason and justification were available, and that these standards demonstrated that fidelity to liberal political principles were the rational way for people who disagree on religious and other matters to live together. Importantly, they supposed that a political regime based on freedom was the best route to an orderly and cooperative society, for reason works through freedom to yield agreement.

In the face of the sustained challenges to the Enlightenment View, however, contemporary liberals cannot be as sanguine that shared public reasoning tells us how to accommodate divergent private or non-public reasoning. If the strongholds of public reason – science and basic moral principles – can be attacked, if it can be alleged that the very concept of reason itself is cultural, and so not universal, then perhaps all of life is solely subject to private reasoning, or reasoning from some perspective that is not shared by all citizens. If so, liberalism seems doomed. For liberalism requires that there are public political truths, and that first among these truths is that each individual's freedom must be guaranteed. If there are no moral truths, or no public principles endorsed by reason, liberal freedom may merely lead to chaos. Liberal freedom would then be 'wild, lawless freedom'.[47] We would be confronted with simply a clash of individual, or 'perspectival', reasons, with no way to adjudicate among the individuals or perspectives. We would be left in a lawless 'state of nature' or perhaps confronted with a 'clash of cultures' or of 'civilizations', each of which is guided by its own reason and moral principles, but none of which get a grip on the others.

This possibility was recognized by Carl Schmit, a German legal scholar who became an apologist for Nazism. As one commentator understands Schmit's position, he insisted that

> there is no truth or rational adjudication in post-Enlightenment ethics and politics. Rather, politics is a matter of conviction, akin to theological fervor. He concluded, not that the beliefs of all must be respected, but that politics is a battleground between self-defined friends and enemies where the strongest win.[48]

In the absence of any moral truth to which reason leads, Schmit insisted that life is simply a struggle between the strong and the weak. If there is no moral or political truth on which all rational inquirers will converge, if values are plural and conflicting, and the choice between them is not determined by our shared reason, it looks as if political life is about choosing values, and so choosing sides in the conflict of values and ways of life. As Schmit himself says, it would seem that 'each has to decide for himself whether in the concrete situation the otherness of the stranger signifies the negation of his own way of life so that he has to be fended off and fought in order to preserve the way of life that is existentially important'.[49] As Cheryl Misak, a contemporary philosopher, asks:

> If there is no objective right or wrong in moral matters, then what prevents one from adopting Schmit's line rather than the line of tolerance? What can the hands-off liberal say to the Schmitian? If nothing can be said, then that is an indictment of that kind of liberalism. For the problem that presses at us from all sides is that the response to pluralism and to the absence of a universal basis of adjudication has too often been intolerance, an intolerance which has sometimes culminated in genocide.[50]

Two liberal responses to the erosion of the Enlightenment View

Our question, then, is whether liberalism can be sustained in the light of the accumulation of criticisms of Enlightenment universalism. In Gray's language, can there be a post-Enlightenment liberalism? As John Rawls, the greatest liberal philosopher of the twentieth century worries, given that 'Enlightenment liberalism' failed to appreciate the diversity of reasonable views,[51] can we develop a liberal theory that takes seriously the fact of reasonable pluralism?

We can distinguish two broad liberal responses to attacks on the Enlightenment View. First, a good deal of contemporary liberal theory can be understood as defending versions of the Enlightenment View against the challenges we have been exploring. A number of contemporary political and moral philosophers have sought to show that rational reflection can produce agreement on the good life for all humans and on appropriate political principles, just as many philosophers of science have upheld the traditional view that scientific inquiry is the best way to expand our discovery of the truth about the world.[52] William A. Galston, a leading contemporary liberal theorist, explicitly upholds a liberalism based on a conception of rational inquiry as transcending mere local opinion to arrive at the truth.[53] Such liberals are, then, *defenders of the Enlightenment View* insofar as they seek to meet and turn back the challenges we have been dealing with. Liberals such as Galston, Joseph Raz, George Sher, Douglas B. Rasmussen and Douglas J. Den Uyl thus endeavor to show that we can arrive at universal moral truths about morality and the perfection of human beings.[54]

My concern in this book is with another, more worried response, to the attacks on the Enlightenment View. I call this 'Post-Enlightenment liberalism'. This liberalism is *not* 'post-Enlightenment' in the sense that it rejects the Enlightenment's conviction that freedom is a public political principle endorsed by reason, or that a political order based on freedom can yield peaceful cooperation. Its post-Enlightenment feature is that its main task is to explain how there can be such principles in a world where the exercise of reason so often leads to divergence and disagreement. Post-Enlightenment liberals do not suppose that there is a moral truth that reason uncovers; indeed, to striking extent they are uncertain that moral truth can be appealed to in politics at all. As Rawls puts it, disagreement about what is good and how one should lead one's life is the 'normal result of the exercise of human reason within the framework of free institutions of a constitutional democratic regime'.[55] The task of Post-Enlightenment liberalism is to show that our reason does not *always* lead us to disagree. Although rational disagreement is pervasive, it is bounded by a public reason justifying a political order based on freedom.

By 'Post-Enlightenment' liberalism, then, I do not mean a liberalism that rejects the Enlightenment, but one that accepts many of the challenges to the Enlightenment View, yet argues that the main conclusion of Enlightenment liberalism is correct: reason can lead us to converge on public principles securing human freedom. Post-Enlightenment liberals, we shall see, tend to stress different aspects of the liberal tradition than do (what I have called) 'defenders of the Enlightenment View'. The defenders are apt to look to John Stuart Mill (especially his theory of human perfection), Kant's moral theory, the ideas of perfection, personal autonomy and even Aristotle. Post-Enlightenment liberals, we shall see, look elsewhere. They are more apt to be inspired by Hobbes, the romantic philosophers, Locke and Jean-Jacques Rousseau. Moreover, we shall see that Post-Enlightenment liberals all jettison important parts of the Enlightenment View, while hoping to secure its central claim: that reason, freedom and peaceful social cooperation all march hand in hand.

1.4 Seven Post-Enlightenment liberalisms

Contemporary theories of liberalism

This book focuses on seven Post-Enlightenment liberalisms.

Chapter 2, which forms an introductory discussion, examines Isaiah Berlin's account of plural values, and the way in which it has often been tied to a defense of a liberal political order. Berlin's view is clearly the place to begin. If he is right, the recognition of the plurality of values, and so the recognition that there is no single truth verified by reason in the matters with which politics deals, is the starting point of liberalism, not a challenge to it. Liberalism, he suggests, is founded on the recognition that reason leads us to no shared truth about what is of value.

Chapters 3 and 4 comprise a pair of analyses of broadly 'Hobbesian' approaches to public reason. Gray, who in many ways has been deeply influenced by Berlin, has argued that because there is no truth in political matters, politics is a matter of a *modus vivendi* – a working compromise among inherently clashing views. In developing this view, Gray offers an interpretation of Hobbes's political philosophy, which he believes is the best foundation for a Post-Enlightenment liberalism – a political philosophy with modest aspirations. Chapter 3 examines Gray and other political theorists, who have argued that Hobbes's theory provides the key for understanding how political order arises out of the clash of private reason. Unlike Berlin, Hobbesian theories see pluralism and rational disagreement as a problem to be solved; they argue that the essence of politics is to mitigate the conflict of private reason. We will, in particular, consider Hobbes's claim that we can construct a sovereign, who provides a collective reason that supplants our appeal to private reasoning and allows for cooperative outcomes. Chapter 4 continues analyzing this general Hobbesian proposal, identifying a 'collective' reasoning that allows for cooperation by supplanting private reasoning. We shall examine the core idea that politics is essentially a matter of coordination guided by public reason – but now public reason is not understood as a collective reason supplied by political actors such as the sovereign, but by society and its rules. Chapter 4, then, looks deeper for the roots of public reason. By the close of Chapter 4 we will have considered a radical proposal that all reason is a sort of collective reasoning, and there really is no such thing as individual, private, reasoning at all.

The next two types of theories look elsewhere – to democracy as the key to showing how a public reason can develop out of private reasoning of citizens. Chapter 5 examines 'deliberative democracy', which contends that the essence of a democratic society is the creation of a public, shared, view through public deliberation. We shall focus on the influential formulations of deliberative democracy advanced by Jürgen Habermas and Joshua Cohen. Habermas, we shall see, believes that proper deliberation can yield answers that are 'valid' for all participants and are in some way analogous to truth claims. Whereas Habermas sees deliberative democracy as an alternative to liberalism, Cohen seeks to articulate a liberal deliberative democracy. Chapter 6 then looks at another way democracy might be thought to be the source of liberal public reason. Rather than shared answers arising out of a democratic deliberation, this view sees public reason as aggregated out of individual votes. The people speak through their votes, and the results of an election declare what the public wills, or believes to be just.

The last two approaches to public reason also construct it out of the private reasons of citizens, but they tie public reason more closely to liberalism than to democracy. These are first and foremost liberal theories of public reason. The core of public reason is the principles of a liberal order.

Chapter 7 examines the highly influential doctrine of *political liberalism* as it has been developed in the work of John Rawls. A shared liberal political conception of justice, he argues, can be a 'module' in all reasonable comprehensive views, and thus can form the basis for a common conception of political justice under conditions of modern pluralism. I conclude in Chapter 8 by presenting my favored views, justificatory liberalism and adjudicative democracy; I try to show how they solve some of the main problems raised in our examination of competing accounts. I hope that by that point in the book the reader will be ready to approach my proposals with the same critical eye that I have employed throughout. Our aim is to publicly reason about these issues; only a critical attitude to each proposal will allow us to see if any is an adequate solution to the problems raised by the pluralism of our post-Enlightenment world.

A note on content and method

In contrast to other surveys of contemporary political philosophy, substantive questions of distributive justice, welfare rights, property rights, international justice, women's rights, ethnic autonomy, and so on, do not loom large in this book. This is not to belittle or dismiss these familiar substantive issues, but it is to insist that they are not the alpha and omega of political philosophy. A great deal of contemporary political philosophy is devoted to more fundamental issues of the relation of individual disagreement and shared public principles, how social cooperation is achieved through politics, and how there can be any public principles in our deeply pluralistic world. If one is not acquainted with these debates one has missed the most distinctive issues in contemporary political theory. Moreover, they set the stage for the more familiar substantive questions. For if there is little in the way of shared public reason, this would seem to imply that a legitimate state's sphere of activity is restricted (or else that political legitimacy does not depend on justification to all rational citizens – which is back to the issue of this book). So while our focus is on these fundamental issues of reasoning and agreement, the outcome of these debates has consequences for the more traditional concerns of political theorists about distributive justice and so on.

My aim is to analyze these theories, as far as possible, by isolating the different claims they make and seeing just how they are supposed to hang together. These theories have shaped recent liberal political philosophy but they often tend to be distressingly vague or incomplete at crucial points. As interesting and important as these philosophers are, it can be difficult to get a firm hold on Berlin, Habermas and Rawls. They sometimes appear to assert different things in different writings, and it is not always clear how their writings fit together to form a coherent view. Often, I think, we do best by pausing and asking 'just what claims are being made, and how are the various claims intended to lead to an important conclusion?' In doing so we run the risk of missing some of the richness of these writings of the important figures, but the first step in understanding is to grasp the basic reasoning underlying a view. If that basic reasoning is deeply flawed, more layers of defence and development are unlikely to save the view.

Notes

1 'By definition a liberal is a man who believes in liberty'. Maurice Cranston, 'Liberalism', in Paul Edwards, ed., *The Encyclopedia of Philosophy* (New York: Macmillan and the Free Press, 1967), p. 459.
2 John Plamenatz, *Man and Society* (London: Longman, 1973), vol. I, p. 46.
3 I consider liberalism's devotion of reason in more depth in my *Political Concepts and Political Theories* (Boulder, CO: Westview Press, 2000), Ch. 3.
4 John Milton, *Areopagitica: A Speech for the Liberty on Unlicensed Printing, to the Parliament of England* in *Areopagitica and Other Tracts* (London: Dent, 1925), p. 50.
5 Ibid., p. 61.
6 Ibid., p. 60.
7 John Stuart Mill, *On Liberty*, in John Gray, ed., *On Liberty and Other Essays* (New York: Oxford University Press, 1991), p. 26 (Ch. 2, para. 7).
8 Ludwig von Mises, *Liberalism in the Classical Tradition* (San Francisco: Cobden Press, 1985), p. 7.
9 See here James H. Fetzer, *The Philosophy of Science* (New York: Paragon House, 1993), pp. 148–149.
10 John Passmore, *The Perfectability of Man* (London: Duckworth, 1971), p. 200.
11 von Mises, *Liberalism in the Classical Tradition*, pp. 5–7.
12 For an examination of this 'harm principle' see my *Social Philosophy* (Armonk, NY: M.E. Sharpe, 1999), Ch. 8.
13 Mill, *On Liberty*, p. 63. (Ch. 3, para. 1).
14 Immanuel Kant, *Foundations of the Metaphysics of Morals*, Lewis White Beck, trans. (Indianapolis: Bobbs-Merrill, 1959), p. 44 (Second Section).
15 Ibid.
16 Isaiah Berlin, *The Roots of Romanticism* (Princeton: Princeton University Press, 1997), p. 23.
17 Alasdair MacIntyre, *Whose Justice? Which Rationality?* (Notre Dame, IN: Notre Dame University Press, 1988), p. 6.
18 See John Gray, *Enlightenment's Wake: Politics and Culture at The Close of the Modern Age* (London: Routledge, 1995), pp. 122ff.
19 This is reported by James Rachels, *The Elements of Morality*, 3rd edn (Englewood Cliffs, NJ: Prentice-Hall, 1999), Ch. 2.

20 See here Isaiah Berlin, 'Alleged Relativism in Eighteenth-Century European Thought', in *The Crooked Timber of Humanity*, Henry Hardy, ed. (Princeton: Princeton University Press, 1990), pp. 71–72. For a sensitive examination by a philosopher of a different culture's ethical beliefs, and the extent to which they are ultimately in conflict with European morality, see Richard B. Brandt's classic study, *Hopi Ethics: A Theoretical Analysis* (Chicago: University of Chicago Press, 1954).

21 Rachels, *The Elements of Moral Philosophy*, p. 28.

22 See Ruth Benedict, *Patterns of Culture* (Boston: Houghton Mifflin, 1934). See also Edward Westermarck, *Ethical Relativity* (London: Kegan Paul, 1932).

23 See James S. Fishkin, *Beyond Subjective Morality* (New Haven, CT: Yale University Press, 1984).

24 See my 'Subjective Value and Justificatory Political Theory' in J. Roland Pennock and John W. Chapman, eds. *NOMOS XXVIII: Justification* (New York: New York University Press, 1986), pp. 241–269.

25 John Stuart Mill, *A System of Logic* in *The Collected Works of John Stuart Mill*, J.M. Robson, ed., vols. 7 and 8 (University of Toronto Press, Toronto (1974 [1843]), pp. 766–767.

26 See Donald Davidson, 'Radical Interpretation', *Dialictica*, vol. 27 (1973): 314–328.

27 MacIntyre, *Whose Justice? Which Rationality?*, p. 7.

28 Ibid., p. 4.

29 See Graham Priest, 'Contradiction, Belief and Rationality', *Proceedings of the Aristotelian Society*, vol. 86 (1985–86): 99–116.

30 See Richard Nisbett and Lee Ross, *Human Inference* (Englewood Cliffs, NJ: Prentice-Hall, 1980). See also Daniel Kahneman, Paul Slovic and Amos Tversky, eds, *Judgments Under Uncertainty* (Cambridge: Cambridge University Press, 1982), p. 13.

31 Stephen Stich, *The Fragmentation of Reason* (Cambridge, MA: MIT Press, 1990), p. 13. Emphasis in original.

32 Thomas Kuhn, 'Reflections on My Critics' in Imre Lakatos and Alan Musgrave, eds, *Criticism and the Growth of Knowledge* (Cambridge: Cambridge University Press, 1970), p. 20.

33 I am following here Fetzer, *The Philosophy of Science*, p. 136.

34 Though it is more attractive in biology than in physics. Aristotelian language is far more often encountered in the former, since talk of 'ends' seems consistent with explaining the behavior and development of organisms.

35 Thomas S. Kuhn, *The Structure of Scientific Revolutions*, 2nd edn (Chicago: University of Chicago Press, 1970), p. 185.

36 See Fred D'Agostino, *Free Public Reason* (New York: Oxford University Press, 1996).

37 Isaiah Berlin, 'Two Concepts of Liberty' in his *Four Essays on Liberty* (New York: Oxford University Press, 1969), pp. 167–169.

38 See e.g., P.F. Strawson, 'Social Morality and Individual Ideals', *Philosophy*, vol. 36 (January 1961), p. 3.

39 John Rawls, *Political Liberalism*, paperback edn (New York: Columbia University Press, 1996), pp. 56–57.

40 Ibid., p. xxvi.

41 Anne Robert Turgot quoted in Passmore, *The Perfectability of Man*, p. 195.

42 Passmore, *The Perfectability of Man*, p. 204.

43 See John Locke, *A Letter Concerning Toleration*, James H. Tully, ed. (Indiana: Hackett, 1983), p. 32. See William A. Galston, *Liberal Purposes* (Cambridge: Cambridge University Press, 1991), p. 259.

44 Immanuel Kant, *Metaphysical Elements of Justice*, John Ladd (trans.) (Indianapolis: Bobbs-Merrill, 1965), p. 76 (section 44). Emphasis in original.

45 John Gray, *Enlightenment's Wake: Politics and Culture at The Close of the Modern Age* (London: Routledge, 1995), p. 66.

46 Immanuel Kant, 'What is Enlightenment?' in Lewis White Beck, ed., *On History* (Indianapolis: Bobbs-Merrill, 1963), p. 3.

47 Kant, *Metaphysical Elements of Justice*, p. 81 (section 47).

48 Cheryl Misak, *Truth, Politics, Morality: Pragmatism and Deliberation* (London: Routledge, 2000), p. 10.

49 Carl Schmit, *The Concept of the Political* (New Brunswick, NJ: Rutgers University Press, 1976), p. 27.

50 Misak, *Truth, Politics, Morality*, pp. 11–12.

51 Rawls, *Political Liberalism*, pp. xl, 36.

52 On the latter see H.W. Newton-Smith, *The Rationality of Science* (London: Routledge and Kegan Paul, 1981).

53 See Galston, 'Peirce's Cable and Plato's Cave' in his *Liberal Purposes*, Ch. 2. Galston's view has evolved in a more pluralistic direction. See his *Liberal Pluralism* (Cambridge: Cambridge University Press, 2002).

54 Joseph Raz, *The Morality of Freedom* (Oxford: Clarendon Press, 1986); George Sher, *Beyond Neutrality: Perfectionism and Politics* (Cambridge: Cambridge University Press, 1997); Douglas B. Rasmussen and Douglas J. Den Uyl, *Liberty and Nature* (La Salle, IL: Open Court, 1991).

55 Rawls, *Political Liberalism*, p. xviii.

2

Pluralistic Liberalism: Making Do Without Public Reason?

2.1 Berlin's Post-Enlightenment liberal project

In contemporary liberal theory, the most eloquent and influential critic of the Enlightenment View has been Isaiah Berlin. He depicts it thus:

> Only the 'constant, the general, the universal' is real, and therefore only this is 'truly human'. Only that is true which any rational observer, at any time, in any place, can, in principle, discover. Rational methods – hypothesis, generalization, deduction, experimental verification where it is possible – can solve social and individual problems, as they have triumphantly solved those of physics and astronomy, and are progressively solving those of chemistry, biology, and economics; philosophy, that is ethics, politics, aesthetics, logic, theory of knowledge, can and should be transformed into a general science of man – the natural science of anthropology; once knowledge of man's true nature is attained, men's real needs will be clear: the only remaining tasks are to discover how they may be satisfied, and to act upon this knowledge.... [T]he triumph of the scientific spirit will sweep away the forces of prejudice, superstition, stupidity and cruelty, too long concealed by the mumbo-jumbo of theologians and lawyers.[1]

Berlin's depiction of the Enlightenment View tends towards exaggeration,[2] but underlying the exaggeration is real insight: the Enlightenment View's devotion to universal reason manifested itself in the conviction that just as science discovered the universal laws of nature, rational reflection could discover the universal laws of human nature and society, and universal principles of ethics and politics. On this view, Berlin insists, in human affairs, 'as in the sciences, all genuine questions have one true answer and only one, all the rest being necessarily errors'.[3] And, furthermore, 'true answers, when found, must necessarily be compatible with one another and form a single whole, for one truth cannot be incompatible with another – that we know a priori' (see section 1.2).[4]

The starting point of Berlin's liberalism is the rejection of the Enlightenment View by the diverse intellectual movement known as 'romanticism', the heart of which, on his interpretation, was in Germany in the seventeenth and eighteenth centuries.[5] As Berlin interprets it, this movement 'has permanently shaken the faith in universal, objective truth, in matters of conduct' by showing that 'different ends recognized as fully human are at the same time ultimate and mutually incompatible'.[6] Berlin has repeatedly insisted that the romantics taught us

> that there are many values, and that they are incommensurable; the whole notion of plurality, of inexhaustibility, of the imperfection of all human answers and arrangement, the notion that there is no single answer which claims to be perfect and true … all this we owe to the romantics.[7]

Berlin, then, insists that the value pluralism advanced by the romantics undermined the Enlightenment View: henceforth the starting point of moral and political philosophy is the plurality of correct answers, and the recognition that equally ultimate human values conflict and are incompatible. In opposition to Gray, however (see section 1.3, but see also section 3.1) Berlin suggests – at least at times – that so far from undermining liberalism, the recognition of the ultimate plurality of values, and that we confront incompatible truths, leads us to liberalism. At least on one interpretation of his political thought (see section 2.4) Berlin does not seek a public reasoning that overcomes or limits the plurality of reasoning because pluralism itself endorses liberalism. If Berlin is correct, liberals need not search for a shared public reasoning to overcome or limit the fragmentation of reason, for liberalism is justified *because* of the fragmentation of reason.

We must, then, begin by examining Berlin's pluralistic liberalism, for if he is right, post-Enlightenment liberals are wrong to see the fragmentation of reason as a challenge to be met – it would be a resource to be employed. Because of Berlin's preeminence among pluralistic liberals, I shall concentrate on his specific formulation, though we shall also consider the general idea of a pluralistic liberalism.

2.2 What is pluralism? The plurality of objective values

Plurality

Before examining Berlin's argument linking pluralism to liberalism, we must be clearer about the doctrine of 'value pluralism'. Obviously, the foundation of all pluralist views is that values are many – they are plural (see section 1.2). Pluralism thus rejects the view of Jeremy Bentham, and a host of other utilitarians, that pleasure (or happiness) is the sole good. For Bentham and his followers, all goodness is either pleasure or a means to pleasure. Thus for Bentham a person who wishes to seek what is most good, or what is of most value (these terms can be used interchangeably), simply seeks the most pleasure, for that is ultimately the only thing of value, and more of it is better than less of it. In contrast, the pluralist insists that there are 'qualitatively [and ultimately] different types of goods ... and they are not reducible to each other'.[8] Pluralism is thus the denial that there is a single supreme value from which all other values or goods derive. It should be stressed that pluralists typically adopt a broad conception of 'value'. Moral philosophers often distinguish the concepts of the good (or valuable) and the right. Whereas goodness or value is that which we ought to cherish or seek, duty and obligation concern that which we owe others.[9] In most moral theories, then, value and duty are distinct categories. However, as Berlin and other 'value pluralists' use it, 'value' includes the full range of moral notions, including not only what is to be cherished or would improve the world, but also duties, obligations and rights.[10] Although I shall continue to employ the familiar term 'value pluralism', 'ethical pluralism' or 'normative pluralism' would be more accurate.

Limited plurality and objectivity

Although Berlin's conception of pluralism is expansive, the range of genuine values is not unlimited. Again appealing to the lessons taught by the romantics, Berlin writes:

> We are urged to look upon life as affording a plurality of values, equally genuine, equally ultimate, above all equally objective; incapable, therefore of being ordered in a timeless hierarchy, or judged in terms of some one absolute standard. There is a finite variety of values and attitudes, some of which one society, some another, have made their own, attitudes and values which members of other societies may admire or condemn (in the light of their own value-systems) but can always, if they are sufficiently imaginative and try hard enough, contrive to understand – that is, see to be intelligible ends of life for human beings situated as these men were. In the house of human history there are many mansions.[11]

For Berlin, then, plural values are in some way objective – 'There is a world of objective values'[12] – and, so, the number of plural values is limited. Berlin's view is not, then, subjectivist; i.e., it is not the case that values are plural because whatever a person likes, seeks or desires is ipso facto a value.[13]

Berlin's understanding of objectivity, however, is not pellucid. At the heart of it seems to be the idea, expressed in the above quotation, that the objectivity of values is somehow bound up with the fact that we can imaginatively enter into the lives of others who follow values that we do not. In defending his claim that there is a world of objective values, Berlin insists that although 'forms of life differ' and 'ends, moral principles, are many', they are 'not infinitely many; they must be within the human horizon. If they are not, then they are outside the human sphere'.[14] As Berlin understands it, values are objective in the sense that they express our common human nature and so are within the common human horizon; given the sort of creatures we are, to think of someone as a human being is to think of her in terms of notions such as 'freedom, sense of time and change, suffering, happiness, productivity, good and bad, right and wrong, choice, effort, truth, illusion'.[15] Our common human nature forms the horizon of what we can understand as genuine human values: someone who says that, for example, he can see no difference between poking pins into people and into tennis balls, insofar as each are simply instances of pushing pins into 'resilient surfaces' simply seems mad. Such a person is unintelligible.[16] Berlin rejects what he understands to be relativism: the 'doctrine according to which the values embedded in a given vision or form of life … are seen as totally arbitrary, or at best, opaque, although not necessarily unintelligible'.[17] In contrast, he tells us, that for him, 'pluralism … means that I can imaginatively enter into the situation, outlook, motives, constellation of values, ways of life, of societies not my own'.[18]

Berlin appears to understand the objectivity of values as intimately related to the empirical observation that many people in many places have sought these values. 'I believe', he says,

> that a good many ultimate values have been pursued in common by a great many people in very many places, over very long periods of time; and that it is these alone we call human values. But that is nevertheless an empirical fact, basic, but still only empirical. The condition of recognizing ultimate values, whether my own or those of other cultures or persons, is that I must be able to imagine myself in a situation in which I could myself pursue them, even though they may in fact repel me, and I may be prepared to resist them with all the means that I have at my command.[19]

Moreover, Berlin maintains that in resisting such a basic attack on his values he would believe he has

> an objective duty to do this – not objective in some Platonic or Kantian sense – but such as arises from *my conception* of the minimal degree of decency with

which human life should be lived…. That is *my view*, *my conviction*, and that
of the people I live with and among, and in my opinion of the great majority
of cultures the world has known…. What I mean by 'the human horizon' is a
horizon which for the most part, at a great many times in a great many places,
has been what human beings have consciously or unconsciously lived under,
against which values, conduct, life in all its aspects, have appeared to them.[20]

Objective values and empirical facts of human existence:
what is their relation?

A major problem in interpreting Berlin's pluralism is to understand how
facts about what values humans have actually pursued, and whether I can
see a value as in some way of interest to all humans (or whether, in contrast, some value is 'opaque' to me), relate to the question whether some
particular value is objective. There are two basic ways in which these
factual claims might be related to claims about objectivity. I call them the
constitutive view and the *evidential view*.

The constitutive view   Being in the common human horizon might *constitute*
the objectivity of value. On this interpretation, that an empirical study of
human history shows that value *V* has been valued by most people in most
places constitutes its objective status. This empirical study would show (1)
that *V* is not some mere subjective desire of a specific group of people, (2)
that the pursuit of *V* is always intelligible and not opaque to us and (3) that
a culture, group or person that had no interest at all in *V* would be opaque
to us. Does this show that *V* is objectively valuable? Well, in philosophy the
idea of 'objectivity' is employed in a wide variety of senses; if we mean by
the 'objectivity of *V*' that valuing *V* is (nearly) universal and (almost)
necessary for humans, then Berlin's argument does establish objectivity. And
we get some of the force of 'objectivity' from this interpretation: individuals or even cultures could be 'wrong' about what is valuable because they
do not value what our common human reason tells us must be valued.[21] But
claims of objectivity – of there being a 'world of values' – typically mean
something stronger: when I say that *V* is objectively valuable I am not saying simply that 'everyone does as a matter of fact value it' and 'it is hard to
imagine humans not valuing it' or even 'people who cannot appreciate that
V at least might be valued must be mad'. For there remains the question: is
what everyone *values* truly *valuable*? That all human beings are interested in
being happy does not show that happiness is objectively valuable or part of
an 'objective world of values' – it only shows that all humans that we can
understand have a concern for their own happiness. Berlin seems to be
making an error that is much like that attributed to John Stuart Mill in his
'proof' of utility. According to Mill:

The only proof capable of being given that an object is visible, is that people
actually see it. The only proof that a sound is audible, is that people hear it:

and so of the other sources of our experience. In like manner, I apprehend, the sole evidence it is possible to produce that anything is desirable, is that people do actually desire it.[22]

The fact that everyone desires something does not show that it is desirable in the sense of worthy to be desired: it shows that it can be, perhaps must be, desired. But it does not follow that what we all desire is really worthy of being desired, i.e., desirable. Perhaps at some point in our lives everyone desires to see their enemies suffer; this hardly shows that it is desirable that they suffer – much less that it is somehow objectively desirable that they suffer. So too with Berlin's universal values. Suppose that I conclude that 'at a great many times in a great many places' V has been 'consciously or unconsciously' pursued; suppose further that we can only make sense of people by supposing that they care for V. How does all this show that V is objectively valuable? How can findings about what people have in fact desired show what is in fact desirable?

A possible answer is this: what humans *must* value, what they *must* care for if there is to be human intercourse and society, simply *is* what we mean by 'objectively valuable'. Berlin sometimes intimates that a value is objective if it is necessary for human intercourse or society itself, and being in the common horizon shows that a value is necessary. But problems confront this interpretation of objectivity. Berlin has specifically said in the above passage, a 'great majority' of cultures have upheld these values; presumably a small minority has not. So apparently some cultures have not upheld the values he considers to be objective. If so, how can their recognition be *necessary*? What some get along without cannot be necessary to getting along. Moreover, to show that every society has acknowledged V, does not show that V is necessary for society: humans may be creatures infected with what Freud called a 'death instinct' such that every society values things that are not good or necessary to society. The human instinct for aggression and self-destruction, Freud argued, is deep-seated in our psyche and a constant threat to social life. That many people in many circumstances have upheld a value certainly shows that it is congenial to humanity, but congeniality to humanity is not objectivity. As Freud observed, we do not 'feel comfortable' without satisfying our inclination for aggression.[23] One can agree with Freud that the death instinct is part of all human cultures and still reasonably deny that death, aggression and destruction are objectively valuable. Perhaps we are flawed creatures who crave what is bad. Could the universal craving for what is bad make it good? Perhaps a follower of Berlin might say that even if humans universally *pursue* some bad things, we all *recognize* them as being bad; we couldn't make sense of someone who saw death, aggression and destruction as themselves good, even if they pursue it. But this again seems to equate what everyone *sees* as good with what *is* good, as if it was impossible for all of mankind to be mistaken. But a few hundred years ago, sexual inequality would have been seen by almost everyone human as fitting and proper; that hardly would have shown that it was fitting and proper.

Berlin and his pluralist followers sometimes suggest a slightly different view: that the common human horizon shows what is necessary for a minimally decent or flourishing life.[24] But now it seems all the philosophical work is being done by our conception of a 'decent' or a 'flourishing' life, and it is extremely hard to see how a study of history or anthropology will reveal what is a decent life. If human nature is radically corrupt – infected by original sin – then the ubiquity of the pursuit of V, or the conviction that V is necessary for a truly human life, may be evidence that V is evil, not good. Anthropology and history can tell us whether V is universally pursued, but not whether this pursuit is part of human well-being or corruption.

The evidential view   The other possible interpretation is that V's pursuit in a wide variety of cultures over long periods of time does not *constitute*, but is only a *test* of, the objectivity of its value. This is a reasonable claim: just as humans almost always agree on the description of the physical world because we see the same objective world, we would expect humans to generally agree on the nature of a commonly perceived world of objective values. Berlin, though, repeatedly rejects the idea that his account entails any sort of 'Platonic' or 'Kantian' account of an objective realm of values; it is very hard to reconcile this repeated denial with the idea that being within the common human horizon is simply our test for whether something is in the realm of objective value. Berlin clearly wants to say, somehow, that objectivity is constituted by an empirical generalization about the conditions for human life.

I shall not further pursue Berlin's rather puzzling account of value objectivity. Any overall evaluation of his liberalism must come to grips with these issues; our main concern, however, is the relation of pluralism to liberalism. Let us suppose for now simply that value pluralists such as Berlin insist on three claims: (1) there is a plurality of values; (2) this plurality is limited to (3) values that are (in some sense) objective.

2.3 What is pluralism? The incommensurability of conflicting values

What is incommensurability?

A plurality of objective values is not enough to generate Berlin's value pluralism. In addition, there must be a claim that at least in a wide variety of cases these values are *incommensurable*.[25] Unfortunately, it is by no means clear what is meant by the 'incommensurability of values'. We can identify at least four (there are more) different types of incommensurability claims in ethics:

(I)   Values V_1 and V_2 are incommensurable if there exists no third value V_3, that determines which is to be preferred or chosen.[26]

(II)   Values V_1 and V_2 are incommensurable if they cannot be measured on the same scale in terms of units of value.[27]

(III)   Values V_1 and V_2 are incommensurable if there is no ordering of them according to which one (and only one) of the following holds: (a) V_1 is better than V_2, (b) V_2 is better than V_1, (c) V_1 is equal to V_2.[28]

(IV)   Values V_1 and V_2 are incommensurable if it is the case that *both* (a) V_1 is better than V_2 and (b) V_2 is better than V_1.[29]

We can find passages in which Berlin clearly endorses incommensurability in senses (I) and (II).[30] However, V_1 and V_2 can be incommensurable in sense (I) and yet we still can rationally choose between them. For example, we can rationally compare the relative value of $100 and £100 even if there is no gold standard – no master third value in virtue of which we compare them.[31] The same point applies to (II): we can compare V_1 and V_2 even if we cannot place them on a common scale of units of value. If the two values are very different – say, a happy day for a child and a great painting – we may be totally at a loss how to place the values on a scale, though we still can compare them in the sense that we can say that one is greater than another.[32] A great painting may well be worth more – which is why the painter works rather than spends the day with his child. Such strict senses of incommensurability are too restricted for Berlin's purposes. Even if (I) and (II) apply to some values, rational decisions about comparative value are possible for those values, and so it may be possible to construct a 'hierarchy' of values, that is, make a series of comparative value judgments that leads to a ranking. But Berlin insists that genuine incommensurability excludes the possibility of any such ranking.[33]

What Berlin seems to have in mind is not just strict incommensurability but incomparability, a rational inability to compare two values. The *incompleteness* interpretation – (III) – says that we cannot compare V_1 and V_2 because our value ranking is incomplete: we cannot say either that V_1 is better than, worse than, or just as good as, V_2. Because our ranking of these values is incomplete we cannot compare them. Thus on (III) values V_1 and V_2 are incommensurable in the sense that they are rationally incomparable.[34] On the other hand, our ranking is *overcomplete* as in (IV) if we have inconsistent rankings, such that we rank V_1 as superior to V_2 and we also rank them vice versa.[35] Here it seems not that they are incommensurable because we are unable to form an overall comparison, but because we form two inconsistent overall comparisons, and so cannot settle on a single comparison. I shall focus here on the incompleteness and overcompleteness interpretations of incommensurability.

Incompleteness

Gray holds that the incompleteness interpretation best captures Berlin's conception of incommensurability.[36] On the face of it, this might seem as if it must be wrong, as Berlin often characterizes value pluralism in terms of the conviction that diverse values are 'equally genuine' and 'equally ultimate'.[37] But if V_1 is equal to V_2 they are not incomparable. To say that two things are equal is to compare them; if we can say that V_1 is equal to V_2 then the ranking is not incomplete regarding them. According to clause (c) of (III), the incompleteness conception of incommensurability, in an incomplete ordering we cannot rank the relevant items 'equal to' or 'just as good as' each other. On closer examination, though, it does not appear that Berlin really thinks that diverse values are equal – when he tells us that 'the goals and values of different ways of life are not commensurable' he is not simply saying that they are equally good.[38] Indeed, that all values were equal would simply imply that the choice between them was a matter of indifference. But Berlin clearly thinks it is not a matter of indifference whether, for example, one adopts the life of a Christian or a pagan: such a choice is not at all like choosing between two identical red BMWs at the car dealership. They are different and incomparable demands.

But if V_1 is not better than V_2 (let us write this '$V_1 \not> V_2$'), and if V_2 is not better than V_1 ($V_2 \not> V_1$) doesn't it follow that they are equal? It would seem that if $A \not> B$, and $B \not> A$, then $A = B$. Indeed, in the history of political philosophy, what we might call a *non-preferential conception of equality* has been often advocated according to which 'A and B are equal' means 'neither is to be preferred to the other'.[39] How can we distinguish incompleteness from equality? Joseph Raz has argued that an indication of incommensurability rather than equality is the failure of a set of incommensurable values to meet the condition of transitivity.[40] According to the transitive relation, if $A = B$, and A is better than C, it must also be the case that B is better than C. So, we can say, $(A = B)$ & $(A > C)$, imply that $B > C$. Thus, for example, if Alf and Betty are equal in height, and Alf is taller than Charlie, it must also be the case that Betty is taller than Charlie. Now, Raz argues, the transitivity relation does not hold if A and B are incommensurable. Let us use '$\daleth$' to designate the incommensurability relation. We can then say that $(A \daleth B)$ & $(A > C)$ do not imply $B > C$.[41]

Gray provides an example of this non-transitivity:

Aeschylus and Shakespeare are each great tragic dramatists, but their dramatic art is incommensurable: it is false to say that the one is a greater dramatist than the other. Nevertheless, it may well be true that Euripides is a greater tragic dramatist than Aeschylus, without it following that Euripides is a greater dramatist than Shakespeare. The original pair of dramatists are incommensurable because, though their work falls within a single recognizable genre, yet its content and structure, its styles and themes, the background of

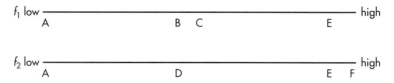

FIGURE 2.1   *Two-dimensional value comparisons*

beliefs and conventions it supposes, and the forms of life it depicts, are too different for them to be comparable in terms of value as exemplars of tragic dramatists.[42]

Let us accept for the present that the incommensurability relation *qua* incompleteness may characterize the relation between some values. Proponents of incommensurability such as Gray, however, make an additional claim: not only are some values incommensurable in this sense, this incommensurability is somehow basic. Quoting Raz, Gray insists 'where there is incommensurability, it is the ultimate truth. There is nothing further behind it'.[43] It seems that for Gray, values that are qualitatively different cannot be compared: Shakespeare and Aeschylus are incommensurable just because they are too different to be compared.

But this cannot be the entire explanation. Consider a dramatist of a low rank, such as the nineteenth-century Austrian Joseph Gleich, who wrote 'improvement plays', which focused on an improvement in a flaw of the main character. Now here too we have a dramatist of a very different genre, yet few would have any difficulty saying that he was a lesser dramatist than either Shakespeare and Aeschylus. But how can we compare such different dramatists? One possibility is that everything Gleich did, Shakespeare and Aeschylus did better. This would be a *dominance* relation: on every relevant dimension Shakespeare and Aeschylus are better than Gleich.[44] But that seems dubious, for given the different genre, Gleich did things they never did. Perhaps he did things they could not do – the great cannot do everything, and writing popular improvement dramas is perhaps one of them.

The category 'dramatist' is multidimensional; a number of factors $(f_1 \ldots f_n)$ might comprise excellence in drama. To simplify, suppose we have simply two dimensions, f_1 and f_2 as in Figure 2.1. Dramatist E dominates dramatist A – everything that A does badly, E does excellently. We would have no trouble comparing A and E. In contrast, F's drama is such that factor f_1 is not relevant to her work; her genre focuses exclusively on f_2. Can we compare dramatists A and F? Obviously we could if we could take the scores on f_1 and f_2 and score them on a single scale, or if there were a third factor that f_1 and f_2 could be reduced to, our comparison would be easy. Because we do not have either of these options we are faced incommensurability in senses (I) and (II) above. But that A and F are incommensurable in senses (I) and (II) does not imply that they are incommensurable in the sense of (III); that we cannot place them on a common metric, or that we cannot evaluate them in relation to a third value, does not show we cannot rank them.[45] Now it seems to me not really contentious to judge (depending on just how we describe the two dimensions) that F is better than A, even though A does do some things (badly) that F does not. If we reflect on their comparative accomplishments, we conclude that F is the more valuable dramatist, even though we cannot commensurate their accomplishments in the senses of (I) or (II).[46] Although more contentious, there is also a case that F is more valuable than both B and C (F is obviously more valuable than D). What, however, about the relative value of B, C, and D? Can we say that B and D are equally good? To do so, we would have to know (1) that f_1 and f_2 are of exactly equal importance in forming a judgment about a dramatist's overall merit and (2) we would have to know that the positions ascribed to B and D on the two dimensions are exact and correct. But both of these are highly uncertain; given uncertainties (1) and (2), we may be unable to compare them; our ranking will thus be incomplete. Given our currently available deliberative resources, we cannot order the options such that either B > D or D > B or D = B. We thus have incommensurability in the sense of (III): there is no ordering of them according to which one (and only one) of the following holds: (a) V_1 is better than V_2, (b) V_2 is better than V_1, (c) V_1 is equal to V_2.

Note that even though we are unable to compare B and D, we still can say that C is better than B so long as the *relative* placements of C and B on the f_1 dimension are correct. We need not be sure whether their exact location is correct, and of course the relative importance of f_1 and f_2 is not an issue. Hence the sources of uncertainty that made the comparison of B and D so difficult do not apply to B and C. So we can conclude that C > B. Yet we still cannot say that C is better than D, for our uncertainties about the relevant merits of B and D do not allow us to say that just because C is better than B it must also be better than D. We thus see the intransitivity of the ⌐ relation: (D ⌐ B) & (C > B) do not imply C > D.

At least in this type of case we can explain the incommensurability of values without resorting to Raz's, Gray's and Berlin's conviction that our inability to compare them is basic and cannot be explained in terms of the uncertainty and vagueness of our criteria.[47] This is important: a claim that values are incommensurable need not be a claim that qualitatively different values are simply impossible to compare, and 'there is nothing further behind it'. Which account, then, is to be preferred: that which takes the noncomparability of qualitatively distinct goods as *basic*, or that which explains incommensurability as *derived* from our uncertainties (about the relative importance of the different dimensions, the precise nature of the score on each of the dimensions, and the vagueness of the criteria of excellence)?[48] There is critical difference between the two, one which I believe strongly favors the derivative over Gray's, Raz's and Berlin's basic analysis. According to the basic view, once we have arrived at an incommensurable judgment *we know that our reasons have run out*. As Raz says, 'if of the options available in typical situations of choice and decision, several are incommensurable, then reason can neither determine nor completely explain their choices or actions'.[49] But if we do not employ our reason in choosing between incommensurable values, what do we do? Raz believes that we use our 'will' rather than our 'reason'. As he sees it, then, our will is not moved by the strongest reason, nor is it the outcome of rational deliberation: the will has autonomy within the space defined by reason. When reasons run out, the will chooses. Berlin's and Gray's views appear similar. At the heart of Berlin's pluralism is what Gray calls 'radical choice' – 'choice without criteria, grounds, or principles'.[50] In some sense we simply choose: as Gray says, if we have to choose between two incommensurable goods, 'we must do so without reason'.[51]

In one sense this conclusion is unavoidable: if right now I must choose between V_1 and V_2 and the $\bar{\mathsf{I}}$ relation holds,[52] then I cannot, ex hypothesi, choose on the basis of reasons. To choose between the incomparable requires that we do so without reasons. But whereas on the basic view I am doomed to reasonless choice, and so there is no reason to further inquire or deliberate on the nature and merits of the values, on the derivative view the incommensurability stems from the uncertainties, complexities and vagueness of my criteria. Therefore rational reflection, deliberation and inquiry are always relevant responses; I cannot know that further deliberation will not reveal the correct ranking. In the face of the incompleteness of our judgments, when we are confronted with a choice between values we cannot compare, the derivative analysis points to inquiry and reflection, not unreasoned acts of will, as the generally proper response. Indeed, if we regularly confront a choice between V_1 and V_2, it is most unlikely that we will continue to see them as incommensurable. Confronted by repeated choices, we will deliberate until we come to a settled decision about what to do.[53] It is hard to imagine a person who frequently has to choose between V_1 and V_2 continuing to understand the options as incommensurable, about which her practical reason is silent.[54] Thus while the derivative view can explain the incommensurability relation, it does not doom us to removing our most difficult value judgments from the realm of rational inquiry and deliberation, and so holds out the hope that we may exercise our intelligence and come to a better and more complete system of value judgments as a response to confronting incommensurable values.

The basic view, we should note, advances a stronger claim than does the derivative account of incommensurability. At the core of the derivative account is the idea that comparing options according to plural criteria is an exceedingly complex business. To employ John Rawls's phrase, in such cases we are reasoning under the 'burdens of judgment' (see section 1.2). It is difficult to come to a decision because we are uncertain how to weigh or rank the different criteria, our criteria are typically vague and require interpretation, the evidence is often conflicting and difficult to evaluate, and it could be – though we can never know for certain – that there simply is no correct decision to be made. Incommensurability thus can result from what I called 'reasonable pluralism' (see section 1.2). The basic view, however, insists that *we know* there is no correct decision to be made; our inability to rank the options is not the result of uncertainties and ignorance, but is the result of the very nature of values. But surely we should hesitate to appeal to such a radical doctrine to explain incommensurability if a more modest one will suffice: to suppose that we are certain there are no correct answers is itself a highly controversial claim, and is itself subject to reasonable disagreement.

Overcompleteness

Although Gray seems to endorse something like the incompleteness interpretation of incommensurability, in other remarks he points to the overcompleteness interpretation. In examining moral choices, Gray argues that the rights of other people 'make conflicting demands on us' and whatever we do in some situations, our action may contain a wrong. And, so, we face 'tragic choices'.[55] To make the point clearer, consider the famous case of

> a politician who has seized upon a national crisis – a prolonged colonial war – to reach for power. He and his friends won office pledged to decolonization and peace; they are honestly committed to both, though not without some sense of the advantages of the commitment. In any case, they have no responsibility for the war; they have steadfastly opposed it. Immediately, the politician goes off to the colonial capital to open negotiations with the rebels. But the capital is in the grip of a terrorist campaign and the first decision the new leader faces is this: he is asked to authorize the torture of a captured rebel who knows or probably knows the location of a number of bombs hidden in apartment buildings around the city, set to go off in the next twenty-four hours. He orders the man tortured, convinced that he must do so for the sake of the people who might otherwise die in the explosions – even though he believes that torture is wrong, indeed abominable, not just sometimes, but always. He had expressed this belief often and angrily in the campaign; the rest of us took it as a sign of his goodness. How should we regard him now? (How should he regard himself?)[56]

Using A for torture and B for not torture, we might say that our politician has two distinct ways of ranking outcomes. If he relies on his principle that it is wrong to torture, he concludes that B > A; on the other hand if he appeals to his concern for saving innocent lives, he concludes that A > B.

FIGURE 2.2   *A two-dimensional moral conflict*

Thus it would seem that both B > A and A > B, giving us incommensurability qua overcompleteness.

Yet there is something odd about this.[57] Consider Figure 2.2, which depicts the conflict. On the anti-torture dimension of moral reasoning, B ranks higher than A; on the saving innocent lives dimension A ranks higher than B. Notice the similarity to Figure 2.1, which also described conflicts between two dimensions of evaluation. In the case described in Figure 2.1, though, this conflict between dimensions resulted in the inability to conclude either that B > D or D > B. Given the uncertainties of the case, we were *unable to arrive at an overall evaluation.* In contrast, in the present case the person *arrives at two, inconsistent, overall evaluations;* each dimension is taken as giving an overall evaluation. The question must be: 'why does the agent take each dimension as constituting an overall evaluation, rather than seeing each as contributing a consideration that, hopefully, can enter into an overall evaluation?'

Perhaps the agent never contemplated the possibility that both dimensions would be relevant to a choice and provide different rankings, so he never developed a way to compare the dimensions. But that would seem to justify incompleteness rather than overcompleteness; if the agent has no idea how to weigh or compare the dimensions, then it seems that he is unable to arrive at an overall evaluation. More promising is Stanley Benn's suggestion that the agent may conceive of each of these dimensions as 'absolute' in the sense that whatever ranking the dimension yields is automatically the overall ranking. Thus if anti-torture is absolute in this sense, its ranking of A over B necessarily constitutes an overall ranking of A over B, and similarly with saving innocent lives. In this case the agent would thus have two, inconsistent, overall rankings. As Benn also recognizes, however, any one with more than one such absolute dimension in his system of values runs the risk of irrationality, and when, as in this case, two absolute dimensions are both relevant, the person is doomed to irrational, inconsistent, decisions.[58] Although he cannot settle on a single comparison, in a way he is committed to choosing A rather than B *and* B rather than A. Thus no matter what he does, he is irrational, because he has *an overall reason to do the opposite.* If we accept overcompleteness as a possible element of a rational system of values, it implies that rational people are necessarily irrational should overcompleteness ever be relevant to their choice. That is, if the agent has an overall evaluation such that A over B is the rational choice, then it must be a violation of rationality to chose B over A. But if both A > B and B > A, then whatever one does *both is required and prohibited by reason*. It is important to stress the contrast with incompleteness: whereas incompleteness tells us that each dimension gives us some reason to choose the option which ranks higher on that dimension, it insists that our inability to compare the dimensions shows that we do not have adequate reason for making a choice. In contrast, overcompleteness tells us that we have two overall evaluations, and so two competing adequate reasons.[59]

I conclude that overcompleteness cannot be a feature of a rational system of values; it demonstrates the impossibility of a rational decision (between the relevant options). Benn seems quite right: when discovering such overcompleteness in his system of values, the rational agent adjusts his commitment to the various dimensions, at least to the extent that he no longer claims that both dimensions automatically yield overall rankings. Doing so, the agent comes to see the possibility of rational choices in situations in which he previously thought a rational decision was impossible. 'That way, indeed, he adds inches to his stature as a rational decision maker, for then he is equipped to deal with further situations he could not have dealt with before'.[60]

Conflict and tragedy: the rejection of monism

We have thus far considered Berlin's doctrine of objective plural values and the idea of incommensurability. One additional element is required to complete the core of the doctrine: namely, the *conflict claim*, according to which values are inconsistent in the sense that we often must forgo one to obtain another – we cannot have all things worth having.[61] According to Berlin

> the ends of men are many, and not all of them are in principle compatible with each other, then the possibility of conflict – and tragedy – can never wholly be eliminated from human life, either personal or social. The necessity of choosing between absolute claims is then an inescapable characteristic of the human condition.[62]

As Berlin says, '[t]hat we cannot have everything is a necessary, not a contingent, truth'.[63] *Monism* – which Berlin associates with the Enlightenment View[64] – is 'the conviction that all positive values in which men have believed must, in the end, be compatible, and perhaps even entail one another'.[65]

Now if monism were correct – if in the end all that is truly valuable can be combined without sacrifice – then even if values were plural, objective, and incommensurable, we would not be doomed to 'tragic choice'.[66] If monism were correct, because we *could* have it all, we would never need to decide which value is greater than another, so incommensurability would not be relevant. But equally, without the incommensurability claim, value conflict would not pose a barrier to rationally ordering all values. Perhaps the most important lesson that economists have taught us is that choice between conflicting values is endemic to human action: whenever we act we seek to secure some valued outcome at the cost of not achieving other values. We must incur 'opportunity costs' – securing one good thing forecloses the opportunity to achieve alternatives. The very idea of rational action presupposes an ability to rank valued outcomes and act on the basis of such rankings. Life is about getting one thing by giving up another. When I buy a house, I forgo the opportunity to take frequent overseas trips, or eat frequently at the best New Orleans restaurants. I choose: I cannot have everything. But mere conflict of values does not create 'tragic choices'. When I sign the contract to buy a house, it is not a tragedy just because I now have given up frequent vacations and great meals. Admittedly, one may sometimes feel regret when one has to give up something important to achieve something else; I may regret that the cost of having a house is all the good food I will miss. However, people who consistently regret the costs they have to pay to get the things they want strike us not as dealing with tragedy, but as immature. When my daughter was around five years old, she would sometimes get money from a relative on a special occasion, and she would promptly go to the toy store. But it was always a tragedy for her: although she desperately wanted the toy, she desperately wanted to keep the money too. She could not bear to pay the cost of the toy, but could not bear to forgo the toy either. Thus typically the trip ended with her breaking into tears. Of course, this was only a tragedy to a young child who had not learned that to get good things we have to give up other good things. Hopefully, Berlin's understanding of the tragedy of choice between values is not simply this sort of immature response to the facts of life.

If values are incommensurable qua overcomplete we can generate an account of the tragedy of choice. If I have a system of values according to which I have an overall evaluation according to which $V_1 > V_2$ and $V_2 > V_1$, then a choice between V_1 and V_2 will indeed be a tragedy. Consider again the case of the politician faced with a choice between torturing a suspect and allowing many innocent people to die in terrorist attacks.[67] If it is overall wrong not to torture and overall wrong to let the innocent people die, then no matter what the politician does he is wrong. He *must not* torture and he *must* save innocent lives, so whatever he does he either fails to do what he must do, or does what he must not do.[68] This seems a real tragedy. However, we have seen that the overcompleteness interpretation of incommensurability dooms us to irrationality. If, as I argued, we reject it as an inherently irrational way to rank values, then the tragedy of such cases arises from the agent's irrationality, not from the plurality of incommensurable values.

The undercompleteness interpretation can, perhaps, show how we might be doomed to tragic choices. According to the undercompleteness interpretation, *none* of the following are part of the agent's value system: $V_1 > V_2$, $V_2 > V_1$, $V_1 = V_2$. Given this, if one is forced to decide between V_1 and V_2 one must forgo a value even though one cannot say that it is of less (or equal) importance to the value one has chosen. Consider the much-discussed case from William Styron's novel *Sophie's Choice*, in which a Nazi forces Sophie, a Polish mother in a concentration camp, to choose which of her children will live and which will die; unless she chooses one, she is told, both will be killed. Sophie proclaims again and again that she cannot choose.[69] This seems the crux of her plight, for until forced to act, she cannot compare the importance of the lives of her children – they are incommensurable in the sense that she simply is unable to compare them, and so is literally unable to choose. To be sure, ultimately the Nazi does coerce Sophie into making a choice by the threat to kill both children if she does not choose one. And she does choose to save one (who also ends up dying in the camp). Given her insistence that she cannot choose between her children, one interpretation of her action is that her rational choice is simply that one child survives rather than both die, rather than expressing a preference for one child over the other. In any case, we can see here a tragedy.

It seems plausible, however, to conjecture that Sophie's anguish stems not from the incommensurability of the value of her children's lives, but from the incredible costs to Sophie no matter what she does. Consider again the case the politician faced with the choice of torturing or failing to save innocent lives. Suppose that he is able to rank the options such that torturing is better than failing to save the lives. Yet, when the costs are extremely high even a mature, rational decision maker may experience anguish – the cost of torturing someone may be so high that it is difficult to bear. Would Sophie be any less anguished if she could commensurate and decide that her son is more valuable than her daughter? It is hard to say. It may be that the inability to rank options between which one must nevertheless choose is especially wrenching when the costs of choice are extremely high. The main factor, however, seems to be the extraordinary 'opportunity costs' of decision. In extreme cases, these costs can be so high that even mature people find it wrenching. Again, though, this cannot be the normal reaction to opportunity costs, for they are part and parcel of almost every significant decision we make, as my daughter came to learn.

Levels of pluralism

Throughout I have been focusing on pluralism as a doctrine about an individual's value system: within an individual's system of values, she

will confront value choices and incommensurabilities. And this is certainly consistent with Berlin's insistence that 'values may easily clash within the breast of a single individual'.[70] Berlin is clear, however, that value pluralism may occur at a variety of levels:

> There are many objective ends, ultimate values, some incompatible with others, pursued by different societies at various times, or by different groups in the same society, by entire classes or churches or races, or by particular individuals within them, and any one of which may find itself subject to conflicting claims of uncombinable, yet equally ultimate and objective, ends.[71]

Thus individuals, groups within a society, or different societies may be said to pursue values, and (within the range defined by the common human horizon, see sections 2.2 and 3.1) these cannot be compared, and ranked superior or inferior to others. Indeed, much of Berlin's thought emphasizes the ways in which the values characterizing different societies are plural and incomparable. Berlin is greatly impressed by Machiavelli, who stresses the incompatibility between pagan and Christian virtues, and insists how different states or regimes are based on these different, conflicting, virtues. 'The combination of *virtù* and Christian values is for him an impossibility. He simply leaves you to choose – he knows which he himself prefers'.[72] This, we shall see, is important; Berlin's insistence that societies pursue incommensurable values is a major obstacle to any attempt to show that his pluralism somehow endorses liberalism.

2.4 Pluralism and liberalism

From pluralism to liberalism?

I have examined in some depth Berlin's understanding of pluralism. We have uncovered serious difficulties. First, the account of the objectivity of values is, at best, unclear and perhaps confused. Second, Berlin's pluralism not only supposes that values can be incommensurable, but that this incommensurability is *basic* rather than derivative. To the extent that it is derivative, Berlin cannot claim that we are doomed to non-rational choice between values, for the use of reason may clear up the uncertainty and vagueness that produces incommensurability. Third, it is not clear in just what way we are doomed to tragic choices between values. Certainly choice of one value over another is not typically tragic, though there may be cases where the costs are so great that anyone will find incurring them wrenching. To be sure, the overcompleteness interpretation of incommensurability provides a foundation for tragic choices, but that appears to reflect an irrational value system.

Putting aside for now these worries about the doctrine of pluralism (we shall see some of them will again come to the fore) let us turn to its relation to liberalism. It certainly seems that at one point Berlin was convinced that the truth of value pluralism somehow showed that liberty was the supreme political value and/or that liberalism was somehow uniquely justified. We can distinguish four arguments in which Berlin seems to link pluralism to liberalism: the arguments from the importance of choice, from humanity, from the truth of value pluralism, and from the value of diversity.

The simple argument from choice

According to the argument from the value of choice, our recognition that we are doomed to tragic choice between values leads us 'to place an immense value upon freedom to choose'.[73] Indeed, at one point Berlin famously proclaimed that a measure of negative liberty is 'entailed' by pluralism.[74] Thus Berlin says that non-liberal societies, devoted to pursuing some single great value, deny their members basic freedoms to choose between values and thus are less humane than are liberal societies. Liberal societies are consistent with our nature as 'unpredictably self-transforming human beings'.[75]

Berlin never provides a clear formulation of this case.[76] According to the simplest version, because of value pluralism we must choose between competing values, and because liberal societies are superior in protecting our freedom to make such choices, liberal societies are superior to non-liberal societies. This simple argument is, I think, at the root of Berlin's reputation as a liberal: if values are plural and we must choose then the first political value must be liberty. The argument, however, clearly fails. For pluralism, and its insistence that values cannot be ranked, cannot show that choice between values can be ranked higher than a life devoted to a single value. As has been pointed out by others, that choice is necessary does not show that it is valuable, and even if it is valuable, choice and freedom cannot be shown to be superior to other values.[77] Berlin himself seems to argue (at least at times) that liberty is as much subject to pluralistic incommensurability as are other values. 'Freedom is only one value among others'.[78]

The argument from common humanity

In his famous essay on 'Two Concepts of Liberty' Berlin suggests a more subtle argument of the general form:

1   Because of value pluralism, we must choose between competing values;

2   It is the nature of humans as 'self-transforming beings' to make such choices;
3   Only societies that protect our freedom to make such choices are consistent with our common human nature;
4   Societies that are more humane (that are consistent with our common human nature) are objectively superior to societies that are not consistent with this nature;
5   Therefore: Liberal societies are more humane than, and so objectively superior to, non-liberal societies.

Whereas the simple version of the argument contends that choice and liberty are in some way not subject to pluralistic incommensurability, this more complicated version argues that humaneness can be rationally ranked as superior to other values. Now, as Jonathan Riley has argued, this argument seems consistent with Berlin's appeal to a common human nature, and a common moral horizon.[79] As we have seen (section 2.2) Berlin makes extensive appeal to our common human nature; in some way our common human nature identifies what values are objective, and *so the limits of pluralism*. This argument, then, seems to maintain that only 'humane' societies are within our common moral horizon, and because of value pluralism, the necessity of choice and our nature as self-defining beings, only societies with extensive negative liberty – i.e., liberal societies – are humane. Without some modicum of liberty, Berlin tells us, , 'there is no choice and therefore no possibility of remaining human as we understand the word'.[80]

We see the importance, then, of our earlier examination of Berlin's idea of objectivity and the common human horizon; on this interpretation, his case for liberalism rests chiefly on those ideas, not directly on value pluralism. Because we have reason to doubt the plausibility of Berlin's analysis of objective moral values, we cannot accept this case for liberalism, which presupposes it. However, even leaving aside the worries about the account of objectivity presupposed by this argument, three additional observations about this defense of liberalism are important.

First, even if it succeeds, it would not provide us with a case for liberalism tightly based on pluralism. Berlin perhaps recognized this: at one point he goes so far as to deny that pluralism and liberalism are even 'logically connected', much less (as he explicitly said in 'Two Concepts of Liberty') that the pluralism 'entails' a commitment to negative liberty.[81] On the common humanity reading it is the objective ranking of values entailed by our common human nature – that is, the conceptual space in which pluralism does not obtain – that shows the superiority of liberalism. As Berlin himself acknowledges, far from being post-Enlightenment View, this claim harks back to the core Enlightenment idea that because of a common human nature, our shared reasoning about morality leads us to similar conclusions about how political values are to be ranked. Riley insists that Berlin departs from the Enlightenment insofar as Berlin insists that many values cannot be ranked: sometimes public reasoning fails us, and many values are incommensurable. But we have seen that even most Enlightenment Views acknowledge that many non-political values cannot be publicly ranked (section 1.3), so that does not seem enough to distinguish Berlin's argument from the standard Enlightenment View that we share enough common nature and rationality to arrive at similar conclusions about the fundamentals of politics.

Second, this version of Berlin's argument relies on a stronger notion of 'the common human horizon' than we encountered in section 2.1. There the common human horizon was used to delimit the sphere of plural, objective, values; even if we oppose these values we can appreciate them as human. 'The condition of recognizing ultimate values, whether my own or those of other cultures or persons, is that I must be able to imagine myself in a situation in which I could myself pursue them, even though they may in fact repel me, and I may be prepared to resist them with all the means that I have at my command.'[82] '[P]luralism … means that I can imaginatively enter into the situation, outlook, motives, constellation of values, ways of life, of societies not my own'.[83] This would seem to suggest that appeal to the common human horizon tells us whether V is an objective value, but not how it is ranked *vis-à-vis* others: we can recognize something as part of the common human horizon even if we fight against it, while others fight for it. However, on the version of Berlin's argument we are presently examining, the common human horizon not only tells us what are the objective values, but also reveals some objective rankings, such that some degree of liberty is objectively ranked above some other values.

The third worry about this argument is that it identifies liberalism with this part of the common human horizon in which values can be ranked. Riley vigorously defends this claim: he insists that any 'decent' society recognizes core liberal equal rights, especially liberty rights. But this seems manifestly implausible. Even if a 'modicum' of liberty is necessary for us to remain human, it is awfully hard to see how this leads to the structure of equal freedoms of speech, association, property and so on that are fundamental to liberalism. The Romans, the French of the *ancien régime*, the Ottoman Turks, Native American tribes before European conquest, contemporary Iranians – all these have been or are recognizably human, and so have made sufficient choices so that we can say that they are humans. But they were hardly liberal societies. To be sure, Berlin is sufficiently vague about the idea of a 'decent' or 'humane' society such that one could, as Riley does, argue that 'decent' is equivalent to 'liberal'. But then we are confronted with a highly dubious appeal to common human reason: we can all see that the only decent humane society is a liberal society.

Moreover, it is very doubtful that Berlin could consistently embrace such a view. Recall that for Berlin pluralism holds not only within individuals and between them, but between societies. Societies choose values and choose how to order them. Recall from section 2.3 that Machiavelli is a pivotal figure for Berlin as he shows that societies make choices: Machiavelli insists that a society cannot be characterized by both pagan and Christian virtues – it must choose. But if societies can choose, they can choose ways of life in which all are co-opted into a joint pursuit of some great project or value; that is, societies in which *individual* choice is greatly circumscribed by *collective* choice. That, though, must mean that illiberal arrangements can be chosen; indeed, the very idea of mandatory participation in such collective projects seems illiberal. Riley would have it that societies can only choose within the bounds of liberal arrangements. This, though, supposes an extremely tame and limited value pluralism, one that has little to do with the 'tragic' choices so vividly depicted by Berlin: between Christianity and paganism, or between egalitarianism and romantic pursuit of great aesthetic values by the elite, but rather more like the choice between the political regimes of Sweden and the United States.

The argument from the truth of pluralism

In the famous passage from 'Two Concepts of Liberty' that we have been examining, Berlin maintains that negative liberty is not simply a more 'humane', but a 'truer' ideal than

> the goals of those who seek in the great, disciplined, authoritarian structures the ideal of 'positive' self-mastery by classes, or people, or the whole of mankind. It is truer, because it does, at least, recognize the fact that human goals are many, not all of them commensurable, and in perpetual rivalry with one another. To assume that all values can be graded on one scale ... seems to me to falsify our knowledge of men as free agents.[84]

Others have been impressed with this claim. In a dispute between Liberal, who sees his values as a matter of choice, and Traditional, who sees his values as a matter of destiny, one commentator insists that '[c]learly Liberal knows something that Traditional does not. Liberal is right in his beliefs about value, whereas Traditional is wrong'.[85] This goes too quickly. If Traditional sees his values as the ones characterizing *his society*, which reflect the way of life *his society* has chosen, Traditional makes no false claims. And indeed many conservative writers have taken such a view of values, stressing that a society's value system is not objectively correct, but is *its* system that defines *its* way of life. Given that pluralism can operate at the level of societies, Traditional's beliefs are fully consistent with pluralism: they are even consistent with pluralism if he is not 'aware of other values and sets of values' and has 'contempt' toward them.[86] As Gray observes:

A particularistic illiberal regime need not claim, when it imposes a particular ranking of incommensurable values on its subjects, that this ranking is uniquely rational, or even that it is better than others that are presently found in the world. It need only claim that it is a ranking embedded in, and necessary for the survival of, a particular way of life that is itself worthwhile, and that this ranking, and the way of life it supports, would be imperiled by the unimpeded exercise of choice.[87]

More radically, consider a romantic who insists that truth is not a value that she ranks highly. Her romantic endorsement of a society that asserts its own values and ignores whether pluralism is true is itself consistent with the truth of value pluralism, for according to this romantic, her society has ranked truth below, say, human self-assertion. Unless we are to hold that truth is a value to be ranked above all other values, we cannot say that in some way this society is objectively inferior to liberal society.

The argument from diversity

Some value pluralists influenced by Berlin have argued that the fact of value pluralism shows the value of a diversity of values and, so, of a free society. 'If there are many and competing genuine values, then the greater the extent to which a society tends to be singled-valued, the more genuine values it neglects or suppresses. More, to this extent, must mean better'.[88] Thus, since the primacy of freedom in liberal society allows citizens to choose a wide diversity of values, it seems that pluralism gives unique support to a free society.

Now we can formulate an argument that leads from a sort of value pluralism to the value of diversity, and so to liberalism. At least two additional assumptions are necessary. (1) Instead of pluralism being committed to the *incommensurability or incomparability* of values, we would have to interpret it as insisting on the *equality* of all true values, a view that, we have seen, Berlin sometimes suggests (section 2.3). (2) In addition, we would have to accept the following principle:

> *Decreasing marginal value*: For any value V, getting additional increment of the amount secured by moving from the n to $n + 1$ unit, always yields less additional value than was obtained by moving from $n - 1$ to n.

Figure 2.3 gives a graphic representation of this principle for the case of equality. Distinguishing between the amount of equality and its value, we can see that the move from $n - 1$ to n yields much more value (the y-axis) than does the move from n to $n + 1$. If these two assumptions held, a society with a rich diversity of value would certainly have more value

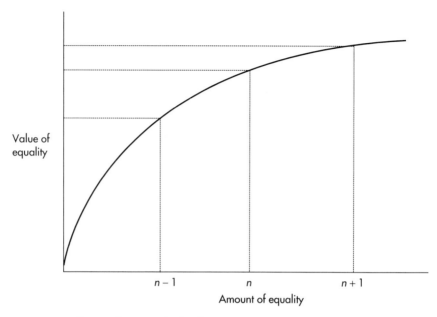

FIGURE 2.3   *Decreasing marginal value*

than a 'singled-value' society. For as we get a reasonable amount of, say equality, to pursue even more of it will yield less and less additional value; thus it would do better at that point to switch to another value, such as liberty, of which we do not have much, and so will yield great additional value per unit.

These are very strong assumptions; they serve to demonstrate just how hard it is to generate a case from pluralism to the value of diversity. To the extent that values are incomparable rather than equal, we cannot say that a society with many values is superior to a singled-value society; for if we are unable to compare the value of, say, liberty, equality, justice and beauty, we simply cannot say that a society with liberty (L), equality (E) and justice (J) is better than a society with only beauty (B). For the diversity argument to succeed under incommensurability, it would have to be the case that even though L ⌐ E, E ⌐ J, L ⌐ J, L ⌐ B, E ⌐ B, J ⌐ B, nevertheless L & E & J > B. It is difficult indeed to see how all that incommensurability could give rise to an objective ranking in favor of liberty, equality and justice. Moreover, the second assumption is also necessary. For unless amounts of a value are characterized by decreasing marginal value, it would be possible for some society to compensate for neglecting liberty, equality and justice by having fantastic amounts of beauty.

An additional objection confronts the argument from diversity to liberalism. Even if we assume that it is objectively more valuable to have a world characterized by the pursuit of diverse values, it by no means follows that a world of liberal states would accomplish this. Again, it is crucial that much of Berlin's writings concern value pluralism between societies. If all the world is composed of liberal states, then some structures of values will not be pursued – structures that only arise in societies that pursue a common, non-liberal, way of life. The values inherent in the collective pursuit of a traditional Islamic way of life cannot be fully captured in a liberal society, with its strong secularist commitments. If the aim is to keep alive the greatest possible diversity of values – a sort of world-wide value zoo – it hardly seems plausible that every society should adopt a liberal political structure. Thus, not only should we doubt the argument from pluralism to the value of diversity; we have grounds to reject the next step, from the value of diversity to the justification of liberal societies as uniquely suitable to value pluralism.

Berlin's dilemma

Our analysis of Berlin's liberal pluralism points to a dilemma. On the one hand, we can interpret Berlin as a radical pluralist, stressing the incommensurability of plural values as by far the most important feature of our moral lives. Certainly this is the feature of Berlin's philosophy that is most distinctive, and it formed the major theme of his writing throughout his long life. It is understandable to think – for one reason, because he seems to say so in numerous places – that Berlin believes that this fundamental feature of our moral experience somehow directly or easily leads to the justification of a free society. But, as has been widely noted, and as we have seen in this section, this project fails. Radical pluralism of values does not lead to the primacy of freedom or liberalism. Although Berlin denied it, his radical pluralism points to what might be called a 'post-modern ethic' – the view that moral positions are inherently plural and incommensurable, and we are thus unable to privilege any one as uniquely true or correct.[89] Rather than developing a Post-Enlightenment liberalism, Berlin's radical pluralism appears to undermine the justification of liberalism as a superior form of political organization.

Of course Berlin is a liberal, but far from following from his pluralism, his liberalism derives from the non-pluralist parts of his thought. These elements of his political thought are not at all post-Enlightenment; they suppose that there is a common human nature, and humans reasoning on the basis of what is required for a decent life will see the truth of liberalism as part of the common human horizon which identifies an objective world of value. What looked like a unique and particularly modern defense of liberalism turns out to be highly traditional, turning on claims about how liberalism best accords with our common human nature.

Thus, it seems that to the extent Berlin is a pluralist, he is not a liberal; and to the extent he is a liberal, he is not a pluralist.

2.5 Summary and conclusion

In the first chapter of this book I argued that one of the most important challenges to the Enlightenment View is pluralism, a group of doctrines according to which there are many values that cannot be ranked, and so the application of human reason to such values fails to yield common answers. In this chapter we have examined the possibility – sometimes suggested by Isaiah Berlin – that the appreciation of the incommensurability of plural values rationally entails liberalism. We began (sections 2.2–2.3) by considering just what is meant by the claim that we confront incommensurable plural values. I expressed serious reservations about the account of objectivity – which, we have just seen, is basic to Berlin's liberalism. I also maintained that Berlin's pluralism not only supposes that values can be incommensurable, but that this incommensurability is *basic* rather than derivative. I argued, however, that to the extent to which it is derivative, Berlin cannot claim that we are doomed to non-rational choice between values, for the use of reason may clear up the uncertainty and vagueness that produces incommensurability. In any event it is not clear in just what way we are 'doomed' to tragic choices between values. Certainly choice of one value over another is not typically tragic, though there may be cases where the costs are so great that anyone will find incurring them wrenching.

Having considered what is meant by the incommensurability of objectively plural values, we turned in section 2.4 to examine Berlin's daring doctrine that pluralism leads to liberalism; however, we could not reconstruct a sound argument to support this doctrine. Indeed, Berlin himself, though suggesting this doctrine, ultimately abandons it: his considered view endorses a pluralism limited by rationally agreed-upon moral truth, or what Riley has called a 'liberal rationalism'. And, we have seen, to the extent his doctrine endorses liberalism, it is not his pluralism, but his 'rationalistic' conviction that we can uncover common objective truths, that does the philosophical work.

Two main lessons emerge from this chapter. The main conclusion is that the sort of objective pluralism envisaged by Berlin, with a basic incommensurability of values, cannot provide the basis for liberal political principles. Thoroughgoing pluralism undermines the justification of liberal politics. Berlin himself recognizes this, and retreats to a much more traditional, if not entirely convincing, justification of liberalism, one with its roots in the Enlightenment View. The second lesson, however, is that we need not embrace a strong conception of pluralism. The claims that values are objectively plural, that we are doomed to tragic choice, and that there is a basic incommensurability of different values, are all highly contentious claims. As we saw (section 2.3), we can account for cases of incommensurability by appealing to our uncertainty and the complexity of choice. It *could* be that there simply is no correct choice to be made, and incommensurability might be basic rather than derivative, but it is certainly reasonable to dispute this.

Notes

1   Isaiah Berlin, 'Alleged Relativism in Eighteenth-Century European Thought' in Henry Hardy, ed., *The Crooked Timber of Humanity: Chapters in the History of Ideas* (Princeton: Princeton University Press, 1990), pp. 70–71. [citation omitted]
2   Eric Mack makes this point in 'Isaiah Berlin and the Quest for Liberal Pluralism', *Public Affairs Quarterly*, vol. 7 (April 1993): 215–230, p. 217.
3   Isaiah Berlin, 'The Pursuit of the Ideal' in *The Crooked Timber of Humanity*, p. 7.
4   Ibid., p. 6.
5   See, e.g., Berlin, *The Roots of Romanticism* (Princeton: Princeton University Press, 1999), pp. 34ff.
6   Isaiah Berlin, 'The Apotheosis of the Romantic Will' in *The Crooked Timber of Humanity*, p. 237.
7   Berlin, *The Roots of Romanticism*, p. 146.
8   John Kekes, 'Pluralism and Conflict in Morality', *The Journal of Value Inquiry*, vol. 26 (January 1992): 37–50, p. 37.
9   I explain this distinction in my *Social Philosophy* (Armonk, NY: M.E. Sharpe 1999), Chs 1, 3. For a more systematic treatment, see my *Value and Justification* (Cambridge: Cambridge University Press, 1990).
10 See Berlin, 'The Pursuit of the Ideal', pp. 11–12; Bernard Williams, 'Conflict of Values' in his *Moral Luck* (Cambridge: Cambridge University Press, 1981), pp. 71–82. See Mack, 'Isaiah Berlin and The Quest for Liberal Pluralism'.
11 Berlin, 'Alleged Relativism in Eighteenth-Century European Thought', p. 79.
12 Berlin, 'The Pursuit of the Ideal', p. 11.
13 On Berlin's commitment to the objectivity of values, see John Gray, *Isaiah Berlin* (Princeton: Princeton University Press, 1996), pp. 46ff; Glen Newey, 'Value Pluralism in Contemporary Liberalism', *Dialogue*, vol. 37 (1998): 493–522. Eric Mack observes a shift in Berlin's early work, in which values were said to be 'created', to his later writings in which they are 'discovered'. 'Isaiah Berlin and The Quest for Liberal Pluralism', p. 219.
14 Berlin, 'The Pursuit of the Ideal', p. 11.

15 Isaiah Berlin, 'Does Political Theory Still Exist?', in *Philosophy, Politics and Society*, second series, Peter Laslett and W.G. Runciman, eds (Oxford: Blackwell, 1962), p. 26. See also Daniel Weinstock, 'The Graying of Berlin', *Critical Review*, vol. 11 (Fall 1997): 481–501, p. 489.

16 Isaiah Berlin, 'Reply to Ronald H. McKinney', *The Journal of Value Inquiry*, vol. 26 (1992): 557–560, p. 560.

17 Ibid., p. 557.

18 Ibid.

19 Ibid., p. 557.

20 Ibid., p. 559. Emphases added.

21 See Gray, *Isaiah Berlin*, pp. 71ff.

22 John Stuart Mill, *Utilitarianism* in John Gray ed., *On Liberty and Other Essays* (New York: Oxford University Press, 1991), p. 168 (Ch. 4, para. 3). Text slightly altered.

23 Sigmund Freud, *Civilization and its Discontents*, James Strachey, ed., trans. (New York: W.W. Norton, 1962), p. 61.

24 See Jonathan Riley, 'Interpreting Berlin's Liberalism', *American Political Science Review*, vol. 95 (June 2001): 283–297; Richard Wollheim, 'The Idea of a Common Human Nature' in *Isaiah Berlin: A Celebration* (Chicago: University of Chicago Press, 1991), pp. 64–79. Cf. John Gray's similar, but also puzzling, claim to deduce conclusions about human perfection from anthropology: 'The human good harbours rival perfections. This is a claim of anthropology'. 'Where Pluralists and Liberals Part Company', *International Journal of Philosophical Studies*, vol. 6 (1): 17–36, p. 19. On this point see Marcus Roberts, 'The Endurance of History? Reflections on John Gray's Post-Enlightenment Pluralism', *Res Publica*, vol. 3 (1997): 185–212, pp. 193ff.

25 This point is stressed by Gray, *Isaiah Berlin*, p. 47.

26 See Williams, 'Conflict of Values', p. 77.

27 See, e.g., Ruth Chang, 'Introduction' to her edited collection, *Incommensurability, Incomparability and Practical Reason* (Cambridge, MA: Harvard University Press, 1997), p. 1; Bernard Williams, 'Conflicts of Value', p. 77; Fred D'Agostino, 'Incommensurability and Commensuration: Lessons from (and to) Ethico-Political Theory', *Studies in the History and Philosophy of Science*, vol. 31 (2000): 429–447.

28 See D'Agostino, 'Incommensurability and Commensuration;' Joseph Raz, 'Value Incommensurability: Some Preliminaries', *Proceedings of the Aristotelian Society*, vol. 86 (1985–86): 117–134.

29 See Riley, 'Interpreting Berlin's Liberalism', pp. 286ff; Amartya Sen, *On Ethics and Economics* (Oxford: Blackwell, 1987), pp. 61ff.

30 See, e.g., Berlin, 'Alleged Relativism in Eighteenth-Century European Thought', p. 70; Berlin, 'Two Concepts of Liberty' in his *Four Essays on Liberty* (Oxford: Oxford University Press, 1969), p. 171.

31 S.I. Benn, *A Theory of Freedom* (Cambridge: Cambridge University Press, 1988), p. 49.

32 See W.D. Ross, *The Right and the Good* (Oxford: Clarendon Press, 1930), p. 144. I deal with incommensurability in this sense in my 'Backwards Into the Future: Neo-Republicanism as a Post-Socialist Critique of Market Society', *Social Philosophy and Policy*, vol. 20 (Winter 2003): 59–91.

33 See Robert A. Kocis, *A Critical Appraisal of Sir Isaiah Berlin's Political Philosophy* (Lewiston, NY: Edwin Mellon Press, 1989), Ch. 4.

34 See Chang, 'Introduction', pp. 13ff. See also James Griffin 'Incommensurability: What's the Problem?' in Chang, ed., *Incommensurability, Incomparability and Practical Reason*, pp. 35–51.

35 I am borrowing these terms from Sen and Riley. See note 29 above.

36 Gray, *Isaiah Berlin*, pp. 50ff.

37 Berlin, 'Alleged Relativism in Eighteenth-Century European Thought', p. 79. Newey argues that Raz equivocates as to whether incommensurable values are equal. 'Value Pluralism in Contemporary Liberalism', pp. 496–498, 507.

38 Isaiah Berlin, 'The Apotheosis of the Romantic Will', p. 224.

39 See my *Political Concepts and Political Theories* (Boulder, CO: Westview Press, 2000), Ch. 6.

40 See Raz, 'Value Incommensurability: Some Preliminaries'.

41 Raz argues that the 'mark of incommensurability ... is failure of transitivity'. Ibid., p. 120. Newey is certainly correct, however, that the failure of transitivity cannot be used to establish incommensurability. See Newey, 'Value Pluralism in Contemporary Liberalism', p. 498.

42 Gray, *Isaiah Berlin*, p. 51.

43 Ibid., p. 53. See Raz, *The Morality of Freedom* (Oxford: Clarendon Press, 1988), p. 327.

44 This dominance relation is stressed by Fred D'Agostino in his account of commensurability. See his *Free Public Reason* (Oxford: Oxford University Press, 1996).

45 See Michael Stocker, *Plural and Conflicting Values* (Oxford: Clarendon Press, 1990), pp. 176ff.

46 See here Sir David Ross, *The Right and the Good*, pp. 142ff. See also Donald Regan, 'Value, Comparability and Choice' in Chang, ed., *Incommensurability, Incomparability and Practical Reason*, p. 135.

47 For an excellent analysis of incommensurability in terms of vagueness see John Broom, 'Is Incommensurability Vagueness?' In Chang, ed., *Incommensurability, Incomparability and Practical Reason*, pp. 67–89.

48 This last source of uncertainty did not arise in the artificial example considered in the text, which assumed that we knew just what f_1 and f_2 were, and indeed that there was no other relevant factor.

49 Joseph Raz, 'Incommensurability and Agency' in Chang, ed., *Incommensurability, Incomparability and Practical Reason*, p. 112.

50 Gray, *Isaiah Berlin*, p. 61. Berlin, in an essay jointly written with Bernard Williams denies this, and adamantly insists that we can rationally compare values. On my view, this joint essay presents a view uncharacteristic of Berlin's philosophy. As interpreted in this essay, the crucial claim of pluralism seems to be that there is no value such that in all cases and at all times it prevails over others – a weaker conception of pluralism than is generally defended throughout Berlin's writings. 'Pluralism and Liberalism: A Reply', *Political Studies*, vol. 41 (1994): 306–309.

51 John Gray, *Two Faces of Liberalism* (Oxford: Polity Press, 2000), p. 42.

52 And I have no other, third, consideration or principle that dictates a choice.

53 I owe this point to Fred D'Agostino.

54 For studies of how actual agents make such comparisons see Philip Tetlock, 'Coping with Trade-Offs: Psychological Constraints and Political Implications', in Arthur Lupia, Matthew D. McCubbins and Samuel L. Popkin, eds, *Elements of Reason: Cognition, Choice and the Bounds of Rationality* (Cambridge: Cambridge University Press, 2000).

55   Gray, *Two Faces of Liberalism*, pp. 113–116.
56   Michael Walzer, 'Political Action: The Problem of Dirty Hands', *Philosophy & Public Affairs*, vol. 2 (1973): 160–180, pp. 166–167.
57   As Sen recognizes, 'it may, in fact, appear straightforwardly bizarre in terms of the standard requirements of internal consistency'. *On Ethics and Economics*, p. 66.
58   See Benn, *A Theory of Freedom*, pp. 56ff.
59   Sen, I believe, does not appreciate this difference. See *On Ethics and Economics*, p. 67.
60   Benn, *A Theory of Freedom*, p. 63.
61   For an excellent, though somewhat different analysis, see Newey, 'Value Pluralism in Contemporary Liberalism', pp. 500–504.
62   Berlin, 'Two Concepts of Liberty', pp. 168–169.
63   Ibid., p. 170.
64   See Berlin, 'The Apotheosis of the Romantic Will'. See also Mack, 'Isaiah Berlin and the Quest for Liberal Pluralism'.
65   Berlin, 'Two Concepts of Liberty', p. 167.
66   Berlin, 'The Pursuit of the Ideal', p. 13.
67   I consider this type of case more fully in my essay on 'Dirty Hands' in Christopher Heath Wellman and Ray Frey, eds, *Blackwell Companion to Applied Ethics* (Oxford: Blackwell, 2003), pp. 169–79.
68   The rationality of this interpretation of the politician's plight is defended by Bernard Williams, 'Ethical Consistency' in his *Problems of the Self* (Cambridge: Cambridge University Press, 1973), pp. 166–186.
69   For a conflicting analysis of this case see Stocker, *Plural and Conflicting Values*, p. 19. I criticize Stocker's analysis in my essay on 'Dirty Hands'.
70   Berlin, 'The Pursuit of the Ideal', p. 12.
71   Berlin, 'Alleged Relativism in Eighteenth-Century European Thought', pp. 79–80.
72   Berlin, 'The Pursuit of the Ideal', p. 8. See also Berlin's 'The Originality of Machiavelli', in H. Hardy, ed., *Against the Current* (Oxford: Oxford University Press, 1981), pp. 25–79.
73   Berlin, 'Two Concepts of Liberty', p. 168.
74   Ibid., p. 171.
75   Ibid.
76   Which, disturbingly, did not always stop him from writing cutting replies to those whom he thought misinterpreted his vague and often inconsistent writings. See, e.g., Berlin and Williams, 'Pluralism and Liberalism: A Reply' and Berlin, 'Reply to Robert A. Kocis', *Political Studies*, vol. 31 (1983): 383–385.
77   See Gray, *Isaiah Berlin*; Crowder, 'Pluralism and Liberalism'.
78   Isaiah Berlin, 'The Bent Twig' in *The Crooked Timber of Humanity*, p. 259.
79   See Riley, 'Interpreting Berlin's Liberalism'.
80   Berlin, 'The Pursuit of the Ideal', p. 12.
81   As reported in R. Jahanbegloo, *Conversations with Isaiah Berlin* (London: Peter Halban, 1992), p. 44.
82   Berlin, 'Reply to Ronald H. McKinney', p. 557.
83   Ibid.
84   Berlin, 'Two Concepts of Liberty', p. 171.
85   Weinstock, 'The Graying of Berlin', p. 491.

86 Ibid.
87 Gray, *Isaiah Berlin*, p. 153.
88 Bernard Williams quoted in Crowder, 'Pluralism and Liberalism', p. 300.
89 See Ronald H. McKinney, 'Towards a Postmodern Ethics: Sir Isaiah Berlin and John Caputo', *The Journal of Value Inquiry*, vol. 26 (1992): 395–407. See Berlin's 'Reply to Ronald H. McKinney'.

3

Hobbesian-inspired Liberalism: Public Reason Out of Individual Reason

CONTENTS

3.1 Liberalism as a *modus vivendi*: another route from pluralism to liberalism? *56*
3.2 Hobbesian public reason *67*
3.3 Substantive public reason as a solution to the Hobbesian paradox *74*
3.4 Summary *79*

3.1 Liberalism as a *modus vivendi*: another route from pluralism to liberalism?

Gray on pluralism, liberalism and modus vivendi

In the last twenty years John Gray has journeyed from a staunch supporter, to a harsh critic, of liberalism.[1] In his most recent work, however, he seems to move back a bit toward liberalism, pointing to the resources within the liberal tradition to develop a political theory built upon a conception of pluralism much like Isaiah Berlin's, which we examined in Chapter 2. Gray, however, argues that the truth of pluralism leads to a new appreciation of that part of the liberal tradition inspired by Thomas Hobbes:

> Liberalism has always had two faces. From one side, toleration is the pursuit of an ideal form of life. From the other, it is the search for terms of peace among different ways of life. In the former view, liberal institutions are seen as applications of universal principles. In the latter, they are means to

peaceful coexistence. In the first, liberalism is the prescription for a universal regime. In the second, it is a project of coexistence that can be pursued in many different regimes.[2]

The first 'face' of liberalism is essentially what Rawls describes as Enlightenment liberalism:[3] liberal toleration is based on the supposition that common human reason can reveal a universal understanding of the good life. According to Gray, the second face, which he associates with Hobbes, seeks not universal truth, but a '*modus vivendi*', a working or temporary compromise among competing interests that produces peace. As Gray understands it,

> *modus vivendi* is liberal toleration adapted to the historical fact of pluralism. The ethical theory underpinning *modus vivendi* is value-pluralism. The most fundamental value-pluralist claim is that there are many conflicting kinds of human flourishing, some of which cannot be compared in value. Among the many kinds of good lives that humans can live there are some that are neither better nor worse than one another, nor the same in worth, but incommensurably – that is to say, differently – valuable.[4]

According to Gray:

> The ideal of *modus vivendi* is not based on the vain hope that human beings will cease to make universal claims for their ways of life. It regards such claims with indifference – except where they endanger peaceful coexistence. In this, *modus vivendi* harks back to Thomas Hobbes. A Hobbesian state extends to private belief the radical tolerance of indifference. Hobbes is thereby the progenitor of a tradition of liberal thought in which *modus vivendi* is central.[5]

Furthermore, Gray insists, 'the pursuit of *modus vivendi* is not a quest for some kind of super value. It is a commitment to common institutions in which the claims of rival values can be reconciled'.[6] Thus, he holds, the end of *modus vivendi* is 'reconciling conflicting goods'.[7]

Gray thus suggests a different route from pluralism to liberalism than that advocated by Berlin: those pursuing competing, incommensurable, values would seek a *modus vivendi* – a working compromise that tolerates everyone in the interests of peaceful coexistence. In this chapter I shall explore whether Hobbes's philosophy, including his analysis of public reason, can provide the basis for the justification of liberal political principles and institutions in a world in which the private use of reason leads to different, and incompatible, judgments. Section 3.1 examines Gray's version of Hobbesian-inspired liberalism; section 3.2 analyzes a more genuinely Hobbesian account of public reason recently offered by David Gauthier, while section 3.3 considers Michael Ridge's proposed revision of Gauthier's theory.

The idea of a modus vivendi

A *modus vivendi* is a type of compromise; it supposes that parties have partially conflicting and partially complementary interests or goals. If the interests and goals of the parties were totally opposed, compromise would not occur. Compromise is impossible if the *most* Party A is prepared to offer is *less* then the minimum Party B is prepared to accept. Consider, for example, the simple case of negotiations between Alf-the-seller and Betty-the buyer over whether Betty is to purchase a commodity from Alf. As the seller, Alf has a minimum that he will accept, call it Alf's minimum. Betty as the potential buyer has a maximum that she will pay, call it Betty's maximum. Now unless Betty's maximum is greater than or equal to (≥) Alf's minimum, there will be no agreement. If Betty's maximum offer is less than the minimum that Alf will accept, no compromise is possible. We can, then, define the range of possible compromises as X, where Betty's maximum ≥ X ≥ Alf's minimum. The conflict between Alf and Betty is over where in the X range agreement will occur; as the seller Alf would like it to occur at Betty's maximum offer, as the buyer, Betty would like agreement at Alf's minimum. Although anywhere in the range of X both parties benefit from an agreement, at one extreme the buyer gets the minimal benefit (if she had to pay any more she would walk away from the agreement), while at the other the seller's gets the least he will tolerate from the bargain (any less and he would rather not sell).

Traditionally, the notion of a *modus vivendi* is used in international affairs to describe a treaty resulting from a compromise between different states.[8] Given their conflict, and the fact that neither can secure its most preferred outcome, the states agree to a compromise that gives each at least its minimum. Exactly what the compromise will be – how close each party gets to its maximum or to its minimum – depends on their relative power and bargaining position. Thus *modus vivendi* can be seen a compromise that reflects the relative power of the parties; as long as their power and bargaining position is unchanged, it suits both parties to accept the compromise. Hence a *modus vivendi* is typically seen as a temporary compromise, since change in the relative power of the parties is apt to lead to a revision of the agreement.

It has been said that, at least initially (in the sixteenth century), tolerance between Catholics and Protestants in Europe constituted a *modus vivendi*.[9] Each religion initially held that the best option was to root out the other, but during the course of the religious wars it became clear that in many places this was impossible. Whereas initially the minimum position of each was that the other be repressed (and so no compromise was possible), eventually Catholics came to accept that an acceptable minimum was that they tolerate Protestants if Protestants tolerated Catholics (and, so too, with Protestants). But so long as this was a *modus vivendi* – a compromise that arose out of the inability of each to secure its preferred option of repressing the others – each party would abandon the compromise if their power rose to the point where they could achieve their preferred option, or an arrangement that was closer to it.

In sum, it seems that we can say that agreement X is a *modus vivendi* between agents A and B if and only if:

1   X promotes the interests, values, goals, etc. of both A and B;
2   X gives neither A nor B everything they would like;
3   The distribution of the gains of the compromise (how close X is to A or B's maximum reasonable expectation) crucially depends on the relative power of A and B;
4   For both A and B, the continued conformity by each to X depends on its continued evaluation that X is the best deal it can get, or at least that the effort to get a better deal is not worth the costs.

Conditions (1) and (2) follow from the idea of a compromise: if X is not in the interests of each, it will not be the object of rational agreement. If one or both parties get everything they wish, then the agreement is not a mutual compromise. Condition (3) points to the root of the *modus vivendi*: neither party has sufficient power to impose its most preferred solution. How close each gets to its most preferred solution depends to a large extent on its relative power. If A is strong and B is weak, X will tend to be closer to A's reasonable maximum expectation than to B's. Lastly, condition (4) reflects the idea that a *modus vivendi* is not a binding contract that each agent will respect regardless of future developments: the continued respect for X depends on the continuing evaluation of each that X is something like the best deal it can get in the circumstances. The parties accept X 'on strictly strategic grounds'.[10] As has been observed, according to a liberal *modus vivendi*, 'Groups with different views agree to live and let live, but with the tacit proviso that their agreement will last only as long as the balance of power between them remains the same. Such an agreement is morally superficial; if the balance of power shifts, the dominant group is likely to attempt to renew conflict with its now weaker opponents'.[11]

A modus vivendi *interpretation of Hobbes's theory*

A common interpretation of Hobbes's theory is that it presents a general theory of politics based on *modus vivendi* resolutions of conflicts. According to Hobbes:

> Nature hath made men so equal in the faculties of body and mind as that, though there be found one man sometimes manifestly stronger in body or of quicker mind than another, yet when all is reckoned together the difference between man and man is not so considerable as that one man can thereupon claim to himself any benefit to which another may not pretend as well as he.

> For as to the strength of body, the weakest has strength enough to kill the strongest, either by secret machination or by confederacy with others that are in the same danger with himself.[12]

Consequently, 'From this equality of ability ariseth equality of hope in the attaining of our ends. And therefore if any two men desire the same thing, which nevertheless they cannot both enjoy, they become enemies; and in the way to their end (which is principally their own conservation, and sometimes their delectation only) endeavor to destroy or subdue one another.'[13] Thus our equality gives rise both to our competition and our fear of each other. Now, Hobbes argues, 'it is manifest that during the time men live without a common power to keep them all in awe, they are in that condition which is called war; and such a war as is of every man against every man'.[14]

> Whatsoever therefore is consequent to a time of war, where every man is enemy to every man, the same consequent to the time wherein men live without other security than what their own strength and their own invention shall furnish them withal. In such condition there is no place for industry, because the fruit thereof is uncertain: and consequently no culture of the earth; no navigation, nor use of the commodities that may be imported by sea; no commodious building; no instruments of moving and removing such things as require much force; no knowledge of the face of the earth; no account of time; no arts; no letters; no society; and which is worst of all, continual fear, and danger of violent death; and the life of man, solitary, poor, nasty, brutish, and short.[15]

This last claim is important; not only, Hobbes argues, would we be in a state of war, but an utterly miserable unwinnable war, which every rational person would see as inferior to peace. Thus, while each of us would prefer to win the war, we would all prefer what Gray calls 'toleration' (i.e., peace) to continued war.

It thus seems that rational Hobbesian agents would see that everyone benefits from calling off the war of each against all.[16] Gray does not think that compromise is in any way the right thing to do, or a morally ideal solution. *Modus vivendi*, he tells us, 'does not preach compromise as an ideal for all to follow'.[17] Rather, he seems to be arguing, each seeks his or her own ideals, but the reality of conflict leads to 'a commitment to common institutions in which the claims of rival values can be reconciled'.[18]

Does a 'Hobbesian' modus vivendi *analysis endorse Gray's pluralist vision?*

Gray presents a vision of a pluralist post-Enlightenment world, in which 'liberal states … live with non-liberal states, liberal culture forms with non-liberal culture forms, in peace and harmony'.[19] Liberal states, he tells us, must adopt 'a willingness to share the earth with radically different cultures'.[20] In contrast to Enlightenment liberalism, '[t]he animating project of pluralism is that different cultures should dwell on the earth in peace, without renouncing their differences'.[21] Does Hobbes's theory provide reasons to think that such a world will result from a *modus vivendi*?

Important to Hobbes's argument is the claim that every rational person – or at least, almost every rational person – would see that a compromise is better than continued war. If many prefer war, then any *modus vivendi* that arises will be local, between a few combatants, but it will not be a general solution to the state of war. According to the Hobbesian account, individuals who find themselves in intractable conflict will agree to political institutions that allow them to manage this conflict and so live in peace. Let us try to be clear about just what premises are required to reach the conclusion. The classic version, derived from Hobbes's, runs thus:

1   Individuals put highest value on their lives and personal safety;
2   Individuals (at least generally) seek their own interests;
3   In situations of anarchy – situations unstructured by any enforced laws – individuals, each seeking their own interest, will find themselves in conflict over resources, including each other's bodies and lives;
4   This clash of interests produces a constant potential for violence and often actual violence;
5   No individual can rationally expect to win this war or be immune from violence;
6   Therefore: Individuals will consent to a workable compromise in which all their interests are reasonably protected, and their lives are secure.

Fundamental to Hobbes's argument are the first and fifth premises, that each cares most for her own preservation and that no one can expect to win the conflict – these are what impel the combatants to compromise their conflicting claims so as to get along. Remember, according to the *modus vivendi* account, each would prefer a different outcome – to get all she wants – but each settles for a *modus vivendi* because the prospect of continued conflict is too terrible to contemplate. In the first part of *Leviathan* Hobbes develops a detailed psychological doctrine to support the first premise (that each cares most about self-preservation), and the account of conflict in the state of nature is intended to establish the fifth.

A problem confronting Gray's reliance on Hobbes is that the latter's psychology, and his claim that people place paramount value on self-preservation, seem inconsistent with radical pluralism: it excludes some values and ways of life. Although this is not a problem for Hobbes (who was not a radical pluralist), it should be a worry for a pluralist. As Berlin recognized, the Romantic tradition has disdained placing continued existence above other values (and they have rejected the Hobbesian supposition that the strong cannot defeat the weak). In his review of German eighteenth-century 'Storm and Stress' (*Strum und Drang*) Romantic drama, Berlin observes:

> the substance of all these plays is that there is some kind of insoluble conflict in the world, in nature itself, as a result of which the strong cannot live with the weak, the lions cannot live with the lambs. The strong must have room to breathe, and the weak go to the wall; if the weak suffer, they will naturally resist, and it is right that they should resist, and it is right that the strong should repress them. Therefore conflict, collision, tragedy, death, – all kinds of horrors – are inevitably involved in the nature of the universe.[22]

A *modus vivendi* will be the rational solution to a conflict only when the parties (1) believe that they cannot win without incurring unacceptable costs and (2) a compromise is less costly than continued conflict. Value systems that put a premium on safety of life and limb are more likely to reach such a compromise than are idealistic, assertive, ways of life. For all of Gray's stress on the plurality and tragedy of incommensurable values, underlying his own account is an assumption of what might be called the bourgeois value at the heart of Hobbes's theory – the reasonable person is one who compromises rather than fights.

There is, then, a worry that Gray too quickly takes over Hobbesian conclusions without reflecting on whether the premises of Hobbes's argument are consistent with broader pluralist commitments. However, even if we waive that worry, it still is unclear whether Hobbes's analysis leads to a world order in which different states and nations reach a *modus vivendi*, living in 'peace and harmony'. Gray focuses his *modus vivendi* analysis not – as does our 'Hobbesian' argument – on a *modus vivendi* among individuals, but on one between cultures, states or nations. But Hobbes himself is explicit that his argument for the rational necessity of abandoning war does not apply to war between states. Hobbes observes:

> But though there had never been any time wherein particular men were in a condition of war one against another, yet in all times kings and persons of sovereign authority, because of their independency, are in continual jealousies, and in the state and posture of gladiators, having their weapons pointing, and their eyes fixed on one another; that is, their forts, garrisons, and guns upon the frontiers of their kingdoms, and continual spies upon their neighbours, which is a posture of war. *But because they uphold thereby the industry of their subjects, there does not follow from it that misery which accompanies the liberty of particular men.*[23]

The Hobbesian argument thus does not endorse Gray's pluralist world vision. States *are* perpetually in what Hobbes called a state of war – constant distrust and preparation for conflict that at any time may result in actual conflict. 'For war consisteth not in battle only, or the act of fighting, but in a tract of time, wherein the will to contend by battle is sufficiently known'.[24] The resort of war is always in the background; as Carl von

Clausewitz insisted, 'war is a mere continuation of policy by other means'.[25] Even if states arrive at *modus vivendi* over some issue (say, a border dispute), because the compromise is based simply on the relative power of each party, it is constantly open to challenge and renegotiation in the face of shifting power. It is unlikely in the extreme that such a simple *modus vivendi* will yield, as Gray thinks, a set of universal human rights 'as a set of minimum standards for peaceful coexistence among regimes'.[26] And should states achieve a *modus vivendi* it is hard to see why, if they are simply interested in peaceful coexistence among themselves, they would interfere in each other's internal affairs by insisting on minimum standards of human rights.

Why Hobbes is not a proponent of modus vivendi

We have seen (1) that as a pluralist, it is dubious whether Gray can take over Hobbes's argument, which relies on certain 'bourgeois' values and (2) even if he does take it over, it does not support his pluralist world vision. But these problems pale beside the third: Hobbes simply does not think that peace can be based on a *modus vivendi*. Indeed, his whole theory is aimed at showing why a *modus vivendi* is unworkable as a solution to the problem of conflict. To see why, let us suppose that rational individuals pursuing their self-interest agree to embrace rules that require and promote peaceful coexistence and toleration. Hobbes himself identified such rules, which he called 'The Laws of Nature'. These Laws of Nature 'suggesteth convenient articles of peace upon which men may be drawn to agreement'.[27] Hobbes believes that reason reveals nineteen laws of nature, including 'that a man be willing, when others are so too ... to be contented with so much liberty against other men as he would allow other men against himself', that you exhibit gratitude to those who have benefited you, that each accommodates himself to others, and that no one seeks any right he will not grant to others. Now one might think that if rational individuals accept this set of rules (which are 'dictates of reason' that instruct us how to preserve ourselves) they would achieve a *modus vivendi*. Each person, employing her own reasoning, would see that a compromise, in which each lives according to these rules, would be better than a war in which each breaks them in hopes of seeking to gain advantage for herself. Not so. Hobbes points to two critical problems. First, so long as the agreement is a *modus vivendi*, each will constantly be using her own reason – Hobbes calls this 'natural reason' – to reevaluate the agreement in light of shifting power relations. Thus any agreement would be wrecked by the ever-present knowledge that one's competitors will pull out of the agreement as soon as doing so is to their advantage. This much is common observation. Second, and less obviously, Hobbes insists that though men be never so willing to observe these laws, there may nevertheless arise questions concerning a man's action; first, whether it were done; secondly, if done, whether against the law, or not against the law; the former whereof is called a question of fact, the latter a question of right'.[28]

> All laws, written and unwritten, have need of interpretation. The unwritten law of nature, though it be easy to such as without partiality and passion make use of their natural reason, and therefore leaves the violators thereof without excuse; yet considering there be very few, perhaps none, that in some cases are not blinded by self-love, or some other passion, it is now become of all laws the most obscure, and has consequently the greatest need of able interpreters.[29]

When we employ our 'private reason' there is, says Hobbes, great dispute about the laws – both the Laws of Nature and civil laws.[30] Thus Hobbes insists that the only solution is to institute a sovereign who provides public reasoning, a definitive interpretation of the law. As Hobbes says 'unless the parties to the question covenant mutually to stand to the sentence of another, they are as far from peace as ever'.[31]

Hobbes's important proposal, that we institute a sovereign who provides us with public reasons that override our private reasons, will be the focus of this and the next chapter. For now, however, note how it undermines Gray's interpretation of Hobbes as advocating a *modus vivendi* between conflicting parties. As long as each party employs his private reason to determine what is required by the *modus vivendi* – the Laws of Nature – we are, Hobbes insists, 'as far from peace as ever'. It is not enough to see that a compromise is in our mutual self-interest, for our self-interest will constantly lead us to interpret differently what is required by the compromise. Thus any such arrangement will, on Hobbes's view, degenerate into accusations and counter-accusations of bad faith, duplicity and unfair advantage taking. That is why Hobbes insists that only the institution of a sovereign, who can provide a public, definitive, interpretation, of the laws can bring about an end to war.

We can now appreciate how wrong Gray is to proclaim that a 'Hobbesian state extends to private belief the radical tolerance of indifference'.[32] The whole point of Hobbes's doctrine is the danger of the private use of reason. As a contemporary Hobbes scholar has observed:

> The fundamental problem of human life in a community, according to Hobbes, is that people have different ideas and plans and come into conflict. The central idea involved here is *disagreement*. People have different ideas about what is valuable or what is reasonable, and therefore, different ideas about what natural law requires or allows. Hobbes is clear about this: 'If every man were allowed the liberty of following his conscience, in such differences of consciences, they would not live together in peace an hour'.[33]

So long as each acts on his private reason this problem cannot be solved. Thus, so far from being 'indifferent' and 'tolerant' of private belief, Hobbes insists that:

it is annexed to the sovereignty to be judge of what opinions and doctrines are averse, and what conducing to peace; and consequently, on what occasions, how far, and what men are to be trusted withal in speaking to multitudes of people; and who shall examine the doctrines of all books before they be published. For the actions of men proceed from their opinions, and in the well governing of opinions consisteth the well governing of men's actions in order to their peace and concord.[34]

Why Gray is not a proponent of modus vivendi

I have maintained, first, that insofar as we interpret Hobbes as advocating a *modus vivendi*, his analysis does support Gray's vision and, secondly, Hobbes does not advocate a *modus vivendi* solution to the problem of disagreement and conflict. I shall now maintain that, surprisingly, despite his repeated proclamations of his devotion to *modus vivendi*, Gray does not construct his pluralist political theory on it.

If Gray's theory was genuinely based on a *modus vivendi* it would have to advocate political norms just because they do, or could, manifest an equilibrium of competing views or interests. And to be sure Gray does indeed sometimes maintain that universal human rights are a 'set of minimum standards for peaceful coexistence among regimes that will always remain different'.[35] He describes these standards in more detail:

> The requirements of legitimacy that all contemporary regimes should meet are not free-standing rights of recent liberal orthodoxy. They are enforceable conventions, framed to give protections to human interests that make any kind of worthwhile life impossible. A regime is illegitimate to the extent that its survival depends upon systematic injury to a wide range of these interests.
>
> Regimes in which genocide is practiced, or torture institutionalized, that *depend for the continuing existence on the suppression of minorities, or of the majority, which humiliate their citizens or those who coexist with them in society, which sanction religious persecution, which fail to meet basic human needs in circumstances where it is practically feasible or which render impossible the search for peace among different ways of life* – such regimes are obstacles to the well being of those whom they govern.[36]

Our analysis of Berlin's liberalism (see section 2.4) is relevant here: such a list of essential human interests – the violation of which Gray calls 'the worst universal evils'[37] – cannot be derived from pluralism; many longstanding human values are inconsistent with the protection of such interests, such as Romantic self-assertion, religious unity, highly competitive societies that do not insure that all needs are met, and so on. This list of evils does not arise from a *modus vivendi* – at most, we would get noninterference among certain sorts of regimes – but from Gray's conviction that these are objective, universal, evils. These evils, he tells us, are attacks on 'generically human interests, injury to which is an obstacle to any kind of worthwhile human life'.[38] Alternatively, Gray tells us that these interests are necessary for humans to 'thrive'.[39] The objective moral evil of attacking these interests thus identifies the limits of pluralism and any possible *modus vivendi* – in Berlin's terms, they constitute the common moral horizon.

Gray's argument that these interests identify an objective, non-liberal, criterion of legitimacy requires establishing two key claims. He must show (1) that the protection of these interests is possible outside of liberal regimes and (2) that these interests are commensurable – and are to be ranked above – other human values. The first claim is necessary if Gray's view is not to collapse into liberalism; the second is required if pluralism is not to undermine Gray's version of the common human horizon. Let us consider each claim.

(1) Although Gray devotes great effort to showing that these requirements do not add up to liberalism, this is hardly obvious. The requirement that neither the majority nor minority be oppressed seems to lead to a robust regime of equal rights and the doctrine of equality before the law and the rule of law – all basic parts of liberal political theory. The additional requirements of religious toleration and that, if feasible, basic human needs are met, point again to the contemporary liberal welfare state. It is certainly plausible to conclude that Gray's general argument (though not his specific comments) point to the modern, multicultural, welfare state as his ideal. Whether these requirements are less demanding, more demanding, or perhaps even inconsistent with, liberalism is simply unclear.

(2) Even if we grant Gray his non-liberal claim, his implicit commensurability claim is doubtful. In the course of history many have found appealing the values of personal self-assertion (even if this leads to oppressing others); national self-assertion (even if this leads to oppressing other nations); fighting for one's values (even if this decreases the possibility of international peace); religious unity (even if this means religious persecution); a meritocratic society in which the able get what they deserve and incompetent lose out (even if this means that the basic needs of the incompetent are not met); a society of great artistic or intellectual achievement (even if this means that resources are spent on these achievements that could have gone to meeting the basic needs of citizens). Those devoted to these values will deny Gray's claim that his universal values are to be ranked higher; they will insist that incommensurability applies here too.

Gray insists that Romantics such as Friedrich Nietzsche are simply wrong to reject these universals.[40] Gray's account of how we come to know what values are objective is very much like Berlin's; in some way an empirical study of human nature and human societies reveals the range of genuine modes of human flourishing. We already have examined this idea (see section 2.2) and need not dwell on it again. It is worth stressing, though, that if the study of history and anthropology shows that all acceptable ways of living accord priority to these fundamental interests in human flourishing, Gray seems committed to dismissing, as outside object-ively valuable human experience, the opposing inegalitarian, aggressive and self-assertive values of the Romantics. Oddly, however, these are the theorists who have apparently taught us the truth of value pluralism.[41] While accepting their message about the incommensurability of values, their own values are held to be objectively inferior to others!

Whether or not we endorse Gray's view of objective value rankings, insofar as Gray can identify criteria of political legitimacy, it is because he does, after all, believe that common human reason reveals the principles of political right. It is not pluralism or *modus vivendi* that justifies these principles. Like Berlin, political justification begins when pluralism runs out. For those more deeply inspired by the Romantics – who believe that there are no limits to the incommensurability of values – Gray's view will be seen as a reassertion of the Enlightenment View's conviction that, while human reasoning can sometimes lead us to disagree, its free exer-cise produces convergence on the objective, universal, principles of politi-cal legitimacy. Gray's main claim to be a post-Enlightenment political theorist, then, is in stressing that common human reason will not get us as far as many Enlightenment figures believed, though, as I pointed out, he does seem to come close to justifying a multicultural welfare state.

We must conclude, then, that Gray is unsuccessful in solving the problem posed by pluralism and reasonable disagreement about values. His initial proposal was insightful, and different from Berlin's: Hobbes shows how political order might rest on a compromise, or equilibrium, between com-peting views and interests. If so, we can accommodate irreconcilable differ-ences of private reasoning without appeal to any overall public, shared, reasoning about what we should do. But Hobbes himself rejects this: only a definitive interpreter of public reason can solve the conflict of the state of nature. In the end, Gray holds that our shared reason does lead us to com-mon objective principles of political legitimacy. Ultimately, and despite his own pluralistic commitments, Gray appeals to something akin to the Enlightenment View: our common reason shows us that human flourishing is a regulative human value that gives rise to our objective knowledge of evils that no legitimate political society can tolerate.

3.2 Hobbesian public reason

Hobbes on reason and conflict, again

David Gauthier recently has advanced a reconstruction of Hobbes's account of public reason that provides the basis for a conception of the legal order as expressing public reason. Gauthier distinguishes our capacity to act for reasons from our capacity to assess the adequacy of those reasons, which he calls *rationality*.[42] The first, our capacity to act for reasons, is our ability to be motivated by our representations of the world as it is, or as it might be. This capacity, Gauthier insists, is distinct from our ability to assess these representations, and whether one's actions 'fit' these representations – whether a person's actions adequately cohere with what she takes her reasons to be. Now, Gauthier maintains, Hobbes recognized that our rationality is fallible: 'no one man's reason, nor the reason of any one number of men, makes the certainty'.[43] Rational people aim at what Hobbes calls 'right reason' – rationality – which reveals the truth. However, because our rationality is fallible, we often disagree about what is right reason; the private use of our reason leads to conflict. Although in such controversies each person claims that the use of her own private reason is 'right reason', such claims simply exacerbate the conflict:

> when men that think themselves wiser than all others clamour and demand right reason for judge, yet seek no more but that things should be determined by no other men's reason but their own, it is ... intolerable in the society of men .... For they do nothing else, that will have every of their passions, as it comes to bear sway in them, to be taken for right reason, and that in their own controversies: bewraying [sic] their want of right reason by the claim they lay to it.[44]

Someone who insists that *her* reason is right reason, and so *her* reason should determine the resolutions to disputes, is not only a danger to society, but because she sees 'every passion' of hers as an expression of 'right reason', she is herself *irrational*: she demonstrates want of right reason by the claim she lays to it.

Gauthier observes that in this passage Hobbes points to two different failures of rationality when a person insists that her private reason is necessarily right reason. By confusing her passions with reason, she ignores what Gauthier calls the 'autonomy' of reason: she abandons control of her actions to passions, forsaking reason. However, Gauthier adds

> Hobbes's real concern in this passage ... is surely with interpersonality rather than autonomy. Rationality frees us, not only from dependence on our passions, but, perhaps more remarkably, from dependence on our own considered judgments, in contexts in which that dependence is disadvantageous to us. In this respect, rationality is, as it were, the remedy for its own defects.[45]

Gauthier directly focuses on our concern in this book: can reason itself solve its own limitation? The limitation of the private use of reason is that we disagree on what is right and true, thus engendering disagreement and conflict. Now, says Gauthier, Hobbes suggests an interesting solution. Using our reason, we can see that it is irrational to insist that our own reasoning is equivalent to right reason in these contexts. 'If each demands that his own reason be taken for right reason, then Hobbes's war of every man against every man must result – and this is "intolerable in the society of men"'.[46]

The sovereign as the voice of public reason

Hobbes concludes that, because of the divergence of our private reasoning, and the irrationality of insisting that one's own reason is identical to right reason, 'when there is a controversy in an account, the parties must by their own accord set up for right reason the reason of some arbitrator, or judge, to whose sentence they will both stand'.[47] We can see how far we have traveled from the *modus vivendi* account. Instituting an arbitrator – the ultimate of whom is the sovereign – is not a mere convenient equilibrium of self-interest. It is a requirement of our rationality that each abandons the use of her own private reason in these contexts, and instead authorize an arbitrator whose reason is then accepted as 'right reason'. Thus, Gauthier maintains, 'on Hobbes's account, the individual mode of deliberation, in which each person judges for herself what she has reason to do, is *supplanted* by a collective mode, in which one person judges what we all have reason to do'.[48] Hobbes's social contract in no mere *modus vivendi* of self-interest: individuals give up the right to be guided by their own private reasoning and authorize another to determine what is right reason. Hobbes seeks to do away with the independence of judgment necessary for the fourth trait of a *modus vivendi* (see section 3.1). The reasoning of the sovereign, as articulated in the laws, '*is to every subject those rules which the Commonwealth hath commanded him, by word, writing, or other sufficient sign of the will, to make use of for the distinction of right and wrong*'.[49] The law does not simply instruct us what to *do* – it is the voice of public reason, which we have authorized, about what right reason instructs as right and wrong.

The crucial difference between Hobbes's original version of the argument and Gauthier's recent account concerns the scope of public reason. Hobbes insisted on the need for an unlimited authorization: whatever the sovereign says is public reason is public reason. Hobbes believed that such a sweeping authorization was necessary to avoid unraveling the appeal to public reason; sometimes this is called the 'regress' argument. To see the idea, suppose that there is some limit on public authority. Call the range of disputes for which the sovereign's reason supplants private reason R; within R the sovereign's reason determines right reason, but in any disputes outside R, the sovereign's reason is not definitive. There are two interesting possibilities about what happens outside of R: either (1) there is some other authority that decides those disputes, or (2) individuals are left to their private reasoning. But neither of these options seem acceptable.

Consider the latter. Outside of R, individuals act on their private reasons. Presumably, then, outside of R individuals continue to insist that their private reason is equivalent to right reason, since they act on it and, in situations of conflict, each seeks to induce others to follow her reasoning. But this seems irrational insofar as once again the individual is ignoring the *interpersonal* dimension of rationality. Once again, each is insisting that 'things should be determined by no other men's reason but their own'. It might be argued, in reply, that in some areas of social life it is not 'intolerable in the society of men' for each to claim that everyone should be determined by his own reason. For example, perhaps in disputes about the best pizzas, society can tolerate this. But this reply simply pushes the dispute up a level: we will have disputes about when social life is consistent with determination by private reason and when it is intolerable in society. In essence, we would have disputes about the contours of range R, over which the sovereign's reason is authoritative. But surely, over this issue each cannot be rationally guided by his own reason. For suppose on some issue the sovereign proclaims a law; according to public reason, he says, X is right reason. But you claim that X is outside R, the range of disputes that the sovereign is authorized to decide. Thus you place yourself into a conflict with the sovereign; it is your private reason against his. But this seems precisely the sort of dispute that worries Hobbes. If you set yourself up in opposition to the government, and insist that you shall be guided by your private reason, there will arise disputes, controversies, and at last war. Thus, any time that you dispute the sovereign's claim that he is acting within the range of legitimate disputes, this ipso facto is precisely the sort of dispute in which the clash of reason endangers society, and so it is irrational to insist that your reason is right reason. On this view, then, no limits can be placed on the sovereign's authority: 'he is judge of what is necessary for peace; and judge of doctrines: he is sole legislator; and supreme judge of controversies'.[50]

Hobbes is (famously) insistent that the first option – that the area outside of R is under a different authority – is not only a recipe for continued war, but is absurd.[51] 'For', says Hobbes, 'that were to erect two sovereigns; and every man to have his person represented by two actors that, by opposing one another, must needs divide that power, which (if men will live in peace) is indivisible; and thereby reduce the multitude into the condition of war, contrary to the end for which all sovereignty is instituted'.[52] On this option we would have authorized two different arbitrators to determine right reason; and when they disagreed about their respective jurisdictions we would be committed to accepting two incompatible views as both right reason, which is absurd and, of course, contrary to peace, 'the end for which all sovereignty is instituted'.

It seems, then, that Hobbes's argument must endorse an unlimited authority of the public reason of the sovereign: if the sovereign says that X accords with right reason, then all subjects must take X as right reason. Importantly, however, Hobbes draws back from this view. As Gauthier stresses, Hobbes insists that the law – public reason – must be consistent with natural law and equity. Civil law interprets the laws of nature: 'Theft, murder, adultery, and all injuries, are forbid by the laws of nature; but what is to be called *theft*, what *murder*, what adultery, what an *injury* in a citizen, this is not to be determined by the natural, but by the civil law'.[53] Now, as Gauthier observes, 'introducing a constraint, whether equity or natural law, would seem to give the subject a basis for limiting the extent to which she accepts the subordination of her natural reason to the "right reason" of the sovereign'.[54] If the aim of the subjects is to secure a common interpretation of natural law – if, as Hobbes says, that is the intention of our submission – then it would appear that subjects would refuse to conform to the civil law when it gives wildly erroneous interpretations of natural law. Hobbes is clear that when 'our refusal to obey frustrates the end for which the sovereignty was ordained, then there is no liberty to refuse; *otherwise, there is*'.[55] So if the aim is to secure interpretations of the laws of nature, a sovereign who regularly and manifestly ignores the laws of nature frustrates 'the end for which the sovereignty was ordained' and so it would appear that we are free to disobey. The Hobbesian common-wealth is apparently infected with what Hobbes himself called the 'poison' of a seditious doctrine: '[t]hat every private man is judge of good and evil actions'.[56] Thus the charge made by John Bramhall, one of Hobbes's contemporaries that, so far from justifying unlimited authority of the sovereign, *Leviathan* is a 'rebel's catechism'.[57]

Gauthier, then, holds that the Hobbesian case points to a limited authoriza-tion: 'to take the reason of one individual or assembly as if it were right reason is to risk creating a monster'.[58]

> Each citizen has good reason, in terms of her own deliberative standard, to agree with her fellows to authorize a public person to judge and will in her name, *on those matters and in those respects that significantly affect the interactions of the citizens and the public goods available to them* …. Each citizen through her authorization agrees to treat the judgments and will of the public person in these areas as if they exhibited right reason, and in this way public reason is established.[59]

Gauthier maintains that 'each sets, and must set, limits on the scope of the public person's authority'.[60] Subjects would thus retain 'the right to recon-sider their authorization, should they find their wishes and expectations betrayed. But so long as they lack reason to reconsider, they are subject, in their deliberations as much as in their actions, to the judgments and will of the public person'.[61]

Public reason from natural reason: the Hobbesian dilemma

It has been said that 'the most distinctive feature of Hobbesian accounts is their attempt to derive a conception of public reason from a conception of natural reason'.[62] The fundamental idea is that an individual, Betty, employing her own private reason, comes to the conclusion that in some circumstances, if everyone, including Betty, relies on their private reasoning, it will be disadvantageous to Betty's individual goals. This, it must be stressed, is itself the conclusion of Betty's natural or private reasoning; at this point in the analysis there is nothing but private reasoning. This conclusion leads Betty to the view that she and others need to construct a public reason, which, in these circumstances, everyone will follow and so will advance their individual goals. Within limits, this public reason, as Gauthier says, will 'supplant' the 'individual reason of each citizen'.[63] Hobbes, we have seen, insists that setting any limit on public reason unravels the account by throwing people back on their private reason; Gauthier argues that Hobbes is wrong to endorse an unlimited authorization, and indeed even Hobbes is driven to place some limits on the authorization. The problem is that both are right: any limitation does unravel the account, and some limitation is inherent in the account. The account is thus inherently paradoxical.

To see why this is so, recall that a presupposition of the argument is that no compromise or discussion among merely private reasoners can solve the problem of conflict. That is why we began with the *modus vivendi* interpretation of Hobbes: if that was correct, no public reason is necessary. Hobbes and his followers insist that we cannot escape conflict as long as we rely on private or natural reasoning: we must construct a public reason in the form of the sovereign. However, as Hobbes recognized, any limitation on the proper scope of public reason requires that subjects employ their natural reason to determine whether the sovereign has exceeded his authority. But this throws individuals back on their private reason.[64] If the very problem of political life is that reliance on private reasoning causes conflict, then any solution that limits the realm of public reason that at some point throws people back on the private reason is objectionable. Moreover, as Hobbes recognized, setting limits inevitably leads citizens to employ their private reason against the sovereign; the sovereign will insist that this matter falls within the sphere in which his reason supplants the private reasoning of citizens while the citizen will insist that it is outside of the scope of public reason. But this means that private reasoning is always in control, for in any given individual, it determines whether that individual will conclude that the issue under discussion is within the range of private or public reason. Private reason, we might say, always monitors the situation. But recall that private reason is partial, and through it the individual seeks to pursue her own goals. That means that when private reason monitors the situation, it will not seek simply an impartial or correct determination of whether the current dispute falls within the proper scope of public reason. Private reason will consult the individual's goals, and ask 'will my goals be advanced by following public reason or going my own way?' But if that question is always being asked – remember that private reason must monitor the situation to make sure that public reason is not exceeding its authority – then rather than being supplanted, private reason will always be in control, and will be seeking the individual's advantage. But if all individuals do that, we are in exactly the situation we sought to avoid: conflict based on private reasoners each going their own way.

A Hobbesian might object that this is not a real problem. That sometimes people's private reasoning will lead them to disagree does not mean that private reasoning always leads to disagreement; indeed, Hobbes allows that sometimes natural reason speaks clearly about the content of the law of nature. So perhaps the situation is this: on some range of disputes R natural reason is ambiguous, so we need an arbitrator or sovereign to decide. But on the issue as to whether dispute X is inside or outside of R, people's exercise of natural reason leads them to agree. Thus, for example, it might be that people disagree whether the United States Constitution protects the right to abort, but they agree that the Supreme Court has the right to decide the issue. If this is the pattern of our disagreements, then Gauthier's restricted scope proposal is viable.

The problem, though, is that if (1) individuals are devoted to best pursuing their own goals and (2) they employ their natural reason to monitor whether they should dispute whether X is in R, they will not achieve this pattern of disputes. Assume we are in a situation in which my natural reason tells me that I can obtain an advantage by disputing whether X is in R. Perhaps I am an opponent of abortion, and I predict that if the Supreme Court decides the issue they will come down in favor of abortion rights. In this case, then, I will contest the Supreme Court's right to decide the issue, just because my goals will be advanced by doing so, and a person's private reason always tells him to best advance his goals. Gauthier sees the problem, and so requires that we entirely give up recourse to the dictates of our natural or private reason. But so long as there are limits to the scope of public reason, I must rely on my natural reason to police the limits. Natural reason, though, is not an impartial policing mechanism: it tells me to advance my goals the best way I can.

As Hobbes saw, the only way to avoid this problem would be for the individuals to grant unlimited authority to the sovereign: to allow public reason to police its own limits. But since the Hobbesian seeks to derive a commitment to public reason from private reason, no good Hobbesian could accept granting authority to public reason when it would harm her goals or interests to do so. It is private reason that creates public reason to accomplish its goals, and so it could never create a public reason that thwarts its goals. As Gauthier rightly says, people would not knowingly create a 'monster' as a means to protect themselves. Thus some limit on public reason's authority is intrinsic to the Hobbesian case, but those limits undermine public reason.

The Hobbesian argument – in both the original and Gauthier's new version – is inherently paradoxical.[65] Private reason sees that the only way to solve the problem of conflict is for it to be self-effacing – for it not to speak on some matters and instead defer to public reason. But it cannot be so self-effacing that it gives unlimited reign to public reason, and so it insists on policing the limits of public reason. But then we are, after all, consulting private reason to see if we can gain any advantage by declaring (if only quietly, to oneself) that some issue is outside the scope of public reason.

3.3 Substantive public reason as a solution to the Hobbesian paradox

Natural reasoning about public principles

Michael Ridge has offered a detailed and complex criticism of Hobbesian public reason in general, and Gauthier's in particular. The crux of Ridge's criticism is, as he says, that 'Hobbesian public reason puts the cart before the horse'.[66] The defining feature of Hobbesian public reason, Ridge argues, is that public reason is identified as the reasoning of a person or a group of persons; that is, the private reasoning of some person or group is equated with public reason.[67] Thus, X is a principle of public reason if and only if X is endorsed by the sovereign's private reason. Ridge contrasts this *procedural* to a *substantive* understanding of public reason, which identifies the principles of public reason not by where they came from, but by their content. On this alternative interpretation, people would accept some common rules or norms as defining genuine public reason. When people come into conflict, their commitment to public reason would require them to appeal to these norms in their disputes, as opposed to rules or norms that are endorsed only by their private reasoning.

> The important point is that the two partisans could not only discuss the case in light of the principles of public reason they accept, but they might also be able to resolve controversies about how those principles should be interpreted, or even revised, in terms of the conception [of public reason] itself, rather than being forced to fall back on their natural reason'.[68]

This last point is important. Suppose, Ridge says, people come to agree on a substantive list of moral and political principles that define public reason for their group. Now when they disagree about the principles, their disagreement is still about public reason. But this is puzzling. Basic to Hobbes's theory is his nineteen laws of nature, which are principles that we all can accept as substantive public reason. Hobbes recognizes such substantive reasons, but then insists that the task of interpreting them is a matter of employing our natural reason. It is the reasoning of individuals about what the public principles mean. And this seems right.

When I interpret a law or a principle, I employ my reason to give an account of it. I give my take on it. This is not to say that I do not restrict myself to relevant reasons; but the understanding of what is relevant, and the relative importance of different considerations, derive from my reasoning. The public reason is exhausted by the text of the law and supporting past interpretations, or the canonical statement of the principles. When our interpretations differ, we bring something additional into the debate: the results of our own reasoning about what these principles mean, their relative importance, and so on. This is the disagreement that sets the stage for Hobbesian political theory: the disagreement of private reasoners about the proper interpretation of public principles. (Recall here Kuhn's analysis of scientific disputes, discussed in section 1.2.)

Hobbes, it should be stressed, does not say that people always and necessarily disagree about these interpretations when they apply their natural reason. Recall that, according to Hobbes,

> The unwritten law of nature, though it be easy to such as without partiality and passion make use of their natural reason, and therefore leaves the violators thereof without excuse; yet considering there be very few, perhaps none, that in some cases are not blinded by self-love, or some other passion, it is now become of all laws the most obscure, and has consequently the greatest need of able interpreters.[69]

So the problem is that, as a matter of fact, given people's overriding concerns with their own goals, they are usually blinded by self-love or some other passion, and thus even the clearest of substantive laws that affect people's basic interests is in need of an interpreter. Hobbes, then, would reject Ridge's claim that our debates about the interpretation of laws can somehow be a matter entirely within 'public reason' that does not force people back onto their natural reason.

The regress argument applied to decision procedures

Hobbes, then, insists that the decisive objection against relying on substantive principles rather than a judge or sovereign (what Ridge calls a 'procedure') is that, for any substantive rule, individuals' private reasoning will typically lead them to disagree about its interpretation. A dispute between Alf and Betty about whether, say, this piece of property belongs to Alf or Betty, cannot reliably be resolved by a certain substantive rule of property, since Alf and Betty are apt to simply disagree about the proper interpretation of the rule of property. And, of course, this debate – about the proper interpretation of the proper rule of property – is unlikely to be resolved by, say, an appeal to a substantive conception of justice; Alf and Betty are at least as likely to simply disagree over *that*, or else advance competing interpretations as to what the conception of justice requires in this case. It thus seems that Alf and Betty are caught in a regress: every time they appeal to some general principle to resolve their dispute, they find themselves disagreeing about how to interpret that principle, and so on. Hobbes argues that only a sovereign can stop this regress of disagreement, calling a halt to the dispute once and for all.

The crux of the Hobbesian case for the primacy of an arbitrator as determining public reason (over substantive principles) is the greater scope for disagreement and dispute about rules than about decisions of the arbitrator. Now, Ridge objects, this case defeats itself since the sovereign must rely on rules to communicate his commands:

> The problem is that if rules and edicts are incapable of constraining their interpretations, then the phrasing of the application or interpretation of the rule and edicts will presumably do no better. Suppose that the original edict is X, and the interpretation takes the form, 'In circumstances C, rule X requires conduct A.' Since this interpretation of the original edict is not on the Hobbesian view self-interpreting, it would seem that we have gotten nowhere by having a sovereign with absolute authority around to issue and interpret edicts.[70]

Consequently, says Ridge, 'in assuming that the sovereign is genuinely capable of communicating with his subjects, he seems to be supposing that some edicts or commands (or, at least, some of his clarifications/ interpretations of those edicts or commands) are not particularly subject to competing interpretations'. If, though, this is true, Ridge argues, 'it is no longer obvious that we need a sovereign'.[71] That is, if the commands of the sovereign are not open to a regress of interpretation, then there is no reason to suppose that all substantive principles are open to such endless interpretative controversies.

If it is supposed that Hobbes's argument rests on the claim that all statements or all principles are equally open to diverse interpretations, Ridge's objection is decisive. But if a Hobbesian did hold such a doctrine it would follow that no one would be able to communicate with anyone else, since every statement would be ambiguous or indeterminate. Whether or not Hobbes was tempted by such a view, it certainly is not required for a plausible case for the superiority of an arbitrator over substantive principle. A reasonable Hobbesian would never insist that all types of statements and commands are open to the same degree of interpretative controversy. Commands that contain reference to specific people doing things are less open to interpretative difference than are statements of general rules and principles. The question is: for any given interpretative controversy over any statement, what are we to do? The logic of the Hobbesian arbitrator argument is to appeal to the decision of someone who resolves the interpretative controversy through a command that is *less open to interpretative controversy*. If there is still interpretative controversy at this level, then an arbitrator is again invoked, to decide the controversy through a judgment that is even less open to competing interpretations. Thus constitutions can interpret natural law, legislation can (and does) interpret constitutions, courts can (and do) interpret legislation. Courts ultimately issue specific verdicts, directing specific people to do specific things. While even court verdicts are open to dispute they are not open to the degree of controversy that are moral principles or even customary rules. Court verdicts usually are clear in instructing one party to perform, or abstain from, an action; they are much less clear about the rationale in substantive public reason for the decision – a clue about where the major ambiguity lies. When courts do issue ambiguous findings people may go back to court for a more fine-grained judgment, or within the very constrained limits of the ambiguity, the relevant parties may arrive at an agreement. The important point is that to say that the law is the voice of public reason is not to simply identify legislation as that voice, but the entire legal system, including judges, lawyers and the police.[72]

The core claim of the Hobbesian is that without an arbitrator, there is no tendency for disputes to be resolved through more specific directives. When faced with an interpretative controversy, those who share a substantive conception of public reason but who have no adjudicator are apt to find their controversies spinning out of control; in response to a challenge to my interpretation of a specific law, I appeal to constitutional principles (which are even more subject to controversy), and in response to my constitutional principles you appeal to natural law. Of course, in those cases where there is no controversy, we do not need an adjudicator. But it is no part of a reasonable Hobbesian case that adjudicators are needed for every dispute. The point is more fine-grained: controversies are common, and when they occur only a system of adjudication can direct the controversy 'down' to less controversial statements (i.e., court judgments).

Procedures, principles and Hobbesian public reason

The Hobbesian account of public reason is based on an important insight: not only do we disagree about what we are to do, but even rational consensus on substantive guides to action – such as Hobbes's laws of nature – cannot resolve the conflict. We require some sort of decision procedure or method of adjudication that brings our interpretative controversies down to a decision that resolves the conflict, and instructs us what to do. Ridge, of course, is right that public reason is substantive as well as procedural – after all, Hobbes thought that everyone's reason would converge on the laws of nature. Yet the Hobbesian insight is that substantive agreement is too thin and fragile to regulate day-to-day social life. Crucial to public reason is the authorization of a decision procedure to decide our disputes about what is to be done, even when our reasoning leads us to disagree on the merits of the case.

However, this point also shows the error of Hobbesian public reason. In order for us to resolve our disputes, we require only a publicly defined *decision procedure* that will resolve conflicts about what to *do*. This procedure may, *à la* Hobbes, be the deliberation of one person or it may be a rule by which a group decides what to do (e.g., majority voting, flipping a coin). But, as R.E. Ewin convincingly argues, to accomplish this practical goal does not require that we accept the decision procedure's outcome *as true*, only that it tells us all *what to do*.[73] As Vice President Gore stated in his concession speech after the 2000 American election, *he accepted the verdict of the Supreme Court, though he did not agree with it*. At least on one reading of Hobbes, this would not be enough: to accept the law as the voice of public reason requires accepting it as right reason. Gauthier is more careful, he only requires that we 'treat the judgments and will of the public person ... *as if* they exhibited right reason'.[74] This is still ambiguous;[75] we only need to treat their judgments as if they were right reason in the sense that we do as they instruct us, no matter how wrongheaded we believe them to be.

The standard Hobbesian view that we should accept the reasoning of the sovereign as right reason is unnecessary, and in any event implausible. It is *unnecessary* because, as Ewin shows, what a Hobbesian seeks is a resolution of our disputes, and that is about what we do, not what we think. There is no reason to give up more in the social contract than is necessary, and all that is necessary is to cede authority over one's actions, not beliefs. It is *implausible* because it supposes that one's *epistemic rationality* – what constitutes a rational belief – can be subordinated to *practical rationality* – the pursuit of aims. The crux of the Hobbesian argument is that we accept the sovereign's reasoning that X is true because believing that X is true will be advantageous to us. But we cannot think that something is true just because it would benefit us to think so. Bernard Williams suggests why this is so in discussing a case of a man whose son has, it seems, been drowned at sea, though he does not know this for certain:

> Somebody might say: if he wants to believe that his son is alive and this hypnotist can bring it about that he believes that his son is alive, then why should he not adopt the conscious project of going to the hypnotist and getting the hypnotist to make him believe this; then he will have got what he wants – after all, what he wants is to believe that his son is alive, and this is the state that the hypnotist will have produced in him. But there is one sense – I think the more plausible one – of 'he wants to believe that his son is alive' in which he means that he wants his son to be alive – what he essentially wants is the truth of his belief. This is what I call a truth-centred motive. The man with this sort of motive cannot conceivably consciously adopt this project, and we can immediately see that the project for him is incoherent. For what he wants is something about the world, something about his son, namely, that he be alive, and he knows perfectly well that no amount of drugs, hypnotism and so on applied to himself is going to bring that about.[76]

The father does not simply want to believe that his son is alive, he wants it to be the case that his son is alive, and that is why he wants to believe it. To believe it for some other reason – because it is a useful thing to believe – requires some sort of self-deception: the belief cannot serve its purpose unless the agent believes, or can at least assume, that it is epistemically rational – that the belief seeks in some way to track the truth, or the best evidence. For the father to say, 'I shall hire a hypnotist to make me believe my son is alive, though I shall remain aware that the belief is epistemically irrational' will not do the trick. He needs to convince himself that it *is* epistemically rational – that the belief is true. If he accepts that it is epistemically irrational to believe that his son is alive, he rationally cannot continue to hold it, however beneficial the consequences of doing so may be. And this, I think, is precisely because beliefs are essentially epistemic phenomena: unless they are epistemically well grounded, we cannot accept them into our system of beliefs. The overall rationality of a belief, then – whether or not it is to be included or excluded from one's belief system – turns on its epistemic rationality, our warrant for thinking it is justified.

If this is so, however, Hobbesians cannot agree to accept the sovereign's reason as right reason just because they would benefit from thinking he is right. They would have to believe that he is more likely to be correct or justified in his beliefs than they are. In that case, they would accept his reasoning on epistemic, not practical, grounds.

3.4 Summary

We began this chapter by examining John Gray's notion of *modus vivendi* liberalism, which he traced back to Hobbes. Gray, we saw, is in many ways a follower of Berlin – he also emphasizes the plural and incommensurable nature of values. Gray, however, suggests that a world of plural values can be ordered by a *modus vivendi* – an equilibrium of competing values and interests upholding a public and international order. I advanced three basic criticisms of Gray's proposal. First, it does not seem that a *modus vivendi* can provide a stable order based on respect for a core set of rights; the order of a *modus vivendi* is based on a shifting balance of power, and is not apt to be either stable or especially peaceful. Second, I argued that despite his avowals of endorsing *modus vivendi*, the heart of Gray's notion of political legitimacy depends on a common human conception of universal evils. Like Berlin, his understanding of a legitimate political order flows not from his pluralism, but from his understanding of the limits of pluralism. Third, it seems erroneous to depict Hobbes as a proponent of *modus vivendi*. At the core of Hobbes's theory is his recognition that the convergence of private judgments on a set of shared political principles (the 'laws on nature') is insufficient to yield peace. As long as we each reason privately, Hobbes believes, we will be in a state of war.

We then turned to David Gauthier's recent explication of Hobbesian public reason. Gauthier shows that, to solve the problem of the conflict of private reasoning, Hobbes advocates a social contract in which we authorize the sovereign to reason for us; his reasoning, as expressed in law, is the voice of public reason. And for Hobbes, rationality tells us to abandon our private reasoning and accept the sovereign's public reason as right reason. Gauthier seems attracted to a similar view. It is, he suggests, irrational to rely on one's private reasoning when this frustrates one's aims; reason is interpersonal, and it is irrational to insist that your own private reason is the same thing as right reason. Thus Gauthier appears to advocate a limited Hobbesian contract according to which, over a range of issues, we treat public authority's reason as if it were right reason.

We examined several criticisms of this view, including those of Michael Ridge. Two worries about it should be emphasized. First, authorizing the sovereign to reason for us seems unnecessary to solve the Hobbesian problem of conflict. If we accept Hobbes's depiction of the problem, we need to *do as the sovereign says*; it seems dubious indeed that the only way to do this is to *believe that what he instructs us to do is right*. Second, it seems impossible to consciously believe that the sovereign is right because it is useful to believe it. We believe things because we believe them to be true or well justified – belief is truth-centered. If so, we cannot accept the sovereign's reason as right reason just because it would serve our interests to do so, unless we somehow deceived ourselves – tricked ourselves into thinking that we followed his reason because it was right, when in fact we do so only because it is useful.

Notes

1   See Loren Lomasky, 'Liberal Obituary?', in Tibor Machan and Douglas B. Rasmussen, eds, *Liberty for the Twenty-First Century* (Lanham, MD: Rowman and Littlefield, 1995), pp. 243–258.
2   John Gray, *Two Faces of Liberalism* (Cambridge: Polity Press, 2000), p. 2.
3   John Rawls, *Political Liberalism*, paperback edn (New York: Columbia University Press, 1996), pp. xl, 36.
4   Gray, *Two Faces of Liberalism*, p. 6.
5   Ibid., p. 25.

6 Ibid.
7 Ibid.
8 I am drawing here on Rawls, *Political Liberalism*, p. 147.
9 See Steven D. Smith, 'The Restoration of Tolerance', *California Law Review*, vol. 78 (1990): 304–355, p. 335. See Rawls, *Political Liberalism*, p. 148.
10 See Frank I. Michelman 'Book Review Panel: *Odus Vivendi Postmodernus?* On Just Interpretations and the Thinning of Justice', *Cardozo Law Review*, vol. 21 (May 2000): 1945–1970, p. 1970.
11 George Klosko, 'Rawls's Argument From Political Stability', *Columbia Law Review*, vol. 94 (October 1994): 1882–1987, p. 1883. Cf. Rawls, *Political Liberalism*, p. 147.
12 Thomas Hobbes, *Leviathan*, Michael Oakeshott, ed. (Oxford: Basil Blackwell, 1948), p. 80 (Ch. 13).
13 Ibid., p. 81 (Ch. 13).
14 Ibid., p. 82 (Ch. 13).
15 Ibid.
16 See James Buchanan, *The Limits of Liberty* (Chicago: University of Chicago Press, 1975).
17 Gray, *Two Faces of Liberalism*, p. 25.
18 Ibid.
19 John Gray, *Enlightenment's Wake* (London: Routledge, 1995), p. 156.
20 Ibid., p. 180.
21 Ibid.
22 Isaiah Berlin, *The Roots of Romanticism* (Princeton: Princeton University Press, 1999), p. 56.
23 Hobbes, *Leviathan*, p. 83 (Ch. 13). Emphasis added.
24 Ibid., p. 82 (Ch. 13).
25 Karl von Clausewitz, *On War*, O.J. Matthijs Jolles, trans. (New York: Modern Library, 1943), p. 16 (Book I, Ch. 1).
26 Gray, *Two Faces of Liberalism*, p. 21.
27 Hobbes, *Leviathan*, p. 84 (Ch. 13).
28 Ibid., p. 102 (Ch. 15).
29 Ibid., p. 180 (Ch. 26).
30 Ibid., p. 176 (Ch. 26).
31 Ibid., p. 102 (Ch. 15).
32 Gray, *Two Faces of Liberalism*, p. 25.
33 R.E. Ewin, *Virtues and Rights: The Moral Philosophy of Thomas Hobbes* (Boulder, CO: Westview Press, 1991), p. 27. Citations omitted.
34 Hobbes, *Leviathan*, p. 116 (Ch. 18).
35 Gray, *Two Faces of Liberalism*, p. 21.
36 Ibid., p. 107. Emphasis added.
37 Ibid.
38 Ibid., p. 111.
39 Ibid., p. 21.
40 See, e.g., ibid., p. 66.
41 See John Gray, *Isaiah Berlin* (Princeton: Princeton University Press, 1996), Ch. 5.
42 David Gauthier, 'Public Reason', *Social Philosophy and Policy*, vol. 12 (Winter 1995): 19–42, pp. 19–20. Reprinted in Fred D'Agostino and Gerald F. Gaus, eds, *Public Reason* (Aldershot, UK: Ashgate, 1998), pp. 43–66.

43 Hobbes, *Leviathan*, p. 26 (Ch. 5).
44 Ibid.
45 Gauthier, 'Public Reason', p. 27.
46 Ibid., p. 27. This same point was made earlier, and in more detail, by Ewin in *Virtues and Rights*, Ch. 2.
47 Hobbes, *Leviathan*, p. 26 (Ch. 5).
48 Gauthier, 'Public Reason', p. 31. Emphasis in original.
49 Hobbes, *Leviathan*, p. 173 (Ch. 26). Emphasis in original.
50 Ibid., p. 130 (Ch. 20).
51 See here Jean Hampton, *Hobbes and the Social Contract Tradition* (Cambridge: Cambridge University Press, 1986), Ch. 4.
52 Hobbes, *Leviathan*, p. 122 (Ch. 19).
53 Thomas Hobbes, *De Cive* in Bernard Gert, ed., *Man and Citizen* (New York: Anchor Books, 1972), p. 185 (section VI.16). See Ewin, *Virtues and Rights*, pp. 149–150.
54 Gauthier, 'Public Reason', p. 35. Cf. Michael Ridge, 'Hobbesian Public Reason', *Ethics*, vol. 108 (April 1998): 538–568, p. 548.
55 Hobbes, *Leviathan*, p. 131 (Ch. 15). Emphasis added. See Gauthier, 'Public Reason', p. 35.
56 Hobbes, *Leviathan*, p. 211 (Ch. 29).
57 See Hampton, *Political Philosophy* (Boulder, CO: Westview Press, 1997), pp. 51–52; Hampton, *Hobbes and the Social Contract Tradition*, pp. 197ff.
58 Gauthier, 'Public Reason', p. 37.
59 Ibid. Emphasis in original.
60 Ibid.
61 Ibid.
62 Ridge, 'Hobbesian Public Reason', p. 540.
63 Gauthier, 'Public Reason', p. 38.
64 Ridge, 'Hobbesian Public Reason', p. 560.
65 See Gauthier, 'Public Reason', pp, 33ff; Ridge, 'Hobbesian Public Reason', pp. 546ff; Ewin, *Virtues and Rights*, Ch. 7; Hampton, *Political Philosophy*, pp. 49ff.
66 Ridge, 'Hobbesian Public Reason', p. 558.
67 Ibid., p. 561n.
68 Ibid., p. 564.
69 Hobbes, *Leviathan*, p. 180 (Ch. 26).
70 Ridge, 'Hobbesian Public Reason', p. 557.
71 Ibid.
72 As Randy Barnett stresses, lawyers are critical in helping to communicate public views about justice. *The Structure of Liberty: Justice and the Rule of Law* (Oxford: Clarendon Press, 1998).
73 Ewin, *Virtue and Rights*, p. 31.
74 Gauthier, 'Public Reason', p. 37. Emphasis added.
75 Ewin criticizes Gauthier for interpreting Hobbes as holding that truth is a matter of agreement. *Virtue and Rights*, p. 31.
76 Bernard Williams, 'Deciding to Believe' in his *Problems of the Self* (Cambridge: Cambridge University Press, 1973), p. 150. I have considered this problem more fully in 'The Rational, The Reasonable and Justification', *Journal of Political Philosophy*, vol. 3 (1995): 234–258, reprinted in D'Agostino and Gaus, *Public Reason*, Ch. 8.

4

Collective Reason: Deepening the Social Roots of Public Reason

CONTENTS

4.1 Freeing public reason from private reason

Let us pause to take stock of our inquiry thus far. Chapter 1 argued that, in the face of anthropological discoveries, developments in the philosophy of science, and pluralist accounts of values, the Enlightenment View – that the free use of human reason, which is a natural capacity of humans, leads to ever-increasing convergence on what is rational, true and morally right – struck many as dubious. This book is thus concerned with the search for a shared, public reason, on which to found public principles of political justice in a diverse society. Chapter 2 considered the possibility that, far from posing a challenge to public liberal principles, pluralism and the incommensurability of values is the foundation of the liberal view of politics: pluralism thus is not a problem for liberalism, but its main justificatory resource. However, our examination of the popular doctrine of liberal pluralism indicated that there is no clear path from pluralism to the justification of liberty or liberalism – or indeed any political principles. Although political theorists such as Isaiah Berlin adopt both pluralism and liberalism, the liberal part of the theory starts where the pluralist part ends: at the common human horizon.

Chapter 3 turned to John Gray's pluralism, according to which the ultimate plurality of values shows the wisdom of a Hobbesian *modus vivendi*. We saw that such a working compromise appears unable to provide a stable order based on respect for a core set of rights – a shifting balance of power is not apt to be either stable or especially peaceful. More generally, the concern in Chapter 3 was the Hobbesian proposal that we might circumvent the problems of relying on private reasons by identifying a public reason that is the reason of the sovereign, which becomes the reason of everyone. Hobbesians, we saw, endeavor to derive public reason from our natural, private, reason. But the problem is that, so long as public reason is limited, our natural reason decides the limits, and so ends up ruling our public reason; and there is no plausible way to derive an unlimited public reason from private reason.

The Hobbesian's problem is that, in the end, because public reason derives from natural or private reason, it is hard to see how public reason can ever be a restraint on private reason. Public reason is created by private reasoners as a means to achieve their private goals. If so, why would private reasoners conform to it when it impedes their private goals? As John Stuart Mill said, only a 'pedant' or a 'slave of his formulas' employs a means when he knows it does not produce the desired end.[1] What seems required is a conception of public reason that is freed from private reason – one that provides public reason with the independence to, at least sometimes, restrain private reason. This chapter considers several ways of doing this, ranging from more modest to more radical approaches. The modest approaches begin with the Hobbesian idea that, since strict reliance on private reasoning leads people into conflict, successful cooperation requires some public way of reasoning. Like the Hobbesian theories, the very idea of reason is split into private, individual, reasoning – which tells an *individual* how best to achieve *her* goals – and a distinct, social, reasoning – which tells *us* how *we* best achieve *our* goals. Public reason is then a sort of collective reasoning. The more radical approach does away with the very idea of private reasoning and sees all reasoning as social, collective, reasoning.

4.2 Public reason as cooperative reasoning

The prisoner's dilemma and private reasoning

As Hobbes showed, rational, self-interested people find themselves in intractable conflict; each relying on her private reason leads each to search for advantages over the rest. As contemporary Hobbesians have pointed out, individuals relying on their own private reason, seeking their own individual aims, find themselves in a 'prisoner's dilemma', in which the attempt by each to advance her own goals leads to a situation in which no

Betty

		Don't attack	Attack
Alf	Don't attack	Peace	Betty conquers Alf, takes his property, kills or enslaves him
	Attack	Alf conquers Betty, takes her property, kills or enslaves her	War

FIGURE 4.1   *The prisoner's dilemma*

one achieves their favored outcomes. Figure 4.1 depicts this well-known problem.

Alf reasons: 'If Betty attacks, and I do not, I'll end up conquered and enslaved; if, however, Betty attacks and I also attack – I defend myself – I stand a chance of survival and winning. So I know one thing: *if Betty attacks, I'd better attack too.*' What if Betty does not attack? Alf reasons: 'If Betty does not attack and I do not attack either, we achieve peace; but if Betty does not attack and I do attack, I win and get all the fruits of victory! So *if Betty does not attack, I do best by attacking anyway.*' But now Alf has shown that attacking is a *dominant strategy*: no matter what Betty does, he does best if he attacks. And Betty will reason in a parallel way; she will conclude that no matter what Alf does, she does best by attacking. So they will both attack, and bring about a state of war. Yet each would prefer peace to war. The problem with the Hobbesian state of nature, as we have seen (section 3.1), is that each is driven to prepare for war, a condition that everyone thinks is worse than peace. These rational agents use their own private reason to best promote their own goals: the result is that everyone's goals are set back. And no agreement to end the war will be stable, for each will constantly employ her private reason to reevaluate the agreement, and determine whether it is in her interests to break the agreement.

The Hobbesian account of public reason sought to overcome this problem by supplanting the private reasoning of individuals with public reason – the reasoning of a *political* office holder, procedure or perhaps even substantive principles. Subjects allow their own private reason to be supplanted with the reasoning of a political office holder whom they have authorized, and who commands that they cooperate ('Don't attack'). The problem, we saw, is that if the individuals are constantly consulting their private reason to see if they should follow public reason, they will not be able to overcome their problem. Indeed, they land in another prisoner's

Betty

		Follow public reason	Rely on private reason
	Follow public reason	Peace	Betty takes advantage of Alf, who complies with public rules
Alf			
	Rely on private reason	Alf takes advantage of Betty, who complies with public rules	War

FIGURE 4.2   A prisoner's dilemma: to follow individual or public reason?

dilemma as in Figure 4.2. Private reason instructs each party to rely on private reason no matter what the other does, just as it instructed each party to confess no matter what the other does. It looks as if, so long as private reason is in control, individuals are unable to cooperate in such situations.

If, however, our reason was more social and less individualistic – if it told us not to attack regardless of the private benefits of doing so – then this cause of war would be done away with. We would all do better if, in addition to our individual maximizing rationality, we also were moved by collective rationality – what maximizes my goals given other people's actions. 'Collective rationality goes beyond an appeal to self-interest by being impartial. It is about serving the common good rather than serving the interests of the individual agent'.[2] Rather than focusing only on what you alone can do to pursue your goals (your payoffs), Christopher McMahon, an advocate of a dualist conception of rationality, argues that in a prisoner's dilemma situation, collective rationality instructs each player 'to compare the value of the outcomes produced by two different combinations of actions' – that is, the combinations in which we both defect and both cooperate.[3] The combination in which we both defect is correlated with less value *to me* than the combination where we both cooperate, so collective rationality directs me to cooperate. More precisely, according to McMahon, those following collective rationality in a prisoner's dilemma would 'assign the same payoff to defection [you attack while the other cooperates] that one assigns to the non-cooperative outcome [mutual non-cooperation]'.[4] Notice that McMahon's version of collective rationality does not simply direct that one should do what is

		Betty *C*	Betty *D*
		2	1
Alf	*C*	2	4
		4	3
Alf	*D*	1	3

FIGURE 4.3 *Prisoner's dilemma orderings*

		Betty *C*	Betty *D*
		2	3
Alf	*C*	2	4
		4	3
Alf	*D*	3	3

FIGURE 4.4 *An assurance game ordering*

best for the group regardless of your interests. That indeed would be a strong conception of collective rationality. As McMahon understands it, an agent following collective rationality discounts the possibility of a payoff through defection, treating that payoff as equivalent to a case of mutual defection. Agents following collective rationality will be able to cooperate in competitive games such as the prisoner's dilemma because, in essence, they convert them into cooperative, assurance, games: if Alf (Betty) can be assured that Betty (Alf) will cooperate, then Alf (Betty) does best by cooperating too. That is, an agent following individual maximizing rationality will see the game in terms of Figure 4.3 while an agent following collective rationality will see the 'same game' in terms of Figure 4.4. The numbers represent Alf's (left bottom of each cell) and Betty's (top right) preference orderings for outcomes composed of combinations of cooperate (*C*) and defect (*D*).

The question, though, is in what sense these are the same game. If the payoffs really are those in Figure 4.4, then rather than having an alternative conception of rationality, we simply seem to have people who are still individual maximizers, but order the options differently.[5] McMahon and other advocates of collective rationality maintain that cooperatively-disposed individuals follow a different conception of rationality: they seek to maximize over something rather than their own choices. But if, as we see here, we can depict this as altering their preference ordering so that one sort of game is transformed into another (or they 'see' 4.3 'as if' it were 4.4), it appears that a cooperatively disposed person simply is one that has a more cooperative preference ordering, but still employs private reasoning – individual goal maximization – as her criterion of rational action. This is an important point. Social philosophers seeking to explain the rise of cooperation are apt to take one of two routes. McMahon and other advocates of collective rationality see cooperatively disposed people as abjuring individual maximization for a different sort of rationality – a more social, public or collective conception of what is 'best' to do. In contrast, a different tradition – one that can be traced back to the eighteenth-century philosopher, David Hume – understands a cooperative person in terms of his sentiments or cooperative dispositions. He does not reason differently from the selfish person; he reasons the same but wants different things.

At least in the present context, the latter approach seems more persuasive. Rather than supposing that cooperative people are rational in the sense of being 'we-maximizers' whereas selfish people are rational in a different sense of being 'me-maximizers', it seems both more elegant and plausible (see section 1.2) to say that every rational person seeks to maximize what she sees as the desirable outcome, but a cooperative person has a different notion of a desirable outcome than does a selfish one. Cooperative people manage to be cooperative because they often order the outcomes as they appear in Figure 4.4, whereas others get into conflict because they order outcomes as in Figure 4.3 – they find themselves in lots of prisoner's dilemmas.[6]

Once again the problem seems to be that private reasoning – understood in terms of a person's attempt to maximize what he sees as desirable outcomes – remains firmly in control of our conception of rational action. As Robert Nozick has remarked about individual maximizing reasoning, 'it is the default theory, the theory that all can take for granted, whatever else they think'.[7] The proponents of collective rationality would have us believe that cooperative people reason differently; but if cooperation can be explained in terms of the familiar, basic idea, of individual maximizing reasoning along with the supposition of cooperative goals, we need not have recourse to the idea that sometimes we reason one way, and sometimes we reason in another way. If collective rationality is to be plausible, I think, we must call into question the very idea of individual maximization as the obvious and uncontroversial notion of rationality. So long as we see individual maximization as the basic case, there is a good case for assuming under it so-called collective reasoning.

Cooperation games and political life

Suppose, though, we can identify collective reason with cooperative reasoning along the lines suggested by McMahon. Given this, McMahon advocates a view 'associated with the contractarian tradition in political thought' of the state as 'a form of mutually beneficial cooperation'.[8] Political authority, aided by collective rationality allows us to achieve mutually beneficial outcomes in situations in which we are tempted to compete, but some cooperative strategy advances the interests of everyone. An important motivation behind collective theories of public reasoning such as McMahon's and David Schmidtz's is that they allow us to understand why it is rational to cooperate with others, and the importance of this, in turn, is that it helps to explain government and politics because government and politics can be explained as a sort of cooperation game. To put it bluntly, collective rationality explains cooperation, and cooperation explains politics. Thus far we have examined the tie between collective rationality and cooperation; let us now turn to the tie between politics and cooperation.

A person following collective rationality will be able to achieve cooperation in these contexts because one will have reason to contribute 'to a cooperative venture that produces something that one regards as good if its total value to one when one's contribution is added to those of the others who have contributed or will contribute exceeds the cost to one of contributing'.[9] But why is government necessary to help us secure cooperation? One important reason is that there are often a number of possible ways to coordinate our actions that make everyone better off than non-cooperation, but we disagree on what is the best way to coordinate.[10] For Jeremy Waldron,[11] a leading contemporary liberal, 'the felt need among members of a certain group for a common framework or decision or course of action on some matter, even in the face of disagreement about what the framework, decision or action should be, are *the circumstances of politics*'.[12] Political authority and the law, Waldron insists, presuppose the circumstances of politics. We reasonably disagree not only about conceptions of the good life and value, but about justice and the common good. But because we need to act together, we cannot rest content with each going her own way. We thus have to deal with the fact that we reasonably disagree while achieving some sort of unity of action. Thus our need for political authority and the rule of law. According to Waldron's view of the circumstances of politics, then, we (1) feel a need for a common framework or action yet (2) have intractable, but reasonable, differences as to what that should be. Waldron understands the problem in terms of an impure coordination game as in Figure 4.5. This is Luce and Raiffa's 'Battle of the Sexes' problem.[13] Alf and Betty wish to go out together: Alf wants to go to the fights with her (X, X); she wants to go the ballet with him (Y, Y). Either coordination point $(X, X$ or $Y, Y)$ is preferred by both of them to options in which they fail to coordinate. Thus (X, X) and (Y, Y) are coordinative equilibria.

Waldron clearly thinks all this is important for an analysis of government and the rule of law. He tells us that whether such a coordination game will be solved:

FIGURE 4.5   *An impure coordination problem*

> depends on the circumstances of each case, including how much more each
> prefers his or her own favorite outcome to the less favored [equilibrium
> point], how likely each thinks it is that they will get their favorite outcome by
> holding out, etc. ... I do not want to claim that law *solves* PC [coordination
> games] and that is why we should respect it.[14]

The law, Waldron argues, can make one coordination point more salient
by attaching sanctions, and so make it less likely that people will hold out
for their favorite outcome.

> But before it can do that, the society must have decided which of the coordi-
> native strategies to select as the one to be bolstered in this way. That itself is
> no mean achievement – and I want to say that it is by embodying that achieve-
> ment that law commands our respect.[15]

The idea seems to be that although a specific law contributes to coordination by 'selecting' a specific coordination point, it does not necessarily
'solve' a coordination problem: the 'achievement' of the law is to select
which coordination point should be sought. In any event, it is clear that
Waldron believes that law and legal authority can be modeled on an
impure coordination game:

> We want to act together in regard to some matter M, but one of us thinks it is
> important to follow policy X while others think it is important to follow
> policy Y, and none of us has reason to think any of the others a better judge
> of the merits of M than himself....
>   In these circumstances, the following will *not* be a way of settling on a
> common policy: each does whatever he thinks is important to do about M. We
> must find a way of choosing a single policy in which [we] ... can participate
> despite our disagreements on the merits.[16]

As Waldron understands politics, we will debate and discuss the
merits and demerits of each of the possible coordination points (policies);
since it is an impure coordination game, I prefer a different coordination
point (X, X) than do you (Y, Y), we have something to argue about.

		Betty		
		X	Y	Z
		2	0	0
	X 1	0	0	
		.3	1	0
Y	.3	2	0	
		0	0	.2
	Z 0	0	.2	

FIGURE 4.6   *A coordination game with a non-coordination point Pareto-superior to a coordination equilibrium*

However, we each prefer any coordination point to lack of coordination. In essence, then, Waldron argues that we need to coordinate on some single reasonable policy, even if it is not the one that each of us sees as most reasonable.

Is coordination always better than going it alone?

It is tempting to suppose that the idea of an impure coordination game necessarily implies that, while we have disputes about the preferred coordination point, we must find a way of acting together, since any way of coordinating is better than any uncoordinated outcome. But things are more complicated than this. Following David Lewis, let us define a coordination equilibrium as 'a combination in which no one would have been better off had *any one* agent alone acted otherwise, either himself or someone else'.[17] Given this, it is possible to have a coordination game in which some uncoordinated points (which are not in equilibrium) are better for everyone than some coordinated points. Consider for example Figure 4.6. (Z, Z) satisfies Lewis's definition of coordination equilibrium; no one can be made better off by a move by either. Given Alf's play of Z there is no move that Betty can make that is better for anyone; given Betty's play of Z, there is no way Alf can move that makes things better off for either. Consider, though what happens when Alf selects Y and Betty plays X, which is not a coordination equilibrium; either player can make a unilateral move that makes both better off. Yet Alf Y, Betty X (Y, X)[18] is Pareto-superior to (Z, Z).[19] Both players are better off in an uncoordinated non-equilibrium than in the coordinated equilibrium of (Z, Z). So it does not follow that in every coordination game 'going it alone' is always worse than every way of coordinating.

To be sure, in Figure 4.6 it is rational to coordinate given the play of the other player. (Y, X) is not a stable option; unilateral defection by either player would move them both to an equilibrium that Pareto-dominates it.

Nevertheless, we see in Figure 4.6 that it is not the case that in every impure coordination game it is always better for everyone to coordinate than if they were somehow stuck in an uncoordinated outcome. Suppose we found ourselves in (Z, Z); this could not be justified on the grounds that, while some coordination points are better, it is at least better for everyone than if somehow there was no law that produced coordination. Figure 4.6 does not support the view that legal authority and the law are worthy of respect just because they help select ways of coordinating, *for some ways of coordinating are worse for everyone than some ways of failing to coordinate.* If we are going to make the coordination analysis of government and the law attractive we must add, at the very minimum, the further requirement *that to qualify as a political coordination game* no coordination equilibrium is Pareto-dominated by any non-coordination point.[20] That is, it seems that if political authority is to be *justified* in terms of a coordination game, we need to specify an additional requirement of the game: it must never be the case that rational agents would unanimously agree to move from a coordinated political outcome to an uncoordinated point. (As they would in Figure 4.6, where a move from (Z, Z) to (X, Y) would be endorsed by both Alf and Betty.) To say that politics allows us to coordinate but that we would unanimously agree to return to an uncoordinated situation hardly seems a compelling case for the political order. More strongly, but still very plausibly, we should add that in our legal coordination game every coordination point actually Pareto-dominates every non-coordination point. It must always be the case that it is better for everyone (or, at least, not worse for anyone) to act together than to go it alone in *any* way. Each person does at least as well in every coordination equilibrium as he would in any way of going it alone. Let us call this the *Pareto-dominance of coordination.* Unless this holds, we need to compare different ways of going it alone to different coordination points; some people will rationally prefer some cases of an absence of a political system to some political systems. For them, it would not be true that each doing 'whatever he thinks is important to do about M' is suboptimal *vis-à-vis* every way of coordinating. At least from the perspective of some, coordination would look like a fetish for acting together, which makes them worse off than they might have been.

Coordination on civil society

The most plausible version of a coordinative analysis of politics is to see a specific political order as a coordination point, and so the absence of coordination a state of nature without law or political society.[21] Hobbes's theory is sometimes interpreted in this way. We can depict Hobbes's state of nature as a no-agreement point, and all civil societies as equilibrium points. The power of Hobbes's characterization of the state of nature is that it is so horrible that every conceivable political society is a coordination equilibrium that Pareto-dominates every non-coordinated point. So, by depicting a horrible no-agreement point, Hobbes can show that everyone benefits by any coordinated outcome (type of government). Given that all civil societies are coordination equilibria, no one has any incentive to defect, understood as leaving a coordinated outcome (a civil society) to return to the state of nature.

It is often underestimated just how much an effective coordination account of civil society depends on a Hobbesian-like state of nature story. As soon as we make the state of nature a kinder and gentler place, with perhaps Lockean 'inconveniences' but not constant war, we immediately undermine the claim that all no-agreement points are Pareto-dominated by every social contract. John Locke was no game theorist, but he clearly recognized this. The Hobbesian can only get her result if any agreement is better than no agreement; but if no agreement is inconvenient but not a living hell, then we will be more selective about possible agreements. Some ways of acting together, or some common frameworks, will be seen as worse than no agreement. Thus they are not, in principle, possible solutions to the political coordination game. People are apt to start insisting on clauses to the social contract, excluding 'ways of acting together' (types of civil societies) that they rank as worse than the state of nature. Some may rank regimes without a bill of rights as worse than the state of nature. And the less harsh we make the state of nature, the more civil societies will be rejected by some people because they fail to improve on the state of nature, and so they are disqualified as possible solutions to the legal coordination game.

In Figure 4.7, Option X might be the US Constitution with a Bill of Rights (most preferred by Alf); Option Y, a Parliamentary sovereignty system with an independent judiciary (most preferred by Betty), and Option Z a Hobbesian sovereign. Again, we see accepting a Hobbesian sovereign (Z, Z) is worse than living in a state of nature. The problem here is that (Z, Z) is not a coordination point at all. It is not a coordination equilibrium – indeed it is not an equilibrium solution at all. The intuitive idea of coordination as 'doing the same thing' departs from the formal idea of a coordination equilibrium.[22] In the ordinary language sense it looks as if we coordinate, but (Z, Z) clearly is not in equilibrium, so in the formal sense it is not a coordination equilibrium. Thus the analysis of coordination games does not justify the conclusion that all ways of 'doing the same thing' are better than no coordination because, formally, some types of 'action-in-concert' are instances of non-coordination. Thus, just because we have a common policy Z on some matter, it does not follow that Z is a coordination equilibrium. The less harshly we describe the 'state of nature', the more common policies actually fail to be coordination equilibria. And even if some ways of doing the same thing are genuine coordination equilibria, that is not enough: only Pareto-dominant coordination equilibria provide a plausible case for the authority of law.

		Betty X	**Betty** Y	**Betty** Z
		2	0	0
Alf X	1		0	0
		0	1	0
Y	0		2	0
		0	0	−1
Z	0		0	−1

FIGURE 4.7   *Three social contracts*

The upshot of all this is that other things equal, the more attractive the no-agreement point, the more possible common policies – political systems – will fail to Pareto-dominate the no-agreement points. Assume that we do not embrace a Hobbesian state of nature, but we make the no-agreement points (regarding civil society) less harsh, say people order the outcomes in a way closer to a Lockean story. Given this Lockean sort of ordering, political systems that are understood by some as making them worse off than they are in the state of nature – say because people *believe* such systems violate fundamental rights to life, liberty and property[23] – will not be genuine coordination equilibria at all. Moreover, even if some arise as coordination equilibria because of the choices of others (e.g., (Z, Z) in Figure 4.6), they may not Pareto-dominate all versions of the state of nature. It follows, then, that insofar as the authority of politics and law derives from its role in *improving everyone's lot* by helping to achieve coordination in the face of disagreement, it has no authority if it selects a way of acting together Z that is not Pareto-superior to some state of nature. Z would not be a solution to the political coordination game. Its way of acting together does not improve the lot of some: we cannot expect rational agents to grant authority to a state that fails to improve on a state of nature. Thus, the coordination analysis itself points to a limitation on the justification of legislative authority to violate these rights – excluded ways of 'acting together'.

Legislation as coordination

Waldron's main concern, however, is not a coordination analysis of political life in general, but of politics, and especially of legislation. Waldron is, of course, right that there are some things on which we need to coordinate, and for some matters the coordination account is insightful. We all (or, very nearly all) agree that we need some laws of property, and just about any regime of property rights is better than a free-for-all (though not every possible system is better than anarchy; those that allow property rights in other humans will be rejected by some). Waldron, though, isn't just out to show that some of our current laws are coordination points (again, *vis-à-vis*, say the state of nature), but that we can understand debates about new laws, and then our acceptance of their authority, as impure coordination games. '*A piece of legislation* deserves respect because of the achievement it represents in the circumstances of politics: action-in-concert in the face of disagreement'.[24]

The story, to recap, is this. We are considering a range of possible laws (X, Y, Z) with regard to some matter, M. We rank the alternatives differently (hence our disagreement). If the law enacted, Y, is the solution to a legal coordination game it must be the case that Y Pareto-dominates every no-agreement point. Now it would certainly seem that the obvious way to characterize the no-agreement points is that they all constitute no legislation at all on M. So each acts in her preferred way. Thus, for Waldron to show that new legislation solves the legal coordination problem, it must be the case that 'no law at all on M' ranks below every proposed (possible?) law in everyone's preference ordering. And that appears to be what Waldron does suppose: 'Suppose too', he adds, 'that we all know that M requires a common policy'.[25]

This supposition, though, is manifestly contrary to fact. Overwhelmingly, in debates about new legislation, a significant number of people believe that no common policy on M is required, or at least that no common policy is certainly better than many ways of acting together. On almost any issue there are reasonable citizens who believe that no common policy should be pursued. Debates about abortion, drug laws, environmental policy, trade policy, pornography, affirmative action and stem cell research are all examples: many would insist that some of the proposals offered by their fellow citizens are distinctly worse than no legislation at all. With pornography, for instance, classical liberals would insist that no common policy at all is the preferred option: people can read it, buy it, leer at it or whatever, if doing so is consistent with their other rights (such a property rights). Some people will prohibit it in their buildings, others won't: each going her way is the preferred option.

Over a very wide range of political issues, then, it would seem that for *each and every* proposal P in the set of options, a number of citizens will rank it as inferior to some no-agreement points: (1) those who prefer all no-agreement points to all agreement points, and so rank P and all other laws behind every way of going it alone, such as classical liberals in our pornography case; (2) those who prefer some, but not all, ways of going it alone to all ways of acting together and (3) those who prefer some non-P option to some no-agreements, but prefer some no-agreements to P. It thus seems almost impossible for any new law to be a solution to the legal coordination game.

Ah, one might say, but then no new law – liberty – is the common policy. Allowing porn (or abortion, or not regulating pollution or stem cell research) is itself a policy, so there is no getting away from a common policy. This prima facie tempting reply trivializes the idea of a coordination game and the use of game theory. If we adopt this interpretation, every cell in Figure 4.5 is a coordinated outcome; it is just that sometimes we coordinate by doing things differently. There no longer is a no-agreement point, for every cell constitutes a 'coordinated' outcome. That clearly won't do, for not every cell satisfies the requirements of being a coordination equilibrium.

Let us consider the problem more carefully. Suppose we are now playing a coordination game, and have arrived at an equilibrium, say, a certain set of laws regarding property rights and personal rights. Now assume that a proposal is made to add to the set of laws a statute against selling pornography. Even if the new proposal is Pareto-dominant *vis-à-vis* all uncoordinated outcomes, it does not Pareto-dominate the current coordination equilibrium, since some of the voters will prefer the existing set of laws. It does not solve any sort of coordination problem, *because there already is a coordination equilibrium*. Voters who prefer the status quo have no reason to move to the new proposed coordination point; and since they will not defect to it, even voters who prefer the new laws will not unilaterally desert the status quo in favor of them, because that would produce an uncoordinated outcome.

A factor upsetting the current equilibrium would do the trick.[26] If we are no longer at an equilibrium point, then we do not have to be moved away from one. Thus it has been suggested to me that we might imagine that the current laws regarding property rights are no longer in equilibrium because, say, environmentalists refuse to obey them any longer, believing that they support environmental policies that environmentalists view as wrong. Hence the environmentalists might violate the property rights of logging firms or petroleum companies. Thus we require a new law to regain coordination. Such a situation is depicted in Figure 4.8 (the original game, at time *t*, is the shaded cells, the game at *t* + 1 includes all the cells). Now given Alf's new preferences, the law (*X*, *X*), which what was an equilibrium at *t* no longer is at *t* + 1, and the new law (*Z*, *Z*) is indeed in equilibrium. But this account takes as its starting point that Alf the environmentalist, undergoes a preference change such that he prefers each going their own way, i.e., (*Z*, *X*) to acting together, (*X*, *X*). Notice, though, that *this provides a coordination account of new laws only by undermining Waldron's main claim*: that though we all have different preferred common policies, we all agree that a common policy is better than each going it alone. Alf does not think this in Figure 4.8 at *t* + 1: he now would prefer going it alone unless he gets his preferred outcome – and that is why he violates the property rights of owners under the current regime.

This account of new laws is thus paradoxical. If there is no preference change, the current laws are in equilibrium, and there will be no movement to a new law. On the other hand, there can be movement to new

		Betty		
		X	Y	Z
Alf	X	2 / 1	0 / 0	0 / 0
	Y	0 / 0	1 / 2	0 / 0
	Z	-1 / 1.2	0 / 0	1.5 / 1.5

FIGURE 4.8 *Destabilizing preference change*

laws if some change their preferences and begin to disobey the current laws such that we no longer have coordination. But this requires that some prefer going it alone to having common policies, and that is precisely counter to the 'circumstances of politics'.

Of course exogenous factors may be such that new problems arise. More sophisticated evolutionary models can explain why small changes in circumstances and behavior can lead to new equilibria. I do not wish to insist on a static model. Even in the type of simple games we are considering, we can build in a rationale for changes of equilibria, e.g., when a new law would Pareto-dominate the current law, everyone agrees that the addition of the new law is better, as in Figure 4.9. Again, the current game is in the shaded area, but because of exogenous factors the third row/ column become available. Although (X, X) is still in equilibrium, it is not in *strong equilibrium*[27] as (Z, Z) Pareto-dominates it. We can easily imagine, then, that a political authority might move us from the former to the latter. *This suggests a different model of new legislation: rather than seeing it as selecting coordination points and so solving coordination games, we might see politics and legislation as moving us around the matrix, from one coordination equilibrium to another.* At one point we have (X, X); then we take a vote and move to (Y, Y), which is not Pareto-superior, but simply preferred by a majority. New laws, then, do not solve coordination problems, they move us from one coordination equilibrium to another.

This, I think, is the most attractive interpretation of Waldron's account. But its plausibility depends on the equivocation between 'ways of doing the same thing' and 'coordination equilibria' that I pointed out above. Consider Figure 4.10. Suppose we start at (X, X); as in the previous figure, legislation can move us to a new coordination point, (Y, Y) that Pareto-dominates it. But legislation is majoritarian, so it can also move us to a coordination point in which the majority (Alf's party) endorses egalitarian measures, taking some gains away from Betty's party, hence it can move us to (Z, Z). But for the same reasons it can move us to (W, W),

	Betty		
	X	Y	Z
X	2 1	0 0	0 0
Y	0 0	1 2	0 0
Z	0 0	0 0	2.5 2.5

(Alf = rows)

FIGURE 4.9   *Pareto-dominance of a new law*

	Betty			
	X	Y	Z	W
X	2 1	0 0	0 0	0 0
Y	0 0	3 2	0 0	0 0
Z	0 0	0 0	2.5 2.5	0 0
W	0 0	0 0	0 0	-1 4

(Alf = rows)

FIGURE 4.10   *Legislation versus coordination?*

which is not a coordination equilibrium at all. Once we allow that legislation can move us around the matrix, including from to a point that is Pareto-*inferior* to the status quo, there is no reason to suppose that the legislation will really identify coordination equilibria. Only by erroneously supposing that, by necessity, every way of doing the same thing is a coordination equilibrium could that seem plausible.

Without doubt one of the functions of politics is to help secure our coordination. But it does not follow that the essence of law and politics is coordination. My point here is not the banal one that any model of legal authority is apt to leave something out: as Waldron reminds us, models of authority have to be purchased 'wholesale, not retail'.[28] Rather, I have argued that there are strong reasons to conclude that legal and political issues are not best conceived as coordination games. To be sure, an important part of politics is achieving some sort of unity in action, and the coordination analysis captures that. But on most political issues some citizens would prefer no action to many possible actions; when this occurs politics is not an impure coordination game. Modeling the political as a sort of coordination game fails to appreciate the requirements for a solution to such games – what would have to be true for law to actually be an equilibrium solution – *and how our current understanding of the law would actually be undermined by depicting it as an equilibrium solution*. But if the crux of law and politics is not to solve coordination problems, then we have reason to question whether public reason is essentially cooperative reasoning that allows us to solve such games. If public reason is social, collective reason, we may need a deeper account of its social roots than the coordination game account suggests.

4.3 The social roots of reason: Baier's modified Hobbesian

Kurt Baier, whose work is also deeply influenced by Hobbes, recently has advanced an account according to which reason is a deeply social phenomenon. In his important book, *The Rational and the Moral Order* – subtitled *The Social Roots of Reason and Morality* – Baier rejects the 'dominant conception' of reason, according to which it is an 'individual power, faculty or ability' that 'involves a kind on nonsensory grasp of logical relations (entailments)'.[29] In place of this flawed view that reason is a faculty or individual power, Baier advocates a 'social' conception of reason: reasons are 'guidelines' developed by one's society that allow one to achieve important ends. Consequently, 'one cannot become fully rational ... except in the context of a social order that is also *an order of reason*, that is, one which develops, makes publicly available, tries to improve, and educates its members so as to be able to apply, these guidelines for solving frequently recurring problems'.[30] If reason dictated a social 'guideline' that we cooperate in a variety of prisoner's dilemma situations, then it would be truly the case that reason itself – not the sovereign's reason, but all of our reasoning – points the way to peace and cooperation.

Although Baier sees all reasons as social guidelines, he too sees a fundamental split between individual (or 'self-anchored') and collective (or 'society-anchored') reasons. Individual reasons, Baier says, are 'self-anchored in four ways'.

First, their ground is some agent favoring property of the action for which they are reasons, as, for instance, prudential reasons or those favoring the agent's loved ones. Second, they are independent of other people's actions, as my preventing myself getting run over by the oncoming bus would be. In other words, they are reasons for doing something an agent can do without the help of others and the doing of which confers a benefit on him. Third, they are independent of others' following the same reasons in the same circumstances, as the reason I have for refraining from leaving trash on the beach may not be, since I may have reason to restrain my inclination to leave my trash only if others do likewise. Fourth, the motivating force of such reasons normally is not and should not be reinforced by certain sorts of social sanctions.[31]

Although many of our social guidelines are anchored to the self in this way, Baier insists, many others are not. In addition, we possess society-anchored reasons. Society-anchored reasons include, I think, McMahon's notion of collective rationality: they include guidelines as to how people should act in cases of social interaction in which what is best for one person depends on the actions of others. In a way that is remarkably similar to McMahon's cooperatively disposed individual, Baier's notion of a society-anchored reason is used to defend a 'Limited Conditional Good Will':

> It is limited in that it is not a disposition to promote or protect other people's good on all occasions, but only when it is required by certain coordinative rules that apply to one. And it is conditional in that one's willingness to do so is dependent on a certain contingency, namely, that all others to whom the rules apply do likewise or, if not all do so, that those who don't do not profit. …
> It is … a willingness not to seek to achieve the good life by making the best reply, in those types of situation in which everyone's doing so has suboptimal effects, but instead to follow uniform publicly recognized guidelines, designed to achieve optimal outcomes.[32]

Note that Baier's person of Limited Conditional Good Will does exactly what McMahon's cooperative person does: in a prisoner's dilemma he refuses to rank his unilateral defection as his first option. Following such a society-anchored guideline is better for everyone than a world in which people follow egoistic self-anchored reasons.[33]

The social roots of rationality

In comparison to Gauthier's Hobbesian public reason, Baier's society-anchored reasons seem less liable to collapse into individual reason, since both self-anchored and society-anchored reasons are themselves social guidelines. If all reasons are social guidelines we need not derive collective or public reason from individual reasoning. As Gauthier recognizes in his own reply to Baier, a theorist who puts primacy on individual reason must question Baier's thesis about the social roots of reason.[34]

A difficulty for Baier's account of social reason concerns the precise nature of the relation between any given social guideline (G) and the claim that accepting such a guideline gives us a reason (R). The strongest interpretation would be:

(I) G is an R for Alf if and only if G is endorsed by Alf's society, which is an order of reason.

I think Baier would agree that this is too strong; being endorsed by society is not sufficient for G being an R. As Baier acknowledges, guidelines can be judged by their usefulness in bringing about desired outcomes, so a guideline endorsed by a society that is perverse – which is a barrier to the goal it is supposed to achieve – is a bad reason. And even an order of reason, which aims at improving its guidelines, can have deeply flawed ones. The United States, we might suppose, has been an order of reason, but throughout most of its history it has taught social guidelines upholding racial segregation as the best way to 'cooperate'. Those who opposed racial segregation were quite right to insist that such guidelines provided them with no good reasons at all. Because we can stand back and evaluate any G, to determine whether it is really an R, a G's status as a guideline is not sufficient to show that it is a reason. Another possible interpretation is:

(II) G is an R for Alf only if G is endorsed by Alf's society, which is an order of reason.

This makes G's endorsement by society merely a necessary condition for its being a reason (R): a G must be endorsed by society to be an R, but not every G that is so endorsed will constitute an R. But even this is too strong: sometimes individuals invent radically new ways (formulate new guidelines) to achieve valued ends, ones that are not yet endorsed by their society. It would certainly seem that if G^* is such a new guideline, the inventor, and those to whom he has communicated G^*, have reason to follow it even before it is endorsed by society. Indeed, if it comes to be endorsed by society it would be because society recognizes that it is (already) a good reason. The inventor would seek to get G^* accepted by society by showing others that it provides a good reason to act; but if he does that, clearly being accepted by society cannot be necessary for G^*'s status as R.

It thus does not seem that a guideline must be accepted by one's society if it is to be a genuine reason. Of course, reason might be social in a weaker sense. It is certainly true that, generally, the guidelines accepted by society will be better than those the individual can invent for himself. As Baier rightly stresses, the cognitive resources of society are much greater than those available to any one individual, so we should endorse a social conception of reason in the sense of (III):

(III) A person can only have a good store of reasons insofar as he has access to the accumulated wisdom of others, including wisdom about ways of deliberating.

As Baier says, one could only become 'fully rational' in a social context, in which we benefit in many ways from the reasoning of others. Thus, as he points out, even an intelligent ape – who figures out that by joining two sticks he can reach his desired bananas – is not fully rational: the ape does not have access to the accumulated wisdom and critical resources of a culture. But though Baier surely accepts this, (III) does not require one to be a *member* of a certain social order or culture except in the sense that one has access to its cognitive achievements. Someone who has never left the jungles of Papua New Guinea can be a 'member' of western culture in this sense if she has access to western scientific, philosophic and other guidelines. To have access to the wisdom of a society does not require being a member of it. It appears, however, that Baier wants a tighter connection between rationality and group membership. Baier insists not that our intelligent ape fails to be fully rational, but that he cannot be evaluated as either rational or irrational because 'he is not a *member* of an order of reason and so could not, even if he had the other required abilities, take advantage of the socially provided "machinery" needed to reflect in a regimented way about which of the performances open to him is according, and which [is] contrary to reason'.[35] It is hard to see how this line of reasoning endorses anything much stronger than:

> (IV) Only if Alf is a language user can his performances (actions, beliefs, and so on) be judged in accordance with, or contrary to, reason.

However, this does not tie one's status as a reasoner to membership in a specific social order, and it does not imply that when reasoning one must take our cue from her own society. The analysis of the intelligent ape also suggests:

> (V) Only if others can criticize one's performances as in accordance with, or contrary to, guidelines that one shares with those others can one be a rational creature.

We shall return to this idea later in this chapter (section 4.4), but even if (V) is true it does not support anything so strong as claim (II) above, for people can and do propose new guidelines; so it must mean simply that lots of the time the guidelines one accepts must be accepted by many others if one is to be a rational creature. But (V) is doubtful; suppose like a psychotic, you typically employ extremely idiosyncratic guidelines – you do not share them with other members of a group. But our evaluation would be that you are mad; but a mad person is irrational. So unlike the ape you are still being considered a rational creature qua one who can be deemed irrational. It is not clear that sharing guidelines with others is required to be judged rational *or* irrational. Of course:

(VI) If a person does not share *our* guidelines *we* will judge *her* to be irrational, but it does not mean that she is.

If we are primitive religious mystics, the unintelligible proto-scientific medical guidelines of an innovator among us may be well grounded: we may consider her quite mad, but actually she will be rational.

The primacy of individual reason

As we have seen in the last two chapters, from Hobbes onwards, the problem for this general approach to public reason is that self-favoring agents only have reason to accept 'society-anchored' reasons if doing so advances their own private ends; thus they will reject public reasoning when their private reasoning leads them to conclude that it no longer serves their interests. More generally, what Baier called the dominant conception of reason as an individual power, faculty or ability to recognize logical relations is not easily jettisoned. There is evidence that people do indeed possess natural mental logics; individuals possess a natural power to process information in terms or rules such as '$(p\&[p \to q]) \to q$', '$\{[p \lor q] \to r\} \& p\} \to r$', and '$(p \& q) \to p$'.[36] Although the material on which people exercise their reason is often supplied by society, and it is through social interaction that our reasoning faculties develop, none of this obviates the important point that individuals do their own reasoning. And if their goals are to advance their own interests, it is hard to see how they might somehow alienate their reasoning on some matters to others, such as the sovereign.

Baier sees that so long as we accept the picture of reasoning as something that manifests an innate ability of individuals, it will be very hard to make sense of a person alienating that ability to others. How can one alienate a natural ability such as thinking? Reason, Baier insists, is not an individual power that allows the individual to compute the best path to her own good: it is *constituted* by shared guidelines about how to achieve the good life. And, Baier can argue, society-anchored guidelines that tell us not to attack (or to cheat) are indeed good guidelines, so they are good reasons, and so we do have good reason to be cooperative; someone who acts on these guidelines is not a fool, but is recognizing a genuine reason. Now if (I) above was sound – if reason was thoroughly social – this would be decisive; perhaps even (II) would help a great deal. However, given the modest senses in which we can say that reason is social, it still seems that a *fully rational* person can say – 'Yes, society has developed that guideline, and yes, it would be better if everyone followed that guideline than if no one did, but it is a stupid guideline for me to follow when I can get away with not following it, and given all my cognitive resources and the things I care about, I have access to an alternative guideline that defeats this society-anchored guideline, and will better achieve my goals. Whether others have reason to follow it depends on their values, commitments and so on.' In short, it can still be rational to put aside social guidelines and act on individual ones.

Baier's social account of reason has, then, two main problems. First, as I have tried to argue, it is not really clear in what sense reason is tied to membership in a society. Just how reason has its roots in social life is not, after all, pellucid. Second, like Hobbes and Gauthier, Baier admits that not all reasoning is social (or public) in the sense of 'society-anchored'; but as long as individuals retain their private reasoning, and as long as they can employ this reason to show that they do best by ignoring the dictates of public reasoning, they will rationally set aside public reasoning when it is to their advantage. Indeed, given the first problem – the uncertainty about just how reason is social – it seems that, as in Hobbes and Gauthier, private reasoning remains basic, and ready to throw out collective reasoning when collective reasoning tells the individual to ignore her own calculations about what is the best thing for her to do to advance her own good. Baier's social-ized Hobbesian account does, however, suggest another solution to our problem of uncovering public reasoning. If it could be shown that *all reasoning is social reasoning*, and so individuals have no rational resources to reject 'society-anchored reasons' in favor of 'self-anchored' ones, rational indivi-duals would have to act on social, or public, reason, for that would be the only reason there is. It is to that proposal that we now turn.

4.4 Wittgensteinian-inspired socialized reasoning: is all reason public reason?

The basic argument against 'private rules'

Can we, then, provide an account of collective or social reasoning that avoids Hobbes's and Gauthier's attempts to ground it on individual reasoning and provides a clearer rationale than does Baier as to why there is a sort of social reasoning that is distinct from the exercise of our natural individual deliberative power? A number of theorists of public reason – most important Philip Pettit and Susan Hurley – have been attracted to a collectivistic analysis of *all reasoning* that is inspired by the philosophy of language of Ludwig Wittgenstein.[37] The core idea is that, as Pettit puts it, '[t]o think is to try to conform to the rules which certain propositions represent'.[38] If to think is to follow rules, then we need to know what is involved in following a rule. Pettit adopts a version of Wittgenstein's argument against private rules.

Wittgenstein asks us to consider a case in which you are instructing a student how to employ a rule adding numbers. We start, 'see here is the number 0? Now you see I'll add 2, to get a sum of 2. Then I add another 2, to get 4, another 2 to get 6, another 2 to get 8, and so on. Can you see what I'm doing?' The student then says 'Sure, I see, that's easy'. He then continues on, getting 10, 12, 14, 16, 18, 20, 22. You leave the room, and tell him to keep on going with the series. When we come back we see at the end, '1000, 1004, 1008, 1012'. Wittgenstein writes:

> We say to him: 'Look what you have done!' – he doesn't understand. We say: 'You were supposed to add *two*: look how you began the series!' – He answers: 'Yes, isn't it right? I thought that was how I was meant to do it'. – Or suppose he pointed to the series and said: 'But I went on in the same way'. – It would now be of no use to say: 'But can't you see that … ?' – and repeat the old examples and explanations. – In such a case we might say, perhaps: It comes natural to this person to understand our order with our explanations as *we* should understand the order: 'Add 2 up to 1000, 4 up to 2000, 6 up to 3000 and so on'.[39]

The crucial question for Wittgenstein, then, is how to carry on the rule at this stage, and for that something additional is needed besides the rule itself. To follow a rule we must know the correct way of 'going on' with it, but there are an indefinite number of ways of proceeding. Rules do not interpret themselves: no statement of a rule is self-interpreting. Now Pettit agrees with me that an individual natural power is involved: thinking subjects must possess an 'extrapolative disposition' that prompts them to 'go on' in a certain way given a finite number of instances.[40] However, this disposition to extrapolate and go on is not sufficient for rule following; as we have just seen in our numerical example, there are an indefinite number of ways to extrapolate – to 'go on in the same way'.

What about a proposal that the individual extrapolative agent decides for himself what is the proper way of going on? Wittgenstein famously argues that this cannot be the case. Following a rule – for instance, an inferential norm – requires that one be able to distinguish successfully following the rule from making a mistake. Or, as Hurley, another advocate of the Wittgensteinian approach puts it, one must be able to distinguish eligible from ineligible interpretations of the rule. And, she argues, no thoroughly individualistic account can adequately articulate this difference. Quoting Wittgenstein, she maintains that 'the difference between making a mistake in following a rule … and following a different rule, or none at all, is not to be found among the intrinsic, non-relational, individualistically identified properties, movements, or states of an individual: [as Wittgenstein says] "What, in a complicated surrounding, we call 'following a rule' we should certainly not call that if it stood in isolation" – or in a different surrounding'.[41] The idea, roughly at any rate, is that a rule follower must be able to distinguish getting a rule right from making an error – from going on in the right way rather than the wrong way. Now to do this there must be a distinction between *thinking* you are extrapolating in the correct way and *really* being correct – there must be a possibility that you can have made a mistake. But, the Wittgensteinian says, no purely individual or intrapersonal way of checking the right way to go on can distinguish thinking you have it right from actually having it right.

The upshot of this argument is that the very idea of thinking implies agreement with others. If to think is to follow a rule, and if following a rule means going on in the correct way, and the only way to see if you are going on in the correct way is to check how others go on, then the very idea of being a reasoner implies that one is a social, public or collective, reasoner. All reasons, indeed all thought, is, to use Baier's term, 'society-anchored'. The Wittgensteinian-inspired argument frees public reason from being directed by private reason by undermining the very idea of private reason.

Agreement and interpretation

In evaluating this argument, we need to distinguish two different perspectives from which it can be made: that of the interpreter and that of the rule follower. Now the interpreter – the perspective on which Hurley focuses – must rely on the principle of charity in determining whether another's activity can be understood as following a rule (see section 1.2). If Betty is interpreting Alf's statement *X* as an instance of his application of a rule in certain circumstances, it would appear that she must (1) be able to make some sense of the rule, and (2) she must be able to understand *X* as an eligible or sensible interpretation of the rule in those circumstances, and that requires that she be able to distinguish eligible from ineligible applications. But, says the Wittgensteinian, this cannot be done *simply* by resorting to facts about Alf and his system of reasons and beliefs. This, I think, is entirely correct. Our interpretation of another as following a norm must be intelligible by our own lights (that is what it means to say that it is *our interpretation*), and that very significantly restricts our freedom to attribute to others norms and beliefs that we do not share, and do not believe are justified. But *sometimes* the best way to make sense of a person is indeed to attribute to him beliefs we do not share. Recall Mill's observation (see section 1.2), that an investigator could best understand the magical beliefs of other cultures by attributing to them erroneous beliefs and invalid inferential rules. *Sometimes* the best way to interpret other people's beliefs is to attribute to them beliefs that we think are unjustified, such as a belief in magic or God. So although interpretation requires significant overlap with the beliefs of others – we could not interpret the utterances of people who had an *entirely* different way of 'going on' with rules than do we, interpretation is *sometimes* best advanced by doing precisely that. 'Adequate translation need not lead us to construe our subjects as rational', for we have access to a large body of psychological and other social-scientific theory that tells us that people often fail to act rationally.[42]

In many ways the perspective of the agent can be reduced to the perspective of the interpreter: when the agent is seeking to follow a rule he can be understood as replicating the deliberations of an interpreter, who tries to understand which interpretations are eligible. What Betty can do for Alf – interpret his actions in relation to a rule and its sensible application – he can do for himself. Although the individual rules that Alf employs are not self-interpreting, Alf himself can be a self-interpreter. Prima facie, this contradicts the Wittgensteinian analysis of a person following a rule. If, as Hurley believes, 'Wittgenstein argues … that no course of action can be determined by a rule, because every course of action can be made out to accord with the rule, and also to conflict with it',[43] Alf's efforts at self-interpretation would seem senseless. If Alf's norms, as they are embedded in his current system of beliefs, are really so radically indeterminate, then clearly he needs to go outside of himself to get any handle on how to apply them. But surely this is too simple a picture. At any given time, Alf has a series of precedents to appeal to – past decisions about what the rule calls for[44] – as well as other beliefs about the point of the rule and its justification. And he can draw on these to limit indeterminacy. A person so reflecting on his system of reasons and beliefs engages in what has been called 'constructive' rather than conversational interpretation – interpreting the rule in the light of his beliefs about its purposes and his past interpretations of it.[45] Though, to be sure the constructive interpretation of one's system of beliefs will always be incomplete and approximate, it nevertheless provides significant constraints on eligible interpretations of any single rule or norm.

Some Wittgensteinians insist this solves nothing, because the indeterminacy that plagues the original rule merely replicates itself at other levels. How to interpret our past decisions, general principles, what the point of a rule is – all these, it might be argued, are as indeterminate as the original problem of how to apply the rule. If no single rule interprets itself, neither can a system of rules. This is implausible. Even though, taken one at a time and in isolation, the application of rules may be highly indeterminate, in the context of a system of rules, in which the interpretation of one has consequences for others, the range of eligible interpretations can be greatly reduced. Consider, for example, the statute according to which 'it is a federal crime for someone knowingly to transport in interstate commerce "any person who shall have been unlawfully seized, confined, inveigled, decoyed, kidnapped, abducted, or carried away by any means whatsoever …".'[46] According to this rule, is it a federal crime for a man to persuade a 'young girl that it was her religious duty to run away with him, in violation of a court order, to consummate what he called a celestial marriage?'[47] Taken in isolation, it may seem that either an affirmative or a negative is equally eligible, thus confirming the neo-Wittgensteinian's claim that the rule itself does not tell us how to go on. But in the context of other rules and justificatory principles with inter-locking interpretations, Ronald Dworkin shows, the indeterminacy is greatly reduced, if not eliminated.[48]

It cannot, I think, seriously be maintained that belief systems are radi-cally indeterminate in the sense that, at any given time, a reasoner does not have within her belief system the resources to greatly constrain eligi-ble interpretations of her beliefs and norms. Advocacy of such a radical indeterminacy, I think, presupposes a singularly odd picture of humans as cognizers of their environment. Imagine a species that developed beliefs, including beliefs about the world, but at any particular time, it was always an entirely open question just what these beliefs involve, and only by appeal to the understandings of others could they give one any guidance about *what to do next*. Such creatures, let us say, would be *purely social reasoners* because their private deliberations about their beliefs would be hopelessly indeterminate, and only through some sort of inter-subjective agreement could they lock on to determinate interpretations of their beliefs. Intersubjective agreement would serve as a convention, which identifies one out of an innumerable set of eligible interpretations as the coordination point. (Notice here the link with our earlier discussion in section 4.2 of public reason as a way to solve coordination problems.) A person excluded from the social deliberation would be paralyzed, not possessing the resources, on her own, to decide what to do, or what to believe, next.

Pettit's revised Wittgensteinian 'holism'[49]

Pettit is more careful than Wittgenstein, acknowledging that in principle intrapersonal consistency might be a sufficient check on the correctness of an interpretation of a rule. Pettit, however, stresses the necessity of 'nego-tiating' our interpersonal differences about how to apply rules; he thus adds a requirement that rules of thought be 'commonable'.[50] It is not pre-cisely clear just what this means, but Pettit tells us that it implies that the relevant rules are those 'over which no one individual has a monopoly; they are capable of being claimed as a common possession by any of the individual's fellows'.[51] The upshot of this account of rule following, Pettit argues, is a 'social holism' according to which '[m]y own inclination [about how to follow a rule] must count as an intimation of the commu-nal voice that firms up in the convergence of different extrapolative dis-positions. It must count as an intimation that is validated only in the achievement, perhaps in negotiation, of a concerted response'.[52]

The image that emerges is a person who does not know what to think except by looking to see what others are thinking. Pettit's argument for this common mind, though at times precise and careful, is difficult to follow at crucial junctures. The critical argument for 'commonable rules', for example, seems to mix together the following claims: (1) a thinking subject seeking to follow rule R, who concludes that R calls for response X, should take account of the claims of others that not-X is required by R;[53] (2) that there is a plausible evolutionary story to show that we would give such epistemic weight to the opinions of others;[54] (3) a thinking subject seeking to follow rule R, who concludes that X is required, should give equal epistemic authority to the judgment of another who believes that not-X is required by R;[55] (4) that there is a plausible evolutionary story to show that we would give this status [as in (3)] to the judgments of others;[56] (5) in cases of disagreement such as the one above, we need to seek out a negotiated convergence on X if we are to believe that X is correct or warranted;[57] (6) that for others to be 'scrutable' and 'accessible' to me I must be able to model their thinking that leads them to not-X and (7) that for others to be 'scrutable' and 'accessible' I must actually identify with, and endorse, their thinking.[58]

Some of these are quite sound (1, 2, 6) and others strike me as false (3, 4, 7) while the plausibility of claims about possible convergence (i.e., 5) depend on the specification of the idealized conditions under which we suppose that others should reach the same conclusions: we certainly do not suppose that under actual conditions Alf's belief that X is always unwarranted just because others reject X. Think again (see section 4.1) of an innovator, who has seen a reason that others thus far reject: we cannot say that at the time he comes up with this new idea it is unwarranted just because it is something that everyone else rejects.

Pettit's claim (1) – that any reasonable deliberator will take the disagreement of others as a reason to pause and reconsider his conclusions – is certainly sound. As McMahon rightly notes, there is a perfectly plausible notion of 'collective reasoning' in the sense of a 'pooling of reasons'.[59] When we are confronted with the different conclusions of others, we have good reason to consider their objections and arguments. But, as McMahon stresses, it is ultimately up to the individual to decide what is rational, and this does not depend on his reaching agreement with others. 'An individual facing even widespread disagreement with others should stick to her guns unless she is given good substantive reason to believe that she is wrong'.[60] In contrast, Pettit believes not only that thinking has this sort of social element, but that the conclusions of others are equally authoritative with my own deliberations about what I am to believe (see his claim (3) above).[61] For Pettit, if after deliberation I conclude that R calls for response X while you insist that not-X is required by R, this leaves me entirely at sea about what to believe; if I literally grant *you and myself equal epistemic authority about what I am to believe* the conclusions of my own deliberations do not have any special epistemic status about what I am warranted in believing. I doubt whether thinking agents could sustain such a radically alienating attitude toward their own deliberations; that others matter, and we do not inhabit a solipsistic world, does not immerse us in a common mind in which *my* deliberations are without any privileged epistemic authority in determining what *I* am to believe.

Freedom and the common mind

Pettit believes that this view of reason – and a 'holist' view of society that he develops in conjunction with it – ought to induce us to 'radicalize our liberal commitments in a republican fashion'.[62] By rejecting individualism, Pettit argues, we are no longer tied to the view that individual, 'non-social' values are the touchstone by which we are to evaluate political structures.[63] This, of course, is precisely the problem that plagues Hobbesian accounts of public reason: individual reasoning and values are the touchstone of rationality, and in the end rational individuals evaluate political institutions by how well they promote those individual values. 'They have assumed, to put the matter otherwise, that part of the job of supporting any political arrangement is to show what there is in it for individuals who could logically have enjoyed a solitary existence instead; what there is about that arrangement that makes it superior for such individuals to a solitary existence'.[64] Pettit, though, argues that his non-individualist account grounds truly social values; in particular, he stresses the way it allows us to appreciate the superiority of 'republican' over liberal 'negative' liberty. According to the liberal, Pettit argues, liberty is a purely negative concept: one is free if, as a matter of fact, one is not interfered with by others. It is a conception of liberty appropriate to atomistic, independent asocial beings. Such liberty could be enjoyed in a pre-social, Hobbesian state of nature. However, he argues that negative liberty is an inadequate conception of freedom as it deems Alf free if, as a matter of fact, he is not interfered with by Betty, though at any time Betty *could* interfere with Alf if she so chose, and so he only remains not interfered with by her sufferance. In such a situation, says Pettit, Betty dominates Alf. 'One agent dominates another if and only if they have a certain power over that other, in particular a power of interference on an arbitrary basis'.[65] It is important that, to Pettit, 'what constitutes domination is the fact that in some respect the power-bearer has the capacity to interfere arbitrarily, even if they are never going to do so'.[66]

For the republican, then, whenever Betty has resources that would give her the capacity to exercise power over another and so interfere if she so chose, she dominates the other and so he is not free. And, as Pettit acknowledges, 'the resources in virtue of which one person may have power over another are extraordinarily various: they range over physical strength, technical advantage, financial clout, political authority, social connections, communal standing, informational access, ideological position, cultural legitimation, and the like.'[67] Private property, especially when it is used to offer employment (rather than, say, personal consumption) is a hallmark of such power. Pettit agrees with socialists that unregulated capitalism is inherently a form of 'wage slavery' – 'however little interference workers suffered, it was still the case that they lived under permanent exposure to interference, in particular arbitrary interference'.[68]

At the heart of Pettit's republicanism is an identification of freedom with security from interference: one is only free if one is not subject to interference, and is secure in that: 'freedom means having security against interference, and the measure of freedom is the quality of protection provided'.[69] Combining freedom and security in this way conceptually forecloses the very possibility that the costs of gaining security is to lose freedom. This foreclosure, though, seem dubious. As one builds walls, either literally or figuratively, one may experience great gains in security, but the walls may also limit what you can do. If I live in a gated community my security is enhanced, but I too am constrained in some ways. Moreover, conflating the question whether I am free, with whether my freedom is protected and secured, blurs the distinction between positive and negative rights. To be sure, a negative right (to some sort of non-interference) may only be secure if I also have a positive right to protection; the police have a duty to come to my aid if someone seeks to interfere with my liberty. If, however, my freedom is equated with its security, then freedom itself involves such positive rights to enforcement, and so it makes no sense to ask whether the benefits of enforcement outweigh its costs to liberty.[70]

Pettit believes that his is a much more plausible version of freedom, and only a commitment by liberals to a social atomism could account for their tenacious commitment to negative liberty.[71] Properly understood, we see that social and political institutions do not take away some of our freedom to better protect other parts; the rule of law in no way detracts from our freedom because it provides citizens with *antipower*. The law, says Pettit, neutralizes the power possessed by some citizens that, if left unchecked, would limit the freedom of their fellows. In particular, Pettit stresses how the state protects freedom by regulating the way in which the powerful may employ their resources. Thus, for example, legal regulation of economic decisions by corporations protects the liberty of employees and shareholders.[72]

Rather than insisting that republican freedom follows from his holism, Pettit's main point seems to be that it frees us from the blinders of liberal individualism so that we can appreciate the social basis of freedom. A liberal, though, is apt to worry that Pettit's conception of reasoning has far more collectivistic *political* implications than he or other neo-Wittgensteinains appreciate. The core idea, that to think rationally is necessarily to think as do others, has chilling implications for individual freedom and non-conformity. Recall Winston Smith in George Orwell's novel, *1984.* Throughout most of the novel, Smith is aware of the

irrationality and self-deceptions of his comrades. He appears to stand for
a lone individual reasoner in the midst of an irrational mass. But Smith
turns out to be an experiment of the totalitarian state, which in the end
reigns him in. He loses his power to think for himself – to deploy his
natural reason. In the end he proclaims 'the Party was in the right. It must
be so; how could the immortal, collective brain be mistaken? By what
external standards could you check its judgments? Sanity was statistical.
It was merely a question of learning to think what they thought.'[73] Thus
at the end Smith accepts a version of the Wittgensteinian view: there are
no standards of good reasoning except those supplied by others. Is rationality statistical?

As we saw at the outset (section 1.1), liberalism is first and foremost a
theory about freedom of thought. Although Enlightenment Liberals
insisted that an important ground for freedom of thought is that it leads
to the discovery of truth, a more fundamental ground of freedom of
thought is respect for the reasoning powers of each individual. Each has
a right to believe as his reason dictates. Now typically this is understood
as simply an external moral right not to be interfered with in certain activities related to belief formation and expression. But one of the puzzling
aspects of freedom of thought is that in an important way merely external
restraints typically do stop one from freely thinking. Brainwashing, as in
the case of Winston Smith, does occur, but more commonly one is pun-
ished for communicating or expressing one's thoughts; rarely does this
actually interfere with a person's thinking what he wishes. If in fact it is
actually difficult to interfere with a person's thinking, why do people
claim freedom of thought rather than simply freedom to speak, to publish,
to worship, and so on?

As long as we see *freedom of thought* as purely a moral right involving
external actions, it will seem a misnomer; and it will not respect people's
reasoning, as much as their actions that express their views, and their
rights to gain access to the views of others. The fundamental place of freedom of thought becomes apparent, though, if we do not insist on a sharp
distinction between moral and epistemic rights, what one is warranted in
doing and what one is warranted in *believing*. To respect a person's reason
and his freedom of thought is to grant to him a right to think as he pleases
in the sense not only of external moral rights, but a claim that, at least
normally, *his* deliberations properly determine what *he* ought to believe.
That is, freedom of thought supposes a moral and epistemic right to
believe that on which one has deliberated and has determined to be well-
founded. Or, to stress its epistemic aspect, let us say that one has strong
warrant to believe that to which one's deliberations lead. Let us call this
respect for the people's deliberations: that Betty's deliberations lead her to conclude X rather than not-X, is a strong warrant for Betty believing that X.

Respect for people's deliberations constitutes an explicit rejection of
Pettit's view that you and I have equal epistemic authority about what I

am to believe. Although, as McMahon stresses, the views of others count, they do not count as much as your own conclusions about what you are warranted in believing. To be a rational believer and agent is not simply to be someone who has rationally justified belief; it is to be a producer of such beliefs and actions based on them. Respect for this status of others as producers of beliefs requires that the fact that a deliberator has herself actually produced X rather than not-X gives her an epistemic and moral right to believe X. Consider the denial of this right. Suppose that the fact that as a result of your deliberation that X was the thing to believe, you had no more warrant to believe X than not-X, if another person, equally acquainted with your belief system and equally competent as a reasoner, concluded not-X is what your system commits you to. Your deliberations are not merely, as it were, one consideration in favor of you believing X. They cause you to believe it.[74] One's status as a consumer of beliefs cannot be abstracted from one's status as a producer of beliefs: what one is warranted in consuming depends to a great extent on what one has produced.

By too thoroughly socializing thought, the neo-Wittgensteinians render precarious the principle of respect for the reasoning of actual deliberators. On their view – and on those of allied 'pragmatists' – what is rational to believe is, roughly, what 'we believe'.[75] This solves the problem of showing how rational agreement comes about – it comes close to defining the rational in terms of agreement – but in so doing tends to undermine the very idea that individuals, employing their natural reason, may come to very different though reasonable views. I am not claiming, of course, that these theorists explicitly adopt these illiberal views. They are generally tolerant people, who try hard to push their accounts at least in the direction of liberal freedoms. (Still political proposals worrying to liberals pop us; Pettit tells us, for example, that 'it appears that if we are to have any hope of promoting civic virtue … We must be able to rely on a system in which everyone is a police officer for everyone else'.[76]) Nevertheless, without a robust sense of individual natural reason, and how this can lead a person to reject the group's conclusions about what is rational and true, a theory has great difficulty generating liberal respect for the freedom of thought of deviants.

4.5 Conclusion

This chapter has examined different formulations of the idea that the Hobbesian problem of private reason ruling public reason can be solved by showing that collective reasoning has social roots that gives it independence from individual reasoning. We began with a modest version of this thesis, Christopher McMahon's and David Schmidtz's proposal that, in addition to private individual maximizing reasoning, cooperative people also reason collectively – they think in terms not simply of what is good for me, but what is good for us. They reason in prisoner's dilemmas as if they were coordination games. The problem, we saw, is to show that cooperative people actually reason differently, rather than simply that they want different outcomes. If it is the latter, then all reasoning is individual maximizing reasoning, but cooperative reasoners employ their reason to achieve different ends (they have different preference orderings). But this still leaves individual maximizing reasoning as the heart of all reasoning. I considered at some length the conception of the politics, government and law for which this notion of collective reasoning is supposed to provide the foundation: the idea that politics is a coordination problem, and so political reason is cooperative reasoning. Focusing on Jeremy Waldron's important coordinative theory of law and politics, I questioned whether politics and the law are essentially about solutions to coordination problems.

We then examined Kurt Baier's more socialized Hobbesian account, which seeks to provide a basis for the idea that reasoning has social roots, and so we should not take reason as an individualized, private, mental ability. Baier argues that the very idea of reason involves socially-endorsed guidelines, and given the problems that Hobbes pointed out, many of the guidelines involve 'society-anchored' reasons that instruct us to cooperate. But two problems confront Baier's account. First, he does not show that all reasons are society-anchored, and so individuals seem free to employ 'self-anchored' reasons to override or ignore their more social reasons. Baier would like to show that society-anchored reasons override self-anchored reasons; but if the main argument for the development of society-anchored reasons is that they solve the problems of cooperation, and so are recommended by reasons of self-interest, it seems that reasons of self-interest are more basic. Second, it is not clear in just what are the necessary social roots of reason, and why one must be a member of a society to be a reasoner.

The neo-Wittgensteinians provide a detailed and sophisticated analysis seeking to show why all reasoning is inherently social. To think is to follow rules, and rule following requires social agreement about what is the correct way to 'go on'. We are not split between individual, natural reason and social, public reason: all reason is social reason. I questioned the argument supporting this claim – that the only check on the indeterminacy of rules is social agreement about what they require. I also suggested that, if it was the correct view of reasoning, Pettit's hope that it may radicalize liberal freedom without going so far as to reject it, may be unsustainable.[77] It is plausible to see neo-Wittgensteinianism as having anti-liberal implications about the grounds for respecting the deliberations of idiosyncratic reasoners.

Still, even if all reason cannot be characterized in terms of social agreement, perhaps an important subset of reasoning – the moral and the political – is inherently about interpersonal agreement. We would once again have a split conception of reason: individual reasoning leading to disagreement on personal matters, but a special sort of reasoning presupposing social agreement on political questions. We might think of this as a sort of combination of the Hobbesian and Wittgensteinian views. It is the subject of the next chapter.

Notes

1 See John Stuart Mill, *A System of Logic* (London: Longman, 1947), Book VI, Ch. xii, section 3; Book VI, Ch. xii, section 2.
2 David Schmidtz, *Rational Choice and Moral Agency* (Princeton: Princeton University Press, 1995), p. 196.
3 Christopher McMahon, *Collective Rationality and Collective Reasoning* (Cambridge: Cambridge University Press, 2001), p. 8.
4 Ibid., p. 21.
5 Simon Blackburn argues for this conclusion in his *Ruling Passions* (Oxford: Oxford University Press, 1998), pp. 183–190. Interestingly, McMahon is himself ambivalent about this; he admits that the behavior of a person following collective reason in the prisoner's dilemma can be modeled by standard utility theory, and that the actions of such a person are equivalent to someone who has payoffs that do not correspond to the prisoner's dilemma.
6 For objections to my argument here see Kurt Baier, *The Rational and the Moral Order: The Social Roots of Reason and Morality* (Chicago, IL: Open Court, 1995), pp. 173ff.
7 Robert Nozick, *The Nature of Rationality* (Princeton: Princeton University Press, 1993), p. 133. Nozick adds: 'The question is whether it is the *whole* of rationality'.
8 McMahon, *Collective Rationality and Collective Reasoning*, p. 63.
9 Christopher McMahon, *Authority and Democracy* (Princeton: Princeton University Press, 1994), p. 104.
10 See ibid. Ch. 4, and McMahon, *Collective Rationality and Collective Reasoning*, Ch. 3.
11 It must be stressed that Waldron is not an advocate of collective rationality; he is, though, a leading liberal exponent of the coordinative model of political life.
12 Jeremy Waldron, *Law and Disagreement* (Oxford: Oxford University Press, 1999), p. 102. Emphasis in original.
13 R. Duncan Luce and Howard Raiffa, *Games and Decisions* (New York: John Wiley, 1957), p. 90.
14 Waldron, *Law and Disagreement*, p. 104. Emphasis in original.
15 Ibid.

16 Ibid., p. 107.
17 David Lewis, *Convention* (Cambridge, MA: Harvard University Press, 1969), p. 15. Emphasis in original. See also Jean Hampton, *Hobbes and the Social Contract Tradition* (Cambridge: Cambridge University Press, 1986), p. 138.
18 Henceforth Alf's move is listed first.
19 That is in (Y, X) at least one player is better off, and no player is worse off, than in (Z, Z).
20 This is not the same as saying that each equilibrium point is a strong equilibrium. An equilibrium is in strong equilibrium when no outcome Pareto-dominates it; I am only requiring that no uncoordinated outcome Pareto-dominates any coordinated outcome. See Peter C. Ordershook, *Game Theory and Political Theory* (Cambridge: Cambridge University Press, 1986), p. 305. Cf. Leslie Green's condition (2c): '(almost) everyone prefers that everyone conform to some [norm] R rather than not conform to any'. 'Law, Coordination and the Common Good', *Oxford Journal of Legal Studies*, vol. 3 (Winter 1983): 299–324, p. 302.
21 See Noel B. Reynolds, 'Law as Convention', *Ratio Juris*, vol. 2 (March 1989): 105–120, p. 107 and Green, 'Law, Coordination and the Common Good', p. 301.
22 See Lewis, *Convention*, pp. 10ff.
23 It should be stressed that it only matters what they believe, and so how they order the outcomes. Nothing depends here on the claim that there actually are such rights. See Green, 'Law, Coordination and the Common Good', p. 309ff.
24 Waldron, *Law and Disagreement*, p. 108. Emphasis added.
25 Ibid., p. 107.
26 I thank Jeremy Waldron for suggesting these points to me.
27 See above, note 20.
28 Waldron, *Law and Disagreement*, p. 121.
29 Baier, *The Rational and the Moral Order*, p. 28.
30 Ibid., p. 51. Emphasis in original.
31 Ibid., p. 129.
32 Ibid., p. 188.
33 Ibid., p. 192.
34 See David Gauthier, 'Individual Reason', in J.B. Schneewind, ed., *Reason, Ethics, and Society* (Chicago, IL: Open Court, 1996), pp. 38–57.
35 Ibid., p. 51. Emphasis added.
36 See Lance J. Ripps, 'Cognitive Process in Propositional Reasoning', *Psychological Review*, vol. 90 (1983): 38–71; Martin D.S. Braine, 'On the Relation Between the Natural Logic of Reasoning and Standard Logic', *Psychological Review*, vol. 85 (January 1978): 1–21.
37 Wittgenstein 'communitarian' notions of public reason are mentioned by both David Gauthier, 'Public Reason', *Social Philosophy and Policy*, vol. 12 (Winter 1995): 19–42 and Michael Ridge, 'Hobbesian Public Reason', *Ethics*, vol. 108 (April 1998): 538–568.
38 Philip Pettit, *The Common Mind: An Essay on Psychology, Society and Politics*, with a new postscript (New York: Oxford University Press, 1993, 1996), p. 68.
39 Ludwig Wittgenstein, *Philosophical Investigations*, 3rd edn G.E.M. Anscomb, trans. (New York: Macmillan, 1958), section 185.
40 Pettit, *The Common Mind*, p. 89.

41 Susan Hurley, *Natural Reasons: Personality and Polity* (Oxford: Oxford University Press, 1989), p. 91. The quotation from Wittgenstein is from *Remarks on the Foundations of Mathematics*.

42 David K. Henderson, 'Charity and Interpretation' in Michael Martin and Lee C. McIntyre, *Readings in the Philosophy of Social Science* (Cambridge, MA: MIT Press, 1994): 323–41, p. 329.

43 Hurley, *Natural Reasons*, pp. 93–94.

44 It is worth noting in this regard that one of Wittgenstein's most powerful statements of the argument against private rules asked us to imagine a case where only *one* person followed a rule on only *one* occasion. See *Philosophical Investigations*, section 199.

45 Ronald Dworkin, *Law's Empire* (Cambridge, MA: Harvard University Press, 1986), pp. 52, 88.

46 Ronald Dworkin, *Taking Rights Seriously* (Cambridge, MA: Harvard University Press, 1978), p. 107.

47 Ibid. The case being discussed is *Chatwin* vs *United States*, 326 U.S. 455 (1946).

48 My point is not to defend the thesis that there is always a correct answer to how to go on with such rules, only that systematic considerations greatly reduce the eligible interpretations.

49 Pettit distinguishes 'holist' and 'collectivist' views. I do not distinguish them here. See *The Common Mind*, Chs 3 and 4.

50 Ibid., p, 180.

51 Ibid.

52 Ibid., p. 190.

53 Ibid., p. 191.

54 Ibid., p. 193.

55 Ibid., pp. 190, 353.

56 Ibid., p. 193.

57 Ibid., p. 188.

58 Ibid., p. 352.

59 McMahon, *Collective Rationality and Collective Reasoning*, p. 109.

60 Ibid., p. 116.

61 Pettit, *The Common Mind*, p. 353.

62 Ibid., p. 286. The relation between republicanism and liberalism is a matter of debate in the republican movement. Republicanism and liberalism are seen as alternatives by Pettit and by Michael Sandel, *Democracy's Discontent* (Cambridge, MA: Harvard University Press, 1996), pp. 25–28. Republicanism is seen as a type of, or at least consistent with, liberalism by Richard Dagger, *Civic Virtues: Rights, Citizenship and Republican Liberalism* (Oxford: Oxford University Press, 1997); Nicholas Buttle, 'Liberal Republicanism', *Politics*, vol. 17 (1997): 147–152; and by Cass Sunstein, *Free Markets and Social Justice* (Oxford: Oxford University Press, 1997), p. 95.

63 Pettit, *The Common Mind*, p. 305.

64 Ibid., p. 306.

65 Philip Pettit, *Republicanism: A Theory of Freedom and Government* (Oxford: Oxford University Press, 1997), p. 52. Elsewhere Pettit suggests that it is better to understand domination in terms of more and less, that is, one person dominates another *to the extent* that they have a certain power over that other, in particular a power of interference on an arbitrary basis.

66 Ibid., p. 63.
67 Ibid., p. 59.
68 Ibid., p. 141.
69 Pettit, *The Common Mind*, p. 310.
70 The blurring of negative and positive rights is at the heart of Stephen Holmes and Cass Sunstein, *The Costs of Rights: Why Liberty Depends on Taxes* (New York: W.W. Norton, 1999), esp. Ch. 1.
71 I have criticized Pettit's republican conception of freedom in my 'Backwards into the Future: Neo-Republicanism as Post-Socialist Critique of Market Society,' *Social Philosophy and Policy*, vol. 20 (Winter 2003): 59–91.
72 See Philip Pettit, 'Freedom as Antipower', *Ethics*, vol. 106 (April 1996): 576–604.
73 George Orwell, *Nineteen Eighty-Four, A Novel* (New York: Harcourt, Brace & World, 1949), p. 280.
74 See my *Justificatory Liberalism* (New York: Oxford University Press, 1996), Ch. 2.
75 I have in mind here especially Richard Rorty, whose work combines themes from pragmatism with Thomas Kuhn's philosophy of science (see section 1.2) and Wittgenstein's philosophy of language. See Richard Rorty, *Contingency, Irony and Solidarity* (Cambridge: Cambridge University Press, 1989); and especially Richard Rorty, 'Postmodernist Bourgeois Liberalism' in his *Objectivity, Relativism and Truth* (Cambridge: Cambridge University Press, 1991), pp. 197–202.
76 Pettit, *The Common Mind*, p. 326.
77 Ibid., p. 304.

5

Deliberative Democracy: Public Reason and Political Consensus

5.1 Habermas: discourse and democracy

Limiting the area of intersubjective agreement

The previous chapter examined a radical proposal – that all reason is social reason insofar as all thinking requires some sort of intersubjective agreement on 'how to go on' with rules. In an important sense, to think correctly is to think as others do. This, we saw, appears to dissolve the post-Enlightenment liberal's problem – how can we justify shared political principles in a deeply pluralistic world? – by undermining the basis of much reasonable disagreement. But surely people are private reasoners in a modest, obvious, but nonetheless crucial sense: at any given time, each of us can deliberate on his beliefs and norms and decide for himself what to do or what to believe, and he can sometimes be justified in doing or believing it, even if others would always disagree.

Jürgen Habermas advances a more qualified, and I think more plausible, account linking public agreement with morality and politics. Habermas insists on basic distinctions between: (1) descriptive statements, which can be true or false, (2) normative statements, especially statements about justice, which can be 'valid' or 'invalid'[1] and (3) questions about values, or the good life. Habermas argues that type (2) statements, which are about justice and morality, can be decided rationally and, in principle, can be the object of rational consensus. In contrast, type (3) questions – about the good life – are more intractably pluralistic, and 'are accessible to rational discussion only *within* the unproblematic horizon of a concrete historical form of life or the conduct of an individual life'.[2] This distinction between questions of justice (type 2) and the good life (type 3) prevents Habermas's argument for public convergence on the former from undermining the foundations of reasonable disagreement and pluralism, which focuses on the latter. Let us, then, examine what Habermas means by saying that statements about justice can be 'valid', and how this relates to public reason.

Reactive attitudes and interpersonal validity

One entry into Habermas's moral philosophy is his discussion of certain 'reactive attitudes', in which he follows P.F. Strawson.[3] Indignation and resentment are reactive attitudes (or, we might say, moral emotions), which are directed at others who violate our integrity by refusing to give us our due. Thus, normally, when a person violates one's rights one feels resentment or indignation. As J.R. Lucas says:

> We are angry when we are hurt, but indignant when treated unjustly. We can be angry with enemies or rivals, but scarcely indignant. Indignation, which is the conceptually appropriate response to injustice, expresses, as its etymology shows, a sense of not being regarded as worthy of consideration. Injustice betokens an absence of respect, and manifest a lack of concern.[4]

It is not simply frustrating when someone does you an injustice: it is an affront. When someone acts unjustly towards you she fails to treat you with the consideration that you are due. Importantly, one does not feel resentment or indignation simply when another treats you in a way that you dislike or of which you disapprove. Your neighbor may greatly annoy you by placing garden gnomes all over her front yard, but you will not feel indignant or resentful unless you believe that she had good reasons not to behave in this way. 'She should know better than to be so inconsiderate', you might say. But unless you think something like that, you may dislike them – you might even be angry that you have to see them every time you walk down the street – but you cannot, conceptually, feel indignation or resentment. Emotions, on this view, are not brute feelings, but complexes of feelings and beliefs; resentment and indignation are, then, certain sorts of feelings based on the belief that one has not been accorded due consideration.[5]

Now, suggests Habermas, we feel resentment and indignation at injustice because we believe that the offender should have known better – she had reasons not to act in this way. Thus if you say that another morally ought to do something, you are claiming that she has good reasons for doing it (and to say that you ought to do it, similarly, is to say that you have good reasons).[6] It is in this sense that one is supposing that the norms of justice are 'valid': the norm can be justified to the others, and that is why they ought to conform to it. Only moral norms that are interpersonally valid in this way can ground the reactive attitudes of resentment and indignation. Public norms of justice then must be publicly justified, i.e., be validated.

Argumentation, validity and discourse ethics

Fundamental to Habermas's ethics and political philosophy is his claim that the justification of a moral norm is not a task for one person – even one philosopher – reasoning by herself (he calls this 'monological' reasoning). Instead, Habermas argues, moral justification requires 'real cooperative effort'.[7]

> Moral argumentation ... serves to settle conflicts of action by consensual means. Conflicts in the domain of norm-guided interactions can be traced directly to some disruption of a normative consensus. Repairing a disrupted consensus can mean two things: restoring intersubjective recognition of a validity claim after it has become controversial or assuring intersubjective recognition for a new validity claim that is a substitute for the old one. Agreement of this kind expresses a *common will* .... What is needed is a 'real' process of argumentation in which the individuals concerned cooperate.[8]

To show that a norm is valid is to justify it through real discourse to all those affected.

Habermas does not believe that simply any intersubjective agreement would suffice to validate a norm. Rather only an intersubjective agreement that arises out of the right sort of discourse justifies. Thus, for example, Habermas mentions the following as possible rules of an adequate discourse:[9]

1   No speaker may contradict himself.
2   Every speaker who applies predicate F to object A must be prepared to apply F to all other objects resembling A in all relevant respects.
3   Different speakers may not use the same expression with different meanings.
4   Every speaker only asserts what he believes.
5   A person who disputes a proposition or norm not under discussion must provide a reason for wanting to do so.

6   Every subject with the competence to speak and act is allowed to take part in a discourse.

7   (a)   Everyone is allowed to question any assertion whatever.
     (b)   Everyone is allowed to introduce any assertion whatever into the discourse.
     (c)   Everyone is allowed to express his attitudes, desires and needs.

8   No speaker may be prevented, by internal or external coercion, from exercising his rights as laid down in 6 and 7.

Habermas claims that such rules are necessary for rational discourse: to deny them is somehow to be caught in a contradiction.[10] Insofar as a discourse following these rules produces a consensus, it is a rational consensus, and thus serves to validate the norm. And insofar as we agree, Habermas argues, we are intelligible to each other: we understand each other's reasons.[11]

What norms might be the object of such a rational consensus? We have seen that Habermas does not think that questions of value or the good life are promising candidates, except within a group that already agrees on much.[12] However, rules of justice are excellent candidates, for at the heart of justice is the idea of universalizability, according to which a moral rule must in some way apply equally to all. 'The intuition expressed by the idea of the generalizability of maxims intends something more than this, namely that valid norms must *deserve* recognition by *all* concerned'.[13] Thus, says Habermas, every valid norm must meet the condition:

> (U) *All* affected can accept the consequences and side effects its *general* observance can be anticipated to have for the satisfaction of *everyone's* interests (and these consequences are preferred to those of known alternative possibilities for regulation).[14]

The universal form of justice stressed by Kantian conceptions of morality (see section 1.1), in Habermas's eyes, leads to the idea of discourse ethics.

Discourse and democracy: a first cut

Because Habermas insists that discourse must actually be carried out among the participants, he rejects the ambition of liberal political philosophers – from John Locke to John Rawls – to construct a theory of political justice that would constrain and usurp democratic deliberation.[15] Habermas criticizes 'Liberals [,who] begin with the legal institutionalization of equal liberties, conceiving these as rights held by individualized subjects. In their view, human rights enjoy normative priority over democracy and the constitutional separation of powers has priority over the will of the democratic legislature'.[16] Because actual deliberation is required to validate norms, it seems that only a political order based on actual public deliberation among the citizens can yield valid norms.[17] Norms that are not so validated do not provide reasons for all to embrace them and to act on them; to impose them would simply be to subjugate others to our will. The ideal, then, must be real political deliberation that leads to a rational consensus on norms. Habermas approvingly quotes the German democrat Julius Fröbel:

> We seek the social republic, that is, the state in which happiness, freedom and dignity of each individual are recognized as the common goal of all, and the perfection of the law and power of society springs from the mutual *understanding* and agreement *of all its members*.[18]

We can immediately see the main worry about deliberative democracy: it is hard to understand how modern plural communities could ever achieve consensus on the whole set of laws. Habermas acknowledges that consensus will always be imperfect. In the end, we will always have to take a vote, which means that consensus was not achieved.[19] Nevertheless, he insists:

> Majority rules retains an internal relation to the search for truth inasmuch as the decision reached by the majority only represents a caesura in an ongoing discussion; the decision records, so to speak, the interim result of a discursive opinion-forming process. To be sure, in that case the majority decision must be premised on a competent discussion of the disputed issues, that is, a discussion conducted according to the communicative presuppositions of a corresponding discourse. Only then can its content be viewed as the rationally motivated yet fallible result of a process of argumentation that has been interrupted in view of institutional pressures to decide, but is in principle resumable.[20]

However, it is puzzling how voting can be an indicator – fallible or otherwise – of validity insofar as validity requires that deliberation actually be carried out. To see the problem, consider the difference between two views that have tied correct outcomes to deliberation: let us call these the *counterfactual* and *actual* deliberative accounts. According to the counterfactual deliberative account, a belief is to be justified if it *would be* agreed to *if* discussion were to go as far as it could fruitfully go.[21] We have here a criterion independent of actual deliberation: X is true (right now) if it *would* be agreed to *if* discussion went as far as it could fruitfully go. Thus we might guess what the outcome would be, or take a vote; the vote might be seen as a fallible indicator of what would be agreed to if discussion went as far as it fruitfully could go. But Habermas often insists that validity is not a matter of what would be agreed to under certain hypothetical conditions, but what *actual* discourse under appropriate conditions *does* lead to. Again and again we are told that real, actual, discourse must be undertaken to validate norms. If so, then we cannot achieve validity by guessing the outcome of this discourse; only if we have actually followed the procedure – had the discussion that led to rational consensus – can we claim that our norms are validated.[22] But that seems to undermine the status of the vote as in some way a pointer to the correct deliberative outcome: if there is not yet a correct answer, we cannot have a fallible indicator of what it is. Rather, the vote seems simply to cut-off deliberation and the search for validity.

What could be the aim of voting for an actual deliberative democrat? It might seem that a deliberative democrat would wish the voting procedure to be a totally reliable indicator of the outcome of the actual deliberation – what the deliberation would conclude were it carried to its conclusion. But this seems inconsistent with – or, at least, in tension with – actual deliberative democracy. According to the actual deliberation model, public reason on matter M is a function of suitably idealized citizens' deliberation. Discussion and deliberation will alter many of the citizens' current views, so that at the conclusion of the deliberation most people's, perhaps everyone's, set of beliefs, etc., is apt to be different from that with which they started. Moreover, public reason thus constructed is almost certainly what political scientists call 'path dependent'. Supposing a certain initial set of individual beliefs, etc. $\{b_1 \ldots b_n\}$, the final set of beliefs $\{b_1^* \ldots b_n^*\}$ is apt to depend on the order in which alterations to the initial set are made. An early concession by b_1 may change the terms of the deliberation, producing a different path to a consensus that would have occurred had b_1 resisted alterations of his belief until late in the day.

Because of this, it would be exceedingly difficult to predict where this sort of process would lead. Suppose we take a vote at time t; participants have to not only know the state of their deliberations about M at t, but be good predictors of what paths deliberation will follow after t, so that they could predict the ultimate projected end of the deliberations. Because such estimations are exceedingly difficult to make, the deliberative democrat stresses the need for actual discourse; it is the actual path the discourse takes that determines its outcome. In light of this, the most we can hope for from a vote is evidence of *the state of deliberation at the time of the vote*. If public reason is to be seen as the outcome of the deliberation, and if voting is a way of coping with the fact that we must act before the deliberation has reached its outcome, a deliberative democrat should want the vote to reflect how far the deliberation has proceeded. Given path dependence, all that really can be known about the requirements of public reason at t is the state of the deliberation at t.

Yet this raises a puzzle. If we accept that voting 'cuts short' deliberation, then we know that the proposal has not yet been vindicated by the deliberation; the deliberation has not been completed. If we are not trying to predict what would happen if the deliberation continued to its conclusion, what is the point of voting now? One possibility, not explored in the literature on deliberative democracy, is that we might be aiming at (what I shall call) *quasi-vindication*. Perhaps the most we could achieve is a collective judgment whether at t any consideration has been advanced thus far that shows proposed law L has failed as a candidate for public reason on M. A proposal that is quasi-vindicated at t may fail to be vindicated later in the deliberation: perhaps L will have to be modified to meet an objection (again we confront path-dependence), or dropped altogether. But given that this cannot be known, the best voting procedure for which the deliberative democrat can reasonably hope would be one according to which, if a vote is taken at time t, L will pass if and only if L has been quasi-vindicated at t. To ask more – that it predicts whether at the end of the deliberation the proposal will be finally vindicated is to ask that the voting procedure outpaces actual deliberation.

The alternative to developing some theory of voting as revealing quasi-vindication is to retreat back to a counterfactual view of deliberation – validity is what actual discourse *would* lead to if it were carried out to its conclusion. This preserves the role of voting as an indicator of validity – we vote for L because we think it is (now) valid, it is what a certain sort of discussion would converge on – but this view undermines the necessity of actual democratic deliberation. It is at least possible that on many technical matters the decision of a panel of experts or a Supreme Court (see section 7.5) is a better indication of what would be agreed to by everyone under ideal conditions than is actual democratic discourse; the counterfactual test may justify employing an expert panel rather than democratic deliberation.

Morality and law

Thus far, my analysis of Habermas has been oversimplified: I have assumed that the task of democratic deliberation is simply to arrive at valid norms of justice. Habermas makes clear, though, that law is not simply to be identified with morality or, in his terms, with *norms*. Habermas's aim is to chart a course between two well-established and opposed views of laws. According to *legal positivism* laws are social *facts*: as John Austin put it, they are commands of the sovereign, to other positivists they are patterns of obedience. The important point for positivists is that laws are social realities that guide the behavior of subjects. As such, the study of law is not a study of what law *should be*, or *what is a moral law*, but what law as a social fact is, how it functions, and how it is possible. Thus a legal positivist will argue that L can be a law even though it is highly immoral: the criterion for being a law is independent of the criterion of morality. In contrast, *natural law theory* has held that in order for L to be a law it must be morally justified: an immoral law – or, at least, a grossly immoral law – is no law at all. This makes laws out to be *norms*. The natural law theorist need not hold that every moral rule is also a law: in addition to being morally justified, it is plausible to add that L must have been enacted in a certain way by the proper authorities. Nevertheless, on this natural law theory, law is a subset of morality; in that sense it is derivative of morality.

The interpretation presented thus far depicts Habermas as a natural law theorist, insofar as democratic deliberations about laws are a search for moral validity. Habermas certainly insists that this is an important aspect of law. Following Kant, Habermas tells us that one perspective on laws is to see them as 'laws of freedom'. Rules that are self-imposed – that are validated in the proper sort of discourse – can be understood as being freely accepted by everyone.[23] Habermas, though, maintains that this natural law insight overlooks the other aspect of laws: they are also *social facts* – rights and duties backed up by coercion which structure human action. This is the factual character of law on which the positivists focused.

Habermas's own view of law – as something between facts and norms – is complex, but the core idea is that the rule of law as a system of individual rights and constitutional provisions such as the separation of powers provides the necessary context for what he calls 'rational political will formation' – rational democratic discourse and decisions in both formal political institutions as well as the citizenry at large. '[T]here is a conceptual or internal relation, and not simply a historically contingent association, between the rule of law and democracy'.[24]

> Discourse theory invests the democratic process with normative connotations stronger than those found in the liberal model ... it gives center stage to the process of political opinion- and will-formation, but without understanding the constitution as something secondary; rather ... it conceives of constitutional principles as a consistent answer to the question of how the demanding communicative forms of democratic opinion- and will-formation can be institutionalized. According to discourse theory, the success of deliberative politics depends not only on a collectively acting citizenry but on the institutionalization of procedures and conditions of communications, as well as the interplay of institutionalized deliberative processes, with informally developed public opinion.[25]

The relation between law and normative validity in Habermas's account is clearly complicated. On the one hand, the *fact* of coercive laws in a constitutional regime is a necessary context for a procedure that yields a *normative*, rational will, and so can validate laws. Yet, of course, not just any constitutional regime will do this – only that which is normatively justified, a proper sort of constitutional order, provides the background for a rational democratic procedure. It would appear, then, that the normative character of law is, in the end, fundamental for Habermas, for only the 'fact' of the right sort of law provides the necessary framework for normative discourse.

5.2 Liberal deliberative democracy

The liberty of the ancients and of the moderns

Whereas liberalism views individual rights to liberty as morally prior to democratic decision making, and so circumscribing the area in which democratic decisions are legitimate, egalitarian democratic critics of liberalism insist that individual rights arise out of the democratic, deliberative, process. This debate about the relative priority of democratic political rights and individual rights to liberty is long-standing.[26] Benjamin Constant, a nineteenth-century French political theorist, distinguished two understandings of liberty, the ancient and the modern:

> First ask yourself, Gentlemen, what an Englishmen, a Frenchman, and a citizen of the United States of America understand today by the word 'liberty'.
> For each of them it is the right to be subjected only to the laws, and to be neither arrested, detained, put to death or maltreated in any way by the arbitrary will of one or more individuals. It is the right of everyone to express their opinion, choose a profession and practice it, to dispose of property, and even to abuse it; to come and go without permission, and without having to account for their motives or undertakings. It is everyone's right to associate with other individuals, whether to discuss their interests, or to profess the religion which they and their associates prefer, or even simply to occupy their days or hours in a way which is most compatible with their inclinations or whims. Finally it is everyone's right to exercise some influence on the administration of the government, either by electing all or particular officials, or through representations, petitions, demands to which the authorities are more or less compelled to pay heed. Now compare this to the liberty of the ancients.
> The latter consisted in exercising collectively, but directly, several parts of the complete sovereignty; in deliberating, in the public square, over war and peace; in forming alliances with foreign governments; in voting laws, in pronouncing judgments, in examining the accounts, the acts, the stewardship of the magistrates; in calling them to appear in front of the assembled people, in accusing, condemning or absolving them. But if this is what the ancients called liberty, they admitted as compatible with this collective freedom the complete subjection of the individual to the authority of the community.[27]

On the face of it, it seems that egalitarian versions of deliberative democracy side with the ancients against the moderns, at least insofar as they accord primacy to collective political deliberation. To be sure, democratic egalitarians believe that the liberties of the moderns – religious freedom, freedom of conscience and association – will arise out of a properly functioning democracy; but they insist that these rights are not morally prior to democratic rights and so do not pose limits to a legitimate democratic decision. Robert Dahl, perhaps the most famous contemporary democratic theorist, calls a liberal democracy, in which the personal liberties provide limits on legitimate democratic decisions, 'limited democracy'[28] – a democracy, that is, is limited by the rights of citizens. Dahl is critical of such half-hearted democracy. According to Dahl, the only rights that properly limit the *demos* are the rights intrinsic to democracy itself, such as the right to vote. This, however, implies that democracy is prior to liberalism, and is only contingently related to it.

Liberty and deliberative democracy

Habermas's position is, again, somewhat more complicated: he seeks to mediate between, or to integrate, the liberties of the moderns and ancients. He thus rejects both liberalism and what he calls 'republicanism', which upholds the priority of the liberty of the ancients. Joshua Cohen, another leading theorist of deliberative democracy, is more clearly in the liberal camp, advancing a case for an inherently liberal conception of deliberative democracy: one in which the liberty of the moderns is an inherent and necessary part of a deliberative democracy. According to Cohen, the core of the deliberative conception is 'the ideal of political justification'.[29] An exercise of coercive political power is justified only if it is based on 'free public reasoning among equals'.[30] So at the crux of Cohen's conception of deliberative democracy is the traditional liberal ideal that each person must be respected as free and equal.[31] Citizens are considered free because, given the fact of reasonable pluralism (see section 1.2), each person is *free* to decide for herself what vision of value or the good life she will pursue; the polity is not committed to any specific understanding of the good life to which all citizens must ascribe as a condition of membership. Citizens are *equal* insofar as each is understood to have the capacities for reasoning that allow for equal participation in deliberations about the legitimate exercise of coercive public authority.[32] Cohen thus understands 'the fundamental idea of democratic legitimacy' as the requirement that 'the authorization to exercise state power must arise from … the discussions and decisions of the members [of a society], as made within and expressed through social and political positions designed to acknowledge their collective authority'.[33]

Cohen, though, is sensitive to our post-Enlightenment quandary. Given the fact of reasonable pluralism (section 1.2) – the absence of shared 'comprehensive moral or religious views'[34] – political justification requires that each citizen be given reasons that are acceptable to her in support of political proposals. Cohen is adamant that it is not enough for legitimate democratic decision making that 'the interests of all be given equal consideration in binding collective decisions'.[35] The freedom and equality of each is only respected by a deliberative process in which reasons for proposals are advanced – and they must be seen as reasons from the perspective of all of reasonable citizens. Cohen calls this requirement the 'principle of democratic inclusion'.[36]

Given this, a legitimate deliberative process cannot require some citizens to abandon, ignore or violate deep-seated reasonable beliefs that stem from the comprehensive conception of value and the good life.

> Suppose that our democracy requires that a person accept as sufficient for justification a reason that his religious or moral philosophy compels him to deny as sufficient – 'compelled', because denying the sufficiency of these reasons follows from a religious or a moral philosophy that not unreasonably commands the person's conviction. This is to deny the person standing as an equal citizen – to deny full and equal membership in the people whose collective actions authorize the exercise of power.[37]

That would violate the basic maxim to treat all as free and equal. Given this, Cohen insists that a conception of deliberative democracy under conditions of reasonable pluralism must acknowledge the fundamental place of religious freedom and, by extension, expressive freedoms: freedoms to articulate 'thoughts and feelings on matters of personal or broader human concern'.[38] The upshot is that, given the conditions of reasonable pluralism, the 'liberties of the moderns' are crucial to deliberative democracy; justified deliberative democracy is thus liberal deliberative democracy.

Two worries about Cohen's defense of liberal rights

Cohen's basic argument for the inherent liberal character of deliberative democracy under conditions of reasonable pluralism appears to run along the following lines:

1 A coercive law or public policy is justified only if all reasonable citizens have adequate reasons for embracing it.
2 To treat citizens as free and equal requires that all laws and policies be justified as in (1).
3 A citizen does not have a good reason to embrace a law or policy that requires he ignore or violate a deep reason of his that flows from his basic view of what makes life worth living, such as a religion or a moral philosophy.
4 Thus it follows that no law or policy can require a citizen to ignore or violate a deep reason of his that flows from his basic view of what makes life worth living, such as a religion or a moral philosophy.
5 Under conditions of modern pluralism, every law or policy that seeks to establish a religious view or favor one religion over others will fail to meet the requirement of (4).
6 Thus deliberative democracy under conditions of modern pluralism will effectively require freedom of religion.

This is a powerful argument. However, it is important to point out that Cohen does not believe that this argument establishes absolute rights. Some regulations, he argues, do not impinge 'very deeply' and so apparently can be justified even if they do run contrary to substantial reasons based on comprehensive views of the good life.[39] Cohen focuses on religion because it is 'deeply held' and provides 'substantial reasons'. It thus seems that the strength of a liberal right protecting an interest or belief (I) against a law (L) depends on two factors:

1   How deeply held and substantial is I?
2   How deeply does L impinge on I?

The more deeply held and substantial I is, and the more deeply L would impinge on I, the stronger is a citizen's right against the imposition of L. Although both factors are sensible, and it is hard to see how any reasonable theory of law and rights can avoid asking the second question, the first is more problematic. To answer the first question we must know a good deal about a person's structure of beliefs: we need to know how important I is to him (and how sincere he is in avowing I). This was the approach taken by United States Selective Service Boards in determining whether a potential draftee was a pacifist. The draftee had to show the board that his pacifism was deeply held. It apparently had to be based on a religious conviction, and could not admit of exceptions. The potential draftee would not, for example, be deemed a pacifist, and so exempted from the conscription law, if he held that some wars might be justified – that apparently demonstrated an insufficiently deeply-held pacifism.

Now in one way this appears a reasonable approach. Adopting a reasoning much like Cohen's, the Selective Service Board was sensitive to deeply held and substantial reasons, and that a law might 'compel' some citizens to reject such reasons. Still, we can observe two worrying aspects of this approach. First, it seems to justify intrusive procedures by which citizens are tested for the depth of their opposition. After all, it is not simply a sound objection, but a deeply held sound objection, that constitutes a strong objection. It is thus not enough to publicly deliberate about the soundness of the objection to a law; a biographical matter is also relevant – how deeply held is this reason by the objector? Is he really a deeply religious person? This points to the relevance of the Selective Service Board's inquiry into the depth of one's convictions. Second, and this was clearly the result of the Selective Service Board's procedures, the criterion of depth disadvantages those who are sensitive to complexity while favoring those who adhere to absolutist views. Potential draftees who had objections to military service in the Vietnam War, but could conceive of wars in which their participation would be justified, were held to have insufficiently deep commitments: they were willing to trade off their objections to war for other goods in some circumstances. Given the complexities of the goods at stake in different wars – reflect on the differences between the United States Civil War, The Second World War and the Vietnam War – it hardly seems unreasonable to see participation as warranted in one or two but not the third. Indeed, a view that refuses to see any differences looks somewhat unreasonable, but it was precisely such 'deep' and 'substantial' objections that the Selective Service acknowledged as genuine. On the face of it, it would appear that Cohen would have to be sympathetic to the Board's approach, and its bias towards simple, extreme and deep commitments.

5.3 Is deliberative democracy a consistent ideal?

Three ideals of deliberative democracy

Our explications of Habermas's and Cohen's specific formulations of deliberative democracy indicate that three sub-ideals characterize the general ideal of deliberative democracy. The first, the *Ideal of Reason*, is at the heart of deliberative democracy. As Cohen observes, '[t]he notion of a deliberative democracy is rooted in the intuitive idea of a democratic association in which the justification of the terms and conditions of association proceeds through public argument and reasoning among citizens'.[40] According to the Ideal of Reason, then:

> Deliberation is *reasoned* in that the parties to it are required to state their reasons for advancing proposals, supporting or criticizing them. They give reasons with the expectation that those reasons (and not, for example, power) will settle the fate of their proposal.[41]

In itself, embracing the Ideal of Reason is hardly an innovation. Aristotle and his followers present us with an ideal of collective political choice based on reasoned deliberation; and to one commentator the 'distinguishing feature' of the liberal tradition is reasoned political deliberation.[42] Contemporary deliberative democracy is distinctive, however, in making two further claims. Deliberative democrats insist that deliberation must be public in a radical sense – only reasons that can be embraced by all of us are truly public, and hence justificatory. As Gerald Postema, a contemporary advocate of deliberative democracy, has put it, a public reason must be a shared reason.[43] So according to the *Ideal of Public Justification*, a policy or principle *P* is justified only if it can, in some way, be embraced by all members of the public.

Now most deliberative democrats maintain that, together, the Ideals of Reason and Public Justification lead to what I will call the *Regulative Ideal of Real Political Consensus*. Recall that, for Habermas, validity supposes an 'agreement' that 'expresses a common will' that arises from an actual 'process of argumentation in which the individuals concerned cooperate'. (see section 5.1). Postema expresses this ideal when he tells us that '[a]gree-ment among members of the community is set as the open-ended task or project of ... [the] exercise of practical reason and judgment'.[44] '[T]he aim of the regulative idea is agreement of conviction on the basis of public reasons uttered as assessed in public discourse'.[45] While this basic idea seems clear enough, the Regulative Ideal of Real Political Consensus is difficult to precisely characterize. Both Habermas and Cohen are well aware that complete actual consensus is not a reasonable aim: 'even an ideal deliberative procedure will not, in general, issue in consensus'.[46] Postema, like Habermas, is clear that the deliberations of citizens are not apt to yield a consensus, and so we may have to cut the discussion off by taking a vote.[47] But, he says, no such closure can ever be final – *public dis-cussion must remain open until common conviction is reached*'.[48] But although the regulative goal is not actual complete political consensus here and now, the Regulative Ideal of Real Political Consensus is more than a claim, that, ideally, all rational people should agree. Achieving actual common conviction is the ideal that should regulate political institutions and processes. As Postema stresses, this notion that public discourse can reach consensus is

> not meant merely as a heuristic device, like Rawls' 'original position', describing the reasoning of a hypothetical congregation of abstract, represen-tative, rational, beings whose choice under restricted conditions is supposed to tell us something about the principles we have reason to endorse. Rather, it is intended as a model for real moral discourse in concrete, historical, social conditions. It is an idealization, to be sure, but it is an ideal to which we can demand real social and political institutions to approximate.[49]

One way of expressing this ideal is to insist that healthy democratic politi-cal institutions should generate wide, though not of course complete, actual consensus on political outcomes. This, I think, is true to Jean-Jacques Rousseau, in whose footsteps many deliberative democrats follow (but see also Chapter 6 below). It will be recalled that to Rousseau the breakdown of actual consensus into 'contradictory views and debates' indicates the corruption of the body politic.[50] 'The more concert reigns in the assemblies, that is, the nearer the opinion approaches unanimity, the greater is the dominance of the general will. On the other hand, long debates, dissensions, and tumult proclaim the ascendancy of particular interests and the decline of the state'.[51]

Although deliberative democrats such as Cohen wish to draw back from the ideal of Real Political Consensus, it appears an essential part of their doc-trine. The defining feature of deliberative democratic theories is that public justification is tied to actual discourse; only the outcomes of actual delibera-tions serve to justify coercive laws. 'Outcome', in this context, however, has to mean something like 'actual agreement', for the test of correctness is precisely the tendency of the discourse to lead to convergence.

To be plausible, deliberative democracy's three ideals must be consistent: it must be the case that all three can, at least in principle, be satisfied. Should it be the case – as I believe it is – that it is impossible to simultaneously meet these three ideals, then deliberative democracy is, literally, a chimera – a fanciful hybrid of different parts. I shall argue in this section that, so far from leading us toward the Regulative Ideal of Real Political Consensus, The Ideals of Reason and Public Justification point us away from it.[52] Common conviction, I shall argue, is not a regulative ideal of political discourse aimed at sincere public justification.

Sincerity as Part of the Ideal of Reason

As indicated above, according to the Ideal of Reason '[d]eliberation is *reasoned* in that the parties to it are required to state their reasons for advancing proposals, supporting or criticizing them. They give reasons with the expectation that those reasons (and not, for example, power) will settle the fate of their proposal'.[53] To say that parties are giving 'their reasons' supposes that they are giving what they believe to be *good* reasons. Postema insists that '[p]articipants regard themselves as bound by a principle of *sincerity* to present proposals and evidence, arguments, and interpretations that they can fully endorse'.[54] This, I think, is actually too restrictive. Postema's principle would seem to imply that Betty, who is trying to convince Alf to accept her proposal *P*, can appeal to reason *R* in support of *P* only if Betty actually accepts *R* as a good reason for *her* to endorse *P*.[55] Suppose, though, that Betty proposes the policy that child health care should be funded by the state. And suppose further that Betty, an atheist feminist, supports this policy because she believes it will help empower women. Now when deliberating with Alf, a Roman Catholic who supports right-to-life groups and believes that the proper place for women is in the home, she rightly believes that he will be unmoved by her reason. But suppose she says to Alf 'Your religious beliefs about the sanctity of life justify your support of child health care'. This certainly violates Postema's principle of sincerity, as Betty cannot fully endorse this reason. But if (1) Betty really does have good reasons of her own to endorse child health care, (2) she believes that Alf is justified in holding his religious beliefs and, (3) she believes that Alf's religious beliefs really ought to lead him to support child health care, then her appeal to them does not seem objectionably insincere.[56] After all, she believes that she has good reasons to support the policy and that Alf is justified in entertaining reasons that should lead him to endorse the policy. In this case they have *convergent* reasons for supporting the policy (see section 7.4).[57] I propose, then, a more modest *Principle of Sincerity*:

A reasoned justification must be sincere. Betty's appeal to reason R justifying P to Alf is sincere if and only if (1) she believes that she is justified in accepting P; (2) she believes that Alf is justified in accepting R; (3) she believes that R justifies P in Alf's system of beliefs.

Rational consensus and the pursuit of actual political consensus

Distinctive of deliberative democracy is the conjunction of this Ideal of Reason to an Ideal of Public Justification, or the giving of uniquely public reasons. One does not simply utter reasons that one finds sound, but one's arguments must be directed at what others can see as good reasons. Recall that, according to Cohen, the core of the deliberative conception is 'the ideal of political justification'.[58] Now taken together, the Ideals of Reason and Public Justification lead us to seek what Cohen calls a '*rationally motivated consensus* – to find reasons that are persuasive to all who are committed to acting on the results of a free and reasoned assessment of alternativess'.[59] If (1) I am committed to giving good reasons for my political proposals and (2) I am also committed to the idea that these reasons must (in some sense) be seen as good reasons by every member of the public, I seem committed to the further claim that (3) my proposal P is justified only if, supposing all members of the public were fully rational and reasoned in good faith, all would accept it. For if any rational member of the public does not have a good reason to accept my proposal, it appears that I have not lived up to the Ideal of Public Justification.

Now although the notion of a 'rationally motivated consensus' is not at all the same as the Regulative Ideal of Real Political Consensus, it is easy to see why many would think that they are intimately related. Deliberative democrats often talk of voting as 'cutting the discussion off before rational consensus is achieved', implying that the actual quasi-consensus achieved at the time of the vote was a stopping (or pausing) point on the road to an ideal rational consensus. This is certainly the view suggested above by Habermas (see section 5.1) and Postema (this section). Actual Political Consensus, it is thought, is an approximation of rationally motivated consensus. Thus, if the Ideals of Reason and Public Justification endorse an ideal of a rationally motivated consensus, it is reasoned, they must also endorse its approximation – the Ideal of Real Political Consensus. I believe that this basic supposition of deliberative democracy is mistaken. Although it is indeed the case that the Ideals of Reason and Public Justification commit us to an ideal of a rationally motivated consensus, the same ideals prevent us from embracing the Regulative Ideal of Real Political Consensus.

In order to see why this is so, let us consider more fully how to interpret the crucial Ideal of Public Justification, and how it relates to the idea of a 'rationally motivated consensus'. Three interpretations are worth considering. None, we shall see, combine all three elements of deliberative democracy: The Ideals of Reason, Public Justification and the Regulative Ideal of Real Political Consensus.

Public Justification as Rational Consensus

The most obvious way to interpret the Ideal of Public Justification is to simply articulate it in terms of an ideal rational consensus. Let us call this *Public Justification as Rational Consensus*:

> Principle/policy P is publicly justified if and only if, supposing everyone reasoned in good faith, reasoned perfectly and had perfect information, everyone would accept P. (Or no one would reject P).

Manifestly, this is consistent with the Principle of Sincerity. The 'public' addressed in Public Justification as Rational Consensus is composed solely of purely rational deliberators – they are perfectly rational, well-informed and argue in good faith in the sense that they accept all, and only, what they have good reason to accept. But while Public Justification as Rational Consensus expresses an ideal of sincere public justification, it does not ground the pursuit of actual political consensus. What would be done by fully rational and informed people with unlimited ability to process information does not seem an appropriate benchmark for *our* practice. That demigods would agree hardly seems a reason for us to aspire to actual political consensus. Ours is a condition of scarcity of cognitive resources and information, in which the pursuit of minimal rationality is challenging enough, without seeking to model our practices on what we would do if we had such semi-divine status.[60] And because we know that actual people fall far short of cognitive perfection, one who accepts Public Justification as Rational Consensus should not expect anything even approaching actual consensus on policy P.

Public Justification as Rational Consensus supports the pursuit of actual consensual politics only if we can suppose – as I think Rousseau did – that the pursuit of actual consensus is the best way to track what perfectly rational agents would all accept. But a contrary hypothesis seems equally plausible: as many have pointed out, actual consensus is sometimes, perhaps often, better obtained by advancing arguments that do not meet Public Justification as Rational Consensus.[61] For example, a large body of evidence indicates that most reasoners rely on what Amos Tversky and Daniel Kahneman describe as 'heuristics;' of special interest here are the 'vividness' and 'availability' heuristics.[62] According to the former, people draw on the most vivid or psychologically salient bit of information, typically discounting or altogether ignoring better information;

the latter concerns the way in which people base their judgments on the most readily retrievable information. Thus, for example, one reason that racial or ethnic stereotypes persist is that they focus on vivid and available information. People find these false but simple images compelling and attractive. Consequently, it seems a reasonable conjecture that the political judgments of cognitively imperfect people are more apt to converge (though of course incompletely) on stereotypical characterizations of some groups than fully-informed understandings. A political style that sought to move as far as possible down the road of actual consensus may well employ stereotypes, thus embracing arguments that violate Public Justification as Rational Consensus. A comparison of the deep cleavages in the democracies of the 1930s with the widespread consensus in authoritarian states, which made extensive appeal to ethnic stereotypes to vilify minority groups, suggests that this may well be more than an interesting possibility suggested by psychological research.

It might be responded that, although cognitively flawed arguments could perhaps gain wide approval, they could never be the objects of total consensus. But that seems quite beside the point, for we are never going to achieve complete actual consensus on any interesting constitutional or political issue. Our options are always between conditions of imperfect consensus. Given this, and given the wide attractiveness of heuristics that can lead to results that would be rejected by perfectly rational creatures, there is no compelling reason to suppose that the path to the most justified position according to Public Justification as Rational Consensus is the same path as that which seeks the widest possible consensus among citizens in the actual political world, a fact demagogues are well aware of.[63]

Public Justification as Consensus Among Reasonable People

Perhaps the problem is with the thoroughly rationalistic conception of public justification expressed by Public Justification as Rational Consensus. And, indeed, many deliberative democrats seem to offer a much less demanding conception of *Public Justification as Consensus Among Reasonable People*:

> Principle/policy P is publicly justified if and only if it would be accepted by every reasonable person reasoning in good faith. (Or, it would not be rejected by any reasonable person).

If we explicate 'rationally motivated consensus' along the lines of Public Justification as Consensus Among Reasonable People, the jump from 'rationally motivated consensus' to the Regulative Ideal of Real Political Consensus seems a short one; and thus it seems as if, after all, a deliberative democrat might be able to unite all the ideals. To be sure, Public Justification as Consensus Among Reasonable People does not require the actual consent of everyone before a principle or policy can be justifiably imposed. Objections from unreasonable people need not stop the coercive imposition of law. Clearly, though, those who adopt Public Justification as Consensus Among Reasonable People believe that, overwhelmingly, ordinary reasoners are – or usually are – reasonable in the requisite sense: they are free from gross cognitive defects and typically reason in good faith according to well known and widely accepted canons of thought. Consequently, a practice modeled on this conception of public justification would seem committed to some fairly broad-based actual political consensus; if almost everyone is reasonable (at least most of the time), and if a justified policy must be accepted by every reasonable person (or not rejected by any reasonable person) it is clearly a sign that things are amiss if policies are imposed in the face of actual widespread dissent.

Public Justification as Consensus Among Reasonable People, however, is unacceptable as an explication of the notion of a rationally motivated consensus. It will be recalled that the notion of a rationally motivated consensus derives from the Ideals of Reason and Public Justification. However, *Public Justification as Consensus Among Reasonable People is inconsistent with the Ideal of Reason*, as it accepts arguments inconsistent with the Principle of Sincerity. To see this, consider again Betty's proposal that child health care be provided by the government; suppose again that her atheist-feminist beliefs give her good reason to support the proposal. Alf is a reasonable person – he is cognitively normal and reasons in good faith according to widely embraced canons of thought; once again, he has religious beliefs that lead him also to endorse state-provided health care. According to Public Justification as Consensus Among Reasonable People the proposal would seem to be justified (in the public restricted to Alf and Betty). But let us now suppose that, in Betty's considered opinion, Alf's religious beliefs are not justified: she thinks religious beliefs are nonsense. In this case the Principle of Sincerity implies that she has not engaged in reasoned justification if she appeals to Alf's religious beliefs; but according to Public Justification as Consensus Among Reasonable People the appeal would be justificatory. So, according to Public Justification as Consensus Among Reasonable People an imposed policy of state-supported child health care would be justified, but Betty's commitment to reasoned justification insists that it is not. Public Justification as Consensus Among Reasonable People thus allows that what Betty sees as bad reasons may be justificatory.[64]

Of course this problem would not arise if it was the case that Alf thinking that *R* is a good reason when it is not implies, ipso facto that he is an unreasonable person. But this would essentially drive us right back to Public Justification as Rational Consensus. And, as a matter of fact, it seems that reasonable people have a large number of unreasonable beliefs. Consider, for example, the famous belief perseverance experiments of Lee Ross and his associates, which induced subjects to develop theories and opinions on the basis of information that was later shown to them to be false.[65] In one experiment, subjects were given false feedback when sorting authentic suicide notes from fictitious ones. Based on their 'successes' and 'failures', subjects developed beliefs about their own competency at the task, and their future ability to make such discriminations. Afterwards, subjects were extensively debriefed, and each subject acknowledged that his or her 'performance' was strictly an artefact of the experimenters' manipulation. Nevertheless, even after the experimenters discredited the evidence upon which their beliefs were based, subjects showed marked belief perseverance – subjects tended to believe they were competent at the task even after the evidence for their competency was undermined. Similar results were achieved in an experiment in which subjects were induced, by giving them false evidence, to develop theories about the relation between fire-fighters' professional performance and the fire-fighters' scores on a test for risk taking. Once again, despite being later informed that the scores were fictitious, subjects showed significant perseverance in their theories. The subjects were above normal in intelligence, and their beliefs were subject to far more rigorous criticism than are most of our political beliefs. In spite of all this, subjects continued to hold beliefs that seem manifestly unjustified.[66] Since their evidence in favor of their beliefs was shown by the experimenters to be illusory, the belief that they do not know whether they possess these skills is strikingly more credible than the belief that they do. The subjects have all the information they need to draw that conclusion, yet they do not. The results of this experiment are consistent with a large body of evidence showing that reasonable people often have strikingly unreasonable beliefs.[67]

Public Justification as Agreement in Reasonable Belief

More promising for an account of public justification is to focus on reasonable *beliefs* rather than reasonable *people*, thus *Public Justification as Agreement in Reasonable Belief*:

> Principle/policy *P* is publicly justified if and only if everyone has reasonable grounds for accepting it. (Or no one has reasonable grounds for rejecting it).[68]

The focus here is not on what reasonable *people* accept (or would reject) but whether principles or policies would be accepted or rejected on the basis of reasonable beliefs. A deliberative democrat relying on Public Justification as Agreement in Reasonable Belief could respond to the above case by insisting that Betty's argument is not justificatory even though reasonable Alf accepts it because his acceptance of it is not based on a reasonable belief.

Explications of Public Justification as Agreement in Reasonable Belief must avoid collapsing into either Public Justification as Rational Consensus or Public Justification as Consensus Among Reasonable People. If we characterize a reasonable belief as one that a fully rational, perfectly well-informed person would accept, we move back to Public Justification as Rational Consensus. Even an articulation of 'reasonableness' in terms of what is fully justified (where one can have a fully justified belief that is not what a fully informed person would believe)[69] would seem to share the problem of Public Justification As Rational Consensus: there is no compelling reason to suppose that the pursuit of actual political consensus is the best way to track what would be accepted by beings who always had fully justified beliefs. On the other hand, to hold, as does Cohen, that '[a]n understanding … is fully reasonable just in case its adherents are stably disposed to affirm it as they acquire new information and subject it to critical reflection'[70] drives us back to Public Justification As Consensus Among Reasonable People: a reasonable belief seems very much whatever a reasonable person is disposed to affirm (see section 5.4 below).[71] To avoid these sorts of collapses an explication of Public Justification as Agreement in Reasonable Belief must, I think, appeal to something like a minimally credible belief or reason (see further section 8.2). A reasonable belief, let us say, is one that is sufficiently credible to justify acceptance, assuming that a belief that violates clear maxims of logic or is based on manifestly bad evidence cannot be sufficiently credible. The notion of a sufficiently credible belief is, I think, fundamental to justification. Analyses of cognitive complexity show that human belief systems are far too vast, and processing time much too precious, for us to accept the rule 'Only believe what is best justified'.[72] In order to efficiently cope with such complexity, we typically evaluate beliefs just long enough to decide whether they are sufficiently credible – i.e., they pass some threshold of reasoning/evidence that is sufficient to show that they merit acceptance. And this threshold will be far below what is required to obtain the best (i.e., most justified) belief.[73]

Although attractive – and I believe ultimately correct – this sort of explication of reasonable public justification requires appeal to people's epistemic judgments about what constitutes a minimally credible belief. Although we can expect more consensus on what is a sufficiently credible belief than we can on what is the correct or best justified belief, there is nevertheless bound to be considerable dispute. To some all religious beliefs are unreasonable. Think about Freud's characterization of religion: '[t]he whole thing is so patently infantile, so foreign to reality, that to anyone with a friendly attitude to humanity it is painful to think that the great majority of mortals will never be able to rise above this view of life'.[74] On the other hand, many committed Christians insist that appeals to their religious convictions in political choice is entirely reasonable (as indeed do many liberal philosophers);[75] it is Freudianism, they say, that is preposterous. The same can be said by, and about, Marxism, Eco-Feminism, Deconstructionism, Libertarianism and Fascism. This is not the point that many claim that whatever they believe to be false they also believe to be unreasonable.[76] The point, rather, is that for any one of these doctrines, a large number of citizens firmly believe that they are more-than-a-little crazy; they are not just wrong, but unreasonably so.[77] The problem is that we do not simply live in a society with plural understandings of the good life, but with diverse and conflicting ideologies that insist their competitors are *deeply* misguided. None of this is to say that political life in an ideologically fractured society is impossible. It does, however, strain beyond plausibility the claim that politics ought – even ideally – to aim at actual consensus. If I believe that Eco-Feminism is an unreasonable doctrine, then even accepting Public Justification as Agreement in Reasonable Belief, I will not see myself as having a reason to obtain the assent of an Eco-Feminist, nor see her rejection of my proposal as showing it is not publicly justified.

5.4 Minimizing reason to maximize agreement

A short summary

Let us briefly pause and draw together this somewhat complicated discussion. The problem is this: deliberative democrats seem committed to the ideals that deliberation should be based on genuine reasons, that these reasons should be public insofar as they can be accepted by everyone, and that politics should aim at some approximation to real political consensus. However, I have argued that meeting any two seems inconsistent with achieving the third.

1   The Ideals of Reason and Public Justification can be met by defining public justification in terms of what ideally rational people would accept. But then it seems dubious that Actual Political Consensus is plausible, since what actual people will converge on may greatly differ from what ideally rational people would agree to.
2   The Ideals of Public Justification and Actual Political Consensus can be met by understanding public justification as what all normal reasoners would accept. But we have seen that this is apt to conflict with the Principle of Reason, and especially the Principle of Sincerity.
3   The Ideals of Public Justification and Reason can be united by understanding public justification as the convergence of reasonable beliefs. But even that will result in significant departures from Actual Political

Consensus, since actual people differ about just what constitutes a reasonable belief.

Cohen's circle

The deliberative democrat has a reply to this line of criticism. The second point describes a case in which the Ideals of Public Justification and Actual Political Consensus are united, but conflict with the Ideal of Reason. What, however, if we adopt a minimalist conception of reason, such that whatever a reasonable person accepts is, by definition, a good reason? This idea is suggested by Cohen, who tells us that 'a consideration is an acceptable political reason just in case it has the support of the different comprehensive views that might be endorsed by reasonable citizens'.[78] Thus R is a good reason if and only if it has the support of every reasonable citizen's comprehensive moral or religious view. Obviously, if this proposal suffices, there will not be a conflict between Public Justification as Consensus Among Reasonable People and the Ideal of Reason, since the latter is essentially defined in terms of the former.

How, then, does Cohen understand the core notion of a reasonable person? People are reasonable, we are told, 'in that they aim to defend and criticize institutions and programs that others, as free and equal, have reason to accept'.[79] This, though, seems circular: a good reason (or reasonable belief) was defined as following from the comprehensive view of a reasonable person, but a reasonable person is defined as one who seeks to justify institutions and programs in terms of what others have reason to accept. To appreciate the circularity, suppose a two-person world of Alf and Betty where the only public debate is about law L. Alf wants to know whether consideration R is a reason for Betty to accept law L. In order to know whether R is a reason for her to accept L, he must know whether R follows from Betty's comprehensive view that she holds as a reasonable person. So he must first decide whether Betty is a reasonable person. Betty is a reasonable person only if she seeks to defend or criticize L to Alf in terms of good reasons that Alf accepts. So in order for Alf to determine whether Betty is a reasonable person he must consider whether she seeks to provide Alf with good reasons; so Alf must know what are good reasons to him. Suppose Betty offers R^* as a reason for to him to reject L. Now for Alf to know whether R^* is a reason for him to reject L, he must know whether R^* follows from his reasonable comprehensive view, and whether he is a reasonable person. So Alf needs to answer the question 'Am I a reasonable person?' if he is to know whether R^* is a reason for him. But Alf can only know if he is a reasonable person if he knows that he seeks to provide Betty with good reasons; so he needs to have some way to determine whether R is a good reason. That though, was the question with which he began! His reasoning has led him in a circle. He can only know whether R is a reason for Betty if he already knows whether R is a reason for Betty.

This is a serious flaw. Cohen seeks to show that the notion of a reasonable person and a good reason cannot conflict by reducing each notion to the other. The upshot, though, is that we have no firm idea of what either is, thus undermining the very foundation of deliberative democracy. Cohen perhaps can avoid this circle by insisting that 'seeking' to provide good reasons to others is simply a matter of good intentions; one 'seeks' to provide good reasons simply if one wants to, even if one has no idea what a good reason is. But that, surely, is an implausibly weak notion of a reasonable person to undergird a conception of deliberative democracy.

Reasonable as simply 'tolerant'

At this point it might be insisted that all this rests on a confusion: epistemic and political reasonableness are simply different ideas (I consider this suggestion in more depth in Chapter 7). A view is epistemically reasonable just in case believing it is justified, while a view is politically reasonable (let us say) just in case it tolerates others. If so, then our atheist (see section 5.3) is simply confused or being ambiguous when she asserts that the religious citizen has unreasonable views; if it tolerates other views of the good life and religions it simply *is* politically reasonable, full stop.

'Reasonable' in this sense does not mean 'reasons well' but 'is willing to accord fair terms to others', as we may say that an offer for a house was 'reasonable'. Still, this proposal seems unacceptable. Two options present themselves. (1) This may be advanced as an understanding of a 'reasonable person' but we might still define independently the idea of a 'good reason' or a 'rational belief'. If we do this, the possible conflicts between the Ideal of Public Justification as Consensus Among Reasonable People and the Ideal of Reason noted in section 5.3 remain, indeed are intensified. People may be 'reasonable folks' in this sense yet still act on bad reasons.

(2) So if this conception of the reasonable is to assist the deliberative democrat in replying to the argument of section 5.3, the deliberative democrat would have to follow Cohen in reducing the idea of a good reason to whatever a reasonable person advances (or, alternatively, accepts) as a reason. That is, by definition, R is a good (political) reason if R is espoused (or, alternatively, accepted) by a reasonable (i.e., fairminded or tolerant) person. But surely this stripped-down conception of a reason is entirely inadequate to ground a deliberative conception of democracy. Suppose Alf is a fair-minded person who never makes unreasonable demands of others; he says 'it is morally wrong to have statesupplied health care for the poor'. Then, by definition, he has advanced a reason. And suppose Betty, another tolerant person, says 'It is morally required to have state-supported health care for the poor'. Then, by

definition, she has advanced a reason. What has become of deliberation? Reason has become relativized and all tolerant people give, by definition, good reasons. In response, an advocate of this interpretation might say that a fair-minded person would never make a demand like that. No reasonable person would say that state supplied health care to the poor was unjustified. Notice, now, that we have built into the very idea of reasonableness what is publicly justified. Rather than having a conception of being a reasonable person, and then accepting that whatever proposals such people can all accept are publicly justified, we now have a view of 'being reasonable' in which we have a prior conception of what sort of proposals are 'reasonable' (i.e., justified), and we define a reasonable person as one who would only make such proposals to others.

Deliberative democracy must be based on a substantive conception of good reasons, for only a rich conception of reasons can ground the core ideal of deliberation. Recall Cohen's characterization of 'deliberative democracy' (see section 5.3) as 'rooted in the intuitive idea of a democratic association in which the justification of the terms and conditions of association proceeds through public argument and reasoning among citizens'. Our intuitive notions of argument and reasoning cannot be divorced from our epistemic standards – our ideas of what constitutes good evidence, sound reasoning, relevant objections and so on. Because of this, a plausible conception of deliberative democracy cannot make the Ideal of Reason simply derivative of consensus or our ideas of what constitutes a fair proposal. And so it seems there remains the conflict between the Ideals of Reason, Public Justification and Actual Political Consensus.

5.5 Summary

I began in section 5.1 by briefly explicating Habermas's discourse ethic. Moral discourse, Habermas, argues, aims at 'validity' rather than truth, though Habermas does insist that 'normative claims to validity are *analogous to truth claims*'.[80] The two are analogous as both are vindicated in discourse by good reasons, and both discourses seek a rational consensus. We then saw that, since Habermas maintains that the validation of moral claims requires that actual discourse be carried out, he is led to a deliberative conception of democracy in which citizens and legislators actually engage in deliberation that aims to validate their claims.

Habermasian deliberative democracy, we saw, can be understood as an alternative to liberal democracy, at least insofar as the 'liberties of the ancients' appears to have some moral priority over the 'liberty of the moderns'. Section 5.2 examined Cohen's resolutely liberal conception of deliberative democracy. Cohen's starting point is the liberal conviction that each must be treated as free and equal agents in the modern context of reasonable pluralism. Directly addressing the theme of this book, Cohen argues that treating each as free and equal under the conditions of modern pluralism precludes polities organized around conceptions of the good life or religion. Only a regime in which the laws are justified to each reasonable citizen, by appeal to reasons that she accepts, treats all as free and equal. This requires, Cohen argues, a deliberative democracy in which liberal liberties are embedded.

Section 5.3 presented a somewhat complex criticism of deliberative democracy (summarized at the start of section 5.4). The crux of this criticism is that deliberative democrats are committed to deliberation (which involves a conception of good reasons), public justification and some form of actual consensus. These ideals are in tension, especially the ideals of reason and actual consensus. The more we aim at actual consensus, the more we are apt to find ourselves departing from good reason. The more we focus on the best reasons, the more we are apt to find our arguments unpersuasive to many. There is a wealth of evidence that real people often fail to respond to good reasons; often, indeed, they respond better to bad ones. If so, the ideals of deliberative democracy appear to conflict.

Section 5.4 examined two attempts to reunite the ideals by tying the Ideal of Reason more closely to what actual people will agree to or believe. Cohen's effort, we saw, leads to a circle while the proposal that R is a reason just in case it is a consideration advanced by a fair-minded person undermines the possibility of fruitful deliberation.

Notes

1 Jürgen Habermas, *Moral Consciousness and Communicative Action*, Christian Lenhart and Shierry Weber Nicholson, trans. (Cambridge, MA: MIT Press, 1991), pp. 52ff.
2 Ibid., p. 108.
3 See P.F. Strawson, *Freedom and Resentment and Other Essays* (London: Methuen, 1974).
4 J.R. Lucas, *On Justice* (Oxford: Clarendon Press, 1980), p. 7. I consider this point more fully in my *Value and Justification* (Cambridge: Cambridge University Press, 1990), pp. 281ff.
5 I explore this understanding of emotions in depth in *Value and Justification*, Ch. 2.
6 Habermas, *Moral Consciousness and Communicative Action*, p. 49.
7 Ibid., p. 67.

8   Ibid. Emphasis in original.
9   Ibid., pp. 87–89. I have altered the numbering.
10 Ibid., p. 91.
11 Jürgen Habermas, *Communication and The Evolution of Society*, Thomas McCarthy, trans. (London: Heinemann, 1976), p. 3.
12 On Habermas's notion of a 'lifeworld' see his *Theory of Communicative Action*, Thomas McCarthy, trans. (Boston: Beacon Press, 1984), vol. 1, p. 100.
13 Habermas, *Moral Consciousness and Communicative Action*, p. 65. Emphasis in original.
14 Ibid. Emphasis in original.
15 Ibid., p. 66.
16 Jürgen Habermas, 'Popular Sovereignty as Procedure', William Rehg, trans., in James Bohman and William Rehg, eds, *Deliberative Democracy: Essays on Reason and Politics* (Cambridge, MA: MIT Press, 1997), p. 44 [also published as Appendix I to Jürgen Habermas, *Between Facts and Norms*, William Rehg, trans. (Cambridge, MA: MIT Press, 1996), pp. 463–490].
17 For a criticism of this thesis, see Thomas Christiano, 'The Significance of Public Deliberation' in Bohman and Rehg, eds, *Deliberative Democracy: Essays on Reason and Politics*, pp. 243–277.
18 Julius Fröbel quoted in Habermas, 'Popular Sovereignty as Procedure', p. 46. Emphasis in original.
19 See Jon Elster's 'Introduction' to his edited collection *Deliberative Democracy* (Cambridge: Cambridge University Press, 1998), p. 14.
20 Habermas, *Between Facts and Norms*, p. 179.
21 Cheryl Misak, *Truth, Politics, Morality: Pragmatism and Deliberation* (London: Routledge, 2000), p. 60.
22 See here Christiano, 'The Significance of Public Deliberation', pp. 262ff.
23 Habermas, *Between Facts and Norms*, pp. 31, 457ff.
24 Ibid., p. 449.
25 Ibid., p. 298.
26 Joshua Cohen, 'Procedure and Substance in Deliberative Democracy', in Bohman and Rehg, eds, *Deliberative Democracy: Essays on Reason and Politics*, pp. 409ff.
27 Benjamin Constant, 'The Liberty of the Ancients Compared with that of the Moderns', in *Political Writings*, Biancamria Fontana, ed. (Cambridge: Cambridge University Press, 1988), pp. 310–311.
28 Robert Dahl, *Democracy and its Critics* (New Haven, CT: Yale University Press, 1989), pp. 154–155, 169ff.
29 Cohen, 'Procedure and Substance in Deliberative Democracy', p. 412.
30 Ibid.
31 On the role of these ideas in liberal theory, see my *Political Concepts and Political Theories* (Boulder, CO: Westview Press, 2000), pp. 158–170, 188–206.
32 Joshua Cohen, 'Democracy and Liberty', in Jon Elster, ed., *Deliberative Democracy*, p. 192.
33 Cohen, 'Procedure and Substance in Deliberative Democracy', p. 407.
34 Ibid., p. 408.
35 Cohen, 'Democracy and Liberty', p. 203.
36 Ibid.
37 Ibid., p. 206.

38 Ibid. On the extension of the case for religious freedom to more general freedom of thought and life styles, see my *Justificatory Liberalism* (Oxford: Oxford University Press, 1996), pp. 162ff.

39 Cohen, 'Democracy and Liberty', p. 220.

40 Joshua Cohen, 'Deliberation and Democratic Legitimacy', in Alan Hamlin and Philip Pettit, eds, *The Good Polity: Normative Analysis of the State* (Oxford: Blackwell, 1989), p. 21.

41 Ibid., p. 22.

42 Frederick Watkins, *The Political Tradition of the West: A Study in the Development of Modern Liberalism* (Cambridge, MA: Harvard University Press, 1948), p. 244. See also my *Modern Liberal Theory of Man* (New York: St Martin's Press, 1983), pp. 205ff.

43 Gerald J. Postema, 'Public Practical Reason: An Archeology', *Social Philosophy and Policy*, vol. 12 (Winter 1995), p. 70.

44 Gerald J. Postema, 'Public Practical Reason: Political Practice', in Ian Shapiro and Judith Wagner DeCrew, eds, Nomos *XXXVII: Theory and Practice* (New York: New York University Press, 1995), p. 356.

45 Ibid.

46 Cohen, 'Democracy and Liberty', p. 197.

47 Postema, 'Public Practical Reason: Political Practice', p. 356.

48 Ibid., p. 359. Emphasis added.

49 Ibid., p. 360.

50 Jean-Jacques Rousseau, *The Social Contract* in *The Social Contract and Discourses*, G.D.H. Cole, trans. (London: Dent, 1973): 248 (Book V, Ch. i).

51 Ibid., p. 249 (Book V, Ch. ii). Cf. Cohen, 'When properly conducted, then, democratic politics involves public deliberation focused on the common good'. 'Deliberation and Democratic Legitimacy', p. 19. See section 6.3, this volume.

52 Throughout the chapter, 'the pursuit of actual political consensus' is equivalent to the Regulative Ideal of Real Political Consensus.

53 Cohen, 'Deliberation and Democratic Legitimacy', p. 21.

54 Postema, 'Public Practical Reason: Political Practice', p. 369.

55 See Postema, 'Public Practical Reason: An Archeology', pp. 70ff.

56 I argue this point more fully in *Justificatory Liberalism*, pp. 138ff.

57 See Fred D'Agostino, *Free Public Reason: Making It Up As We Go* (New York: Oxford University Press, 1996), p. 30ff. Cf. Postema, 'Public Practical Reason: Political Practice', p. 350.

58 Cohen, 'Procedure and Substance in Deliberative Democracy', p. 412.

59 Cohen, 'Deliberation and Democratic Legitimacy', p. 23. Emphasis added.

60 See Christopher Cherniak, *Minimal Rationality* (Cambridge, MA: MIT Press, 1986). See also Herbert Simon, *Reason in Human Affairs* (Stanford, CA: Stanford University Press, 1983).

61 See, for example, Susan C. Stokes, 'Pathologies of Deliberation', in Jon Elster, ed. *Deliberative Democracy*, pp. 123–139; Adam Przeworski, 'Deliberation and Ideological Domination' in Jon Elster, ed., *Deliberative Democracy*, pp. 140–160.

62 See Amos Tversky and Daniel Kahneman, 'Availability: a Heuristic for Judging Frequency and Probability', in Daniel Kahneman, Paul Slovic and Amos Tversky, eds, *Judgments under Uncertainty: Heuristics and Biases* (Cambridge: Cambridge University Press, 1982), pp. 163–179. On vividness, see Richard E. Nisbett and Lee Ross, *Human Inference: Strategies and*

Shortcomings of Social Judgments (Englewood Cliffs, NJ: Prentice-Hall, 1980), pp. 55, 15.

63   It may seem that the Condorcet jury theorem, supports the contrary view, i.e., that large majorities are more likely to be correct than are individual voters. I consider this issue in section 6.3.

64   It might be objected that the problem with Public Justification Among Reasonable People is that it depicts the assent of, or non-rejection by, all reasonable people as sufficient for justification; perhaps it is only necessary. I have considered this possibility more fully in my 'The Rational, The Reasonable and Justification', *Journal of Political Philosophy*, vol. 3 (September 1995): 234–258. Reprinted in Fred D'Agostino and Gerald F. Gaus, eds, *Public Reason* (Aldershot, UK: Ashgate, 1998).

65   For summaries, see Lee Ross and Craig A. Anderson, 'Shortcomings in the Attribution Process: On the Origins and Maintenance of Erroneous Social Assessments', in Kahneman, Slovic and Tversky, *Judgments Under Uncertainty*, pp. 129–152. See also Nisbett and Ross, *Human Inference*, Ch. 8.

66   Although Ross and his colleagues certainly believed that the subjects were persisting in unjustified beliefs, some philosophers have recently risen to the defense of Ross's subjects. See for example Gilbert Harman, *Change in View* (Cambridge, MA: MIT Press, 1986), pp. 29ff; Stephen Stich, *The Fragmentation of Reason* (Cambridge, MA: MIT Press, 1991), pp. 8–10.

67   I consider this evidence in more detail in my 'The Rational, The Reasonable and Justification' and *Justificatory Liberalism.*

68   I leave aside the problem of bad-faith rejection here.

69   See my *Justificatory Liberalism*, pp. 38ff.

70   Joshua Cohen, 'Moral Pluralism and Political Consensus', in David Copp, Jean Hampton and John E. Roemer, eds, *The Idea of Democracy* (Cambridge: Cambridge University Press, 1993), pp. 281–282. Cohen attributes this view to Mark Johnston.

71   See my, 'The Rational, the Reasonable and Justification'.

72   See here Cherniak, *Minimal Rationality*.

73   More needs to be said to fully explicate the idea of 'the best belief' – best relative to what constraints? For here, however, the crucial idea is that Betty's belief can be sufficiently credible even if she believes that further reflection would lead her to some different belief (though she does not know what different belief).

74   Sigmund Freud, *Civilization and its Discontents*, James Strachey, trans. (New York: W.W. Norton, 1961), p. 21.

75   See e.g., Kent Greenawalt, *Religious Convictions and Political Choice* (New York: Oxford University Press, 1988).

76   See Cohen, 'Moral Pluralism and Political Consensus', pp. 283ff.

77   'My sister Louise … attended the [1992 National Woman's Studies] conference with me … Having spent several hours with the … conferees, she had doubts about their competence and reasonableness'. Christina Hoff Sommers, *Who Stole Feminism? How Women Have Betrayed Women* (New York: Simon and Schuster, 1994), p. 53.

78   Cohen, 'Democracy and Liberty', p. 195.

79   Ibid., p. 194.

80   Habermas, *Moral Consciousness and Communicative Action*, p. 56. Emphasis in original.

6

Political Democracy: Public Reason
Through Aggregation

6.1 Aggregative democracy

Deliberative and aggregative democracy

In the last chapter we examined 'deliberative democracy', according to which discourse among citizens induces convergence in their political judgments. As Jon Elster has famously described it, the deliberative view conceives of democracy as a 'forum' in which 'preferences' (or judgments) are transformed through public reasoning: as we reason with each other, and respond to each other's arguments, unacceptably biased or unreasonable views give way to those that can form the basis of a public consensus.[1] The problem, I argued, is that a commitment to sincere reasoning often, perhaps typically, prevents us from securing agreement. Sincere reasoners find themselves in principled disagreements, which cannot be negotiated or compromised. The metaphor of a 'negotiation' is appropriate when interests or mere preferences are at stake; but not in discussions aimed at getting things right or the truth. And just as one must be guided by one's own understanding of the truth, so too must one be guided by one's own understanding of reasonableness when applying a principle of public justification. My efforts to sincerely give what I believe to be good arguments that will not be rejected on reasonable grounds inevitably calls *on my own understanding of what constitutes reasonableness.*

Because this is so, we will inevitably have competing judgments about what is publicly justified. Sincere reasoners offering public justifications will constantly differ. They will arrive at conflicting judgments about what is reasonable, about what has met the test of reasonableness, about what is sincere and much else. That is, a political order that embraces the Ideals of Reason and Public Justification will be one of constant arguments and disputes about what is justified, and there is no reason to think that anything remotely like actual consensus will emerge on these issues. Indeed, efforts to give the best justification may well lead one to put forth arguments that block consensus. One can often achieve consensus by splitting the difference, giving something to everyone. However, as philosophers know better than most, this often leads to blurring the dispute and confusing the issue. Philosophers excel at splitting hairs – sharpening differences and making fine distinctions. That is an excellent way to seek the truth (or, that which is best justified), but it is not a particularly good way to achieve consensus.

Elster contrasts the deliberative conception to an *aggregative* view of democracy, according to which the aim of democratic decision making is, taking individual preferences (or judgments) as a given, to aggregate them into a social decision through voting. The aggregative view makes central what the deliberative view pushes to the periphery: that citizens deeply disagree about matters of justice and the common good, and so a vote must be taken to determine the social or public will. The aggregative conception underlies much of our normal thinking about democracy. Many of us talk about elections in terms of finding out what the people think, what the people want, or giving the people's judgment. According to Thomas Jefferson, in collections of people self-government requires following a collection of wills expressed by the majority; the majority, typically although not always through voting, articulates the collection of wills.[2] And famously, while we have seen that deliberative democrats trace their theory back to Jean-Jacque Rousseau's *Social Contract* (see section 5.3), Rousseau's theory seems to accord far more importance than do deliberative democrats to the process of voting. As we shall see, Rousseau often suggests that voting can be understood as a way in which the voice of the people is revealed. So, in light of the persistent disagreement among citizens, perhaps we should explore more carefully the aggregative conception of democracy: that, in some way, voting among citizens who disagree reveals the will of the people. In that sense, the outcome of a vote could be considered the expression of public reason or the public will.

The Voice of the People Thesis

Before exploring different versions of political, aggregative, democracy, and how voting might produce a coherent public will out of diverse private wills, it will help to fix ideas if we focus on a more precise statement of the claim that political democracy – in particular, voting – reveals the voice of the people. Let us, then, work with the *Voice of the People Thesis*:

> Voting on occasion O, under the conditions of (1) universal franchise, (2) equality of votes and (3) additional conditions C, yields decisions that can be plausibly interpreted as revealing what the people or the public want or believe on some issue, i.

A few clarifications are in order. First, the voice of the people thesis leaves open both how we define issues and what the issue under consideration is. This is a simplification, and one that down the road would require a good deal of defense. How issues can be individuated is itself a contentious matter; I have tried to deal with this problem elsewhere, but for now I merely note it, and assume that it can be done.[3] Second, the voice of the people thesis does not tell us whether the issue is about candidates or substantive proposals. Third, the reference to the additional conditions C indicates that any voice of the people theory will provide additional constraints on the way voting and political life must be conducted if voting is to reveal the voice of the people. Famously, Rousseau argued that if factions arise, or if many people abstain from voting, it will no longer be plausible to interpret the outcome of an election as revealing the voice of the people.[4] Of course, accounts of how voting can be interpreted as revealing the voice of the public will be more or less interesting depending on how demanding are conditions C. If a theory builds in extremely demanding conditions – specifying, for instance, the precise nature of the voters' preferences or beliefs – it will not be particularly interesting.[5] In contrast, a theory that imposes modest conditions will be of much more interest, as there is some hope that we can attain them, and so actually interpret a democratic outcome as expressing the voice of the people.

6.2 Popular will theory

Popular will theories

Rousseau tells us that the social contract can be reduced to the following terms: 'Each of us puts his person and all his power under the supreme direction of the general will, and, in our corporate capacity, we receive each member as an indivisible part of the whole'.[6] Rousseau describes the general will as the will of the 'body of the people' or simply 'the will of the people'.[7] Moreover, he insists that if the people deliberate under the proper conditions, their vote will reveal the general will.[8]

It is this feature of Rousseau's thinking that led William Riker to describe him as a 'populist'. According to Riker:

> The fundamental notion goes at least back to Rousseau. There is a social contract, which creates a 'moral and collective body' that has 'life' and 'will', that is, the famous 'general will', the will of the incorporated people, the Sovereign.... The way to discover the general will ... is to compute it by consulting the citizens.[9]

Taking our cue from Riker, let us characterize *Popular Will Theory* thus:

> On occasion O, under the conditions of (1) universal franchise, (2) equality of votes and (3) additional conditions C, a decision procedure D expresses the popular will of the people on some issue, i by (4) aggregating the individual wills of each citizen into a general will.

The general picture, then, is this: (a) there is a group of people; (b) each member of the group has an individual will; (c) this group has a popular or general will; (d) under certain conditions, the voting system computes the popular will by consulting each citizen's individual will; (e) the outcome of voting thus expresses the popular will – the voice of the people.

Riker's requirements for a Popular Will Theory

Riker advances two core requirements for an acceptable popular will theory.

(1) Uniqueness   Let us call the first requirement 'uniqueness' and define it thus:

> Let $\{p_1 \dots p_n\}$ be the set of preference orderings[10] for individuals 1 to n.
> Let P be the social preference ordering.
> *Uniqueness*:   For any given profile of individual preferences $\{p_1 \dots p_n\}$, there is no more than one social preference P.

As is well known, Riker argues that the uniqueness requirement cannot be satisfied. Consider for example the distribution of preferences in Figure 6.1. If we employ the first-past-the-post or plurality system, in which whoever gets the most first-place votes is selected, the winner is w, who gets 9 first-place votes; the next closest is x, with 6 votes. But w does not have a majority: out of 26 votes, candidate w gets only 9. An alternative is the Condorcet method, which votes on every pair of candidates.

Number of voters	First choice	Second choice	Third choice	Fourth choice
9	w	z	x	y
6	x	y	z	w
2	y	x	z	w
4	y	z	x	w
5	z	x	y	w

FIGURE 6.1   *A distribution of preferences which generates different results under different voting rules*

Each candidate meets every other candidate in a one-on-one competition. The Condorcet winner is z: as Figure 6.1 shows: z wins against every other candidate: w – the plurality winner! – loses against every other candidate. Or again, the single transferable majoritarian system, employed in elections to the Australian House of Representatives, selects x.[11] Thus, Riker insists, equally plausible methods of voting yield different results. The same collection of individual wills, then, can generate several, competing, popular wills depending on the aggregation procedure employed, none of which is uniquely the best.

Jules Coleman and John Ferejohn maintain that a populist can reject the uniqueness criterion: 'Populists', they argue, 'may … be committed to a general will, but they need not assert its uniqueness'.[12] In their view, the populist may hold that the derivation of multiple social preference orderings from the same profile of individual preferences would only show that there is more than one acceptable alternative. They thus propose what might be called a *disjunctive interpretation of multiple social preference orderings*. On their view, if the profile of individual wills, $\{p_1 \dots p_n\}$, yields two different social wills, P_1 and P_2, this shows that the popular will is either P_1 or P_2.

The question, though, is why we should assume that the correct interpretation is that the public wills either P_1 or P_2: how do we know that, given a certain profile of preferences $\{p_1 \dots p_n\}$, this shows that the public has a will that 'either P_1 or P_2'? Well, one good way to defend Coleman and Ferejohn's conclusion would be if we could identify a 'meta-decision rule', D^*, which identified the public decision when D_1 and D_2 disagree. Suppose that according to D^*, if D_1 (e.g., first past the post) yields P_1 and D_2 (e.g., the Condorcet method) yields P_2, then the social decision is P_1 or P_2. But this would only show that social preference is for either P_1 or P_2 if there is no plausible alternative meta-decision D^{**} which yields a different public will when D_1 and D_2 clash (such as that, in the case of a conflict, D_1's result is to be chosen over D_2's). If D^* and D^{**} are both plausible and yield different results, then we still do not know what is the public will. But that means, of course, that if this line of reasoning is to support Coleman's and Ferejohn's claim that the popular will is for either P_1 or P_2, D^* must itself meet the uniqueness requirement, the very requirement that they are seeking to reject!

Suppose that Coleman and Ferejohn insist that they do not think that there is any unique 'meta-decision' rule according to which in the case of conflict between D_1 and D_2, the public will is for what either identifies. They might insist that P_1 and P_2 are simply two independent public wills, not linked by any overall 'metarule'. If that is their view, Riker presents the more plausible interpretation. In this case the people simultaneously have at least two distinct wills that are not related to each other by, say, a single 'metawill' – a will about their wills. They are simply independent, competing, collective wills. And this does, I think, suggest an inconsistent, incoherent, confused or – as Riker himself politely says – an ambiguous will. All general will theories maintain that the popular will is at least as coherent, and it is usually said to be more coherent, than the individual wills that compose it; if the popular will is actually two, distinct, incompatible wills, the will of the people seems far too close to a schizophrenic personality to support a plausible theory of democracy.[13] If, within a single 'person' we find independent, competing wills, it is impossible to give 'her' what 'she' wants without also denying 'her' what 'she' wants. If we satisfy P_1, we ipso facto frustrate the will as manifested by P_2, and vice versa. If we are to make sense of the idea of giving the people what they want, or listening to their decision, it looks like we had better accept the uniqueness requirement.

(2) Reasonableness: fairness and logicality But, it might be objected, these voting methods are not all equally plausible ways of aggregating preferences; one is uniquely the best, and that is the one that reveals the true popular will. However, drawing on Kenneth Arrow's general possibility theorem, Riker argues that 'no method of voting can simultaneously satisfy several elementary conditions of fairness and also produce results that always satisfy elementary conditions of logical arrangement';[14] thus every method is flawed and none stands out as uniquely correct.

To appreciate Riker's point, suppose that each individual can rank each political option, and that these rankings are *transitive*. That is, according to transitivity, if Alf

(1) prefers the Labour Party to the Liberal Democrats;
(2) and he prefers the Liberal Democrats to the Tories;
     then it must also be the case that he:
(3) prefers Labour to the Tories.

Transitivity is a requirement of a rational ordering. If you prefer your first choice to your second choice, and if you prefer your second choice to your third choice, transitivity simply requires that you also prefer your first choice to your third choice. Transitivity, then, is a minimal condition for a rational preference ordering.

Now what Arrow showed is that, given two or more individuals who possess transitive rankings of three or more options, no method of aggregating individual preferences can be (1) guaranteed to always produce a rational, transitive, social will and (2) always meet the following conditions:[15]

> *Universal Domain.* There is a popular will for every possible set of individual preference profiles.
> *Monotonicity.* An individual's changing her evaluation from {Y is better than X} to {X is better than Y} cannot itself make X socially less preferred than Y.
> *Non-imposition.* The popular will is always a function of the individual wills.
> *Pareto optimality.* If everyone wills X over Y, the people will X over Y.
> *Independence of Irrelevant Alternatives.* If, given the set of all options Q that are socially ordered in the popular will P, there is a subset of options q (where q is a subset of Q) which are subordered p (where p is a subset of P), the suborder p cannot change unless some individual reorders the options in q.
> *Non-dictatorship.* There is no person whose individual ordering of Q itself generates P.

Together, we can understand these conditions as specifying minimum conditions for a reasonable aggregation procedure. A reasonable aggregation procedure should, firstly, not produce an intransitive popular will. Failure to recognize relations of transitivity is another characteristic of schizophrenics;[16] if the popular will is schizophrenic, there seems precious little reason to pay attention to it. But, in addition, a reasonable method of computing the popular will from a set of individual wills must be non-arbitrary (an important feature of the independence condition), not dictatorial, it must pay attention to the actual preferences of the citizens (non-imposition and the Pareto condition), and voting for a candidate or policy must never count against it (monotonicity). Because Riker concludes that no method of voting can satisfy all these reasonable conditions, he claims that meaning cannot be attributed to the outcome of voting methods, and, so, elections cannot be meaningfully interpreted as revealing a popular will.[17]

Simple popular will theory

If no actual voting system can be guaranteed to satisfy uniqueness and the Arrovian conditions,[18] then Riker shows the implausibility of what we might call *simple popular will theory*, according to which the voting system itself aggregates individual wills into a popular will. If, as Riker shows, no voting system can meet these conditions, then we know that, in principle, there is no unique popular will. At least over a wide range of cases, there will be multiple popular wills; different ways of counting votes will yield different decisions. Looking back to Figure 6.1, if we employ the plurality system (as is done in the UK and USA), we cannot say that w is the popular will, for under other, equally good ways of aggregating votes into decisions, x or z would have been chosen. We must be careful here, though. Riker does not show that it will *always* be the case that different decision rules yield different results from the same set of voter preferences, only that equally plausible systems will sometimes, given certain profiles of preferences, yield different results. So an advocate of simple popular will theory still might argue that, in those cases where all the reasonable rules yield the same results, a unique popular will does emerge. For example, we might take profiles of individual preferences and calculate the outcome under a wide range of different systems; in those cases where all the systems agree, we might then (and only then) say that a popular will emerges. Voting would thus *sometimes* yield a popular will. However, two considerations mitigate the effectiveness of this response to Riker.

First, uniqueness is especially difficult to meet when our concern is an entire electoral system: it is well established that electoral laws have important consequences on electoral outcomes.[19]

Second, voting is subject to strategic behavior: people 'misrepresent' their preferences by voting 'against' their true preferences – say, by voting for their third over their second choice in hopes of attaining their first. For example, consider yet another system of voting, known as the Borda count. This system is often used in deliberations within university academic departments when hiring new academic staff. In this system each voter gives one point to her first choice, two points to her second choice and three to her third choice, and so on; all the voters' points are tallied, and the candidate with the least number of points wins. Given ten voters and three candidates, the lowest possible score is ten (a single point from each voter) and the highest (and so, worst) score is thirty (third choice for everyone). Suppose we have three candidates, Alf, Betty and Charlie. I order the candidates in that order (Alf best, then Betty, then Charlie). However, I have reason to suppose that Betty may defeat Alf; I thus maximize Alf's chance of selection if I vote (1) Alf, (2) Charlie and (3) Betty – which runs counter to my true preference order. Because such 'strategic' voting occurs often, and no system with three candidates is immune to it,

$$f(p)\ \{p_1 \ldots p_n\} \longrightarrow P$$

Expressed through $\downarrow$ $\uparrow$ Evidence of

$$f(v)\ \{v_1 \ldots v_n\} \longrightarrow D$$

FIGURE 6.2   *Sophisticated popular will theory*

we can never be sure that a profile of votes is identical to a profile of voters' true preferences. Moreover, those who understand the subtleties of decision making can, and do, manipulate the procedures in order to achieve their ends; so they may (and do) misreport their preferences in order to intentionally produce intransitive results.[20] Thus even if all the systems of voting produce the same result, we still cannot be confident that this is the true will of the people, based on their sincere preferences. It is, then, very difficult to conclude that the results of an actual election constitutes a popular will.

Sophisticated popular will theory

As Coleman and Ferejohn recognize, however, there is another reply to this criticism of popular will theory. On a more sophisticated Rousseauean view, voting may be *evidence* of what constitutes the general will, but not (pace simple populism) itself constitutive of the general will. To see this better, let us distinguish two different functions:

> Call $f(p)$ the function that takes a set of individual wills – preferences orderings $\{p_1 \ldots p_n\}$ – and aggregates them into a general will or social preference P.
> Call $f(v)$ the function that takes individual votes $\{v_1 \ldots v_n\}$ and transforms them into a social decision, D.

We can thus generate a more sophisticated form of populism that understands voting as simply evidentiary of the popular will as in Figure 6.2 That is, votes are seen as *evidence* of voters' judgments (or preferences) and the final tally is seen as *evidence* about the true popular will. Rousseau seems to advocate such a sophisticated theory. He never actually says that a popular vote *constitutes* the general will but, instead, indicates that it is a reasonably reliable way to *discover what is the popular will*. It thus seems as if Riker only shows what we already knew: the voting function – $f(v)$ – is an imperfect mechanism, subject to a variety of distortions. On the sophisticated view, however, this does not undermine the Rousseauean ideal because voting is only understood as an imperfect procedure for identifying the general will. That different plausible voting rules yield different results from the same set of citizen preferences does not show that the general will is ambiguous, only that the interpretation of elections is sometimes ambiguous.

On reflection, though, this reply to Riker does not suffice: his criticism of the simple popular will theory also applies to more sophisticated popular will theories that take voting as evidentiary, rather than constitutive, of the general will. Although Riker focuses on voting, his point is (or ought to be) that the very idea of the popular will is incoherent because, as he and Arrow show, there is no unique and reasonable $f(p)$ – *no function* that would allow us to aggregate a set of individual wills into a unique popular will. If, then, the aim of voting is to provide evidence of what the public will is, but there is no unique, reasonable will, then popular will theory does look pretty confused. If there is no unique and reasonable public will, then understanding voting as providing evidence about what it is doesn't make much sense. Riker seems right: 'to seek what we know, a priori, we cannot get is like trying to square the circle'.[21]

6.3 Epistemic democracy

Epistemic populism

Although, I have argued, Coleman and Ferejohn fail to turn back the brunt of Riker's attack on popular will theory, the distinction between the voting and preference functions points to an alternative form of aggregative democracy that has gained considerable currency in the last few years. I have distinguished $f(v)$, which aggregates votes into a social decision, and $f(p)$, which aggregates individual preferences into a social preference. The uniqueness and reasonableness requirements, I argued, apply to $f(p)$ – the function that yields the popular will – not $f(v)$, the voting function. The voting function is to be evaluated by different criteria, most especially: given the alternatives, is it a reasonably reliable way to reveal the general will? Now a variety of theorists – most especially Joshua Cohen whom, we have seen, is also an advocate of deliberative democracy (see sections 5.2–5.4) – have endorsed what they call 'Epistemic Populism'.[22] At its core, epistemic populism jettisons any commitment to the idea that there is an aggregation of preferences that yields the will of the people – the troublesome $f(p)$ is abandoned. All that remains is the $f(v)$ function – voting is a reliable, though of course not perfect, way for the people to reveal its judgment on some issue. Let us characterize *epistemic populism* thus:

> On occasion *O,* under the conditions of (1) universal franchise, (2) equality of votes and (3) additional conditions *C,* voting expresses the judgment of the people on some issue, *i.*

Proponents of epistemic populism insist that, on Rousseau's theory, the general will is to be identified with the common good. Writes Rousseau:

> The first and most important deduction from the principles we have laid down is that the general will alone can direct the state according to the object for which it was instituted, i.e., the common good. For if the clashing of particular interests made the establishment of societies necessary, the agreement of these very interests made it possible. The common element in these different interests is what forms a social tie; and, were there no point of agreement between them all, no society could exist. It is solely on the basis of this common interest that society should be governed.[23]

On this view, the general will is not constructed via some aggregation procedure, but is identified with a substantive end: the common good. According to Bernard Grofman and Scott Feld, voting is 'not a means of combining divergent interests but a process that searches for "truth"'.[24] That is, voting is a process that reveals the truth about the question 'What law or policy advances the common good?' The common good, they insist, is not to be found by aggregating preferences; it is a substantively characterized moral goal. As Rousseau said, the general will always aims at the public advantage.

Epistemic populism is something of the rage today – Coleman and Ferejohn, Cohen, Grofman and Feld are just a few of those who have endorsed it as a way to save the 'populist' theory of voting.[25] It seems so attractive because, as Figure 6.3 shows, it rids itself of the troubling idea of the popular will function, and simply takes voting as evidentiary. According to the sophisticated popular will theory, votes are expressions of preferences and the outcome of the election is evidence of the popular will. In contrast, under epistemic populism, the outcome of the election is merely taken as providing evidence about what the people think will promote the common good, is right, or is just. Moreover, for the reasons I canvassed earlier, it seems as if Riker's and Arrow's arguments should not be terribly worrying to an epistemic populist; she can readily acknowledge that the voting function, $f(v)$, is imperfect evidence of the truth about what laws or policies advance the common good. Only if it is very imperfect does it fail to have evidentiary value.

Epistemic democracy and Condorcet's theory theorem

Although to a devoted democrat it may be enough to show that voting can be interpreted as evidence about what the people think is in the

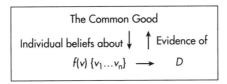

FIGURE 6.3   *Espistemic populism*

common good, or is just, that clearly is not enough for a liberal worried about public reasoning. At a minimum, it must be claimed that voting is not only evidentiary of what the people think is just, but also that what the people think is just is sound evidence for what really is just or conforms to public reason. Imagine an epistemic populism according to which voting reliably revealed what the people thought about justice, but the people were always wrong about what is just. Such a voting would still reveal 'the voice of the people' but it would not tell us anything at all about public reasoning – about what good reasoning about public matters reveals. Because the epistemic populist identifies public reason with a substantive end, such as the truth about what promotes the common good, he must show that voting – asking the people – is a good way to arrive at this truth.

The epistemic populist requires, then, not only the argument that voting reveals what the people think, but also that this, in turn, reveals the truth about public matters. Interestingly, such an argument was advanced by the eighteenth-century mathematician and political theorist, Marie Jean Antione Nicolas de Condorcet, and has been refined by many contemporary proponents of an epistemic understanding of democracy. Rex Martin explains Condorcet's 'jury theorem' this way:

> The argument is probabilistic in form. The argument, put starkly, is that a probability of correctness, for each voter, of greater than half (and for simplicity sake we assume an equal probability for each voter) would yield a majority rule social decision having an even greater probability of correctness (as to which policies were in the perceived interests of an indeterminably larger number of voters). And it could be shown, further, that the probability value of the social decision will increase with an increase in any (or in two or in all) of three factors: (1) the absolute size of the difference between the number of voters and the number of minority voters, (2) the probability of correctness of each individual voter, (3) the size of the majority vote, expressed as a percentage of all votes.[26]

If each voter has more than a 50 percent chance of being right (and assume for a moment that each has the same probability of being right), a majority of voters will have greater chance of being correct than any one person.

If we assume that the average voter is only slightly more likely to be correct than not, say 51 percent likely, and if we require only 51 percent of the vote to carry a proposal, then the probability that a 51 percent majority is correct in its judgment when 100 are voting is 51.99 percent. For an electorate of 500, the probability that a 51 percent majority opinion is correct is 59.86 percent. When 1,000 are voting the probability is 69 percent; and when 10,000 are voting the probability is 99.97.[27]

This appears to give advocates of epistemic democracy precisely what they need: an argument of the form that democratic decisions are good evidence of the truth. Indeed, under apparently modest assumptions, it looks almost certain that the majority will be correct. It would seem that the majority is, after all, the voice of public reason. Although the individual use of reason leads us to disagree, when we take a vote, the majority is almost certain to 'speak the truth'. As Rousseau says, 'From the deliberations of a people properly informed, and provided its members do not have any communications among themselves, the great numbers of small differences will always produce a general will and the decision will always be good'.[28]

The first worry about the jury theorem: competency and multidimensionality

Condorcet's jury theorem, however, is an uncertain support for epistemic democracy. The probability of a correct answer plunges just as dramatically *downward* if the average voter is more likely to be wrong than right. Thus, whether the argument endorses a populist system or condemns it depends on whether the average voter is more or less likely to be correct, and it seems very hard to be sure about this.[29] And if we can identify some class of voters as more likely to be wrong than right, the argument provides grounds for their disenfranchisement. Indeed, depending on the number of remaining voters and the differences in their competencies, the argument can even sanction excluding some of those who are more likely to be right than wrong (e.g., those who do only barely better than chance at selecting the right answer), if their inclusion so drags down the average competency of the group that it decreases overall group reliability.

The problem of the multidimensionality of political issues raises particular worries about the average competency of voters. Democracies seldom have votes on well-defined, specific, issues; voters are usually faced with a choice of parties or candidates; even in referenda, voters are asked whether they support or oppose an action or law, not their specific judgment on an issue. Because of this, there is almost always more than one issue or 'dimension' of dispute that is relevant to a political decision. Take a simple situation in which the people are taking a vote on the 'best' route for a new highway through their town, being faced with a choice between routes *A* and *B*. Condorcet's jury theorem would indicate that, if people are on average more likely to choose the 'better' rather than worse route, a majority in an electorate of, say, 10,000 is almost certain to get the correct answer. But like most issues in politics, 'bestness' is multidimensional. Relevant dimensions include which route will minimize local congestion, which route will be best for local business, which route will cause the least environmental damage, which route will cost less and which route will preserve the most important areas of the town. Now suppose that on each of these issues the average voter will be more likely to be right than wrong. This would by no means ensure that her overall decision is more likely to be right than wrong, for each voter must decide how to order these considerations. Except in the easiest of cases, some considerations are apt to favor route A and some B. So to decide which is the superior route these dimensions must be ordered. But problems of incommensurability are apt to arise (see section 2.3), or at the very least it may be very difficult to provide the correct ordering. Thus, people may have far less than a fifty percent chance of arriving at the correct ordering of the dimensions. So even if on each dimension each person is more likely to be right than wrong, overall each person's judgment on 'what is best' may be more likely to be wrong than right.

Martin is more sensitive than most to this problem. He argues that it is only because the political goal is the common interest that the jury theorem applies. Because we can assume that each person is more likely to be right than wrong about her own interests, we can assume that the aggregation of votes is good evidence about the common interest.[30] But this would only follow if the voting mechanism could take as input each person's judgment about what advances *her own interests* and yield as output a reasonably reliable judgment about *the public interest*. And, to be sure, sometimes Rousseau himself suggests such a view.[31] But the claim that democratic systems operating under something like majority rule function as a sort of political invisible hand – translating votes expressing private interests into the public good – is, at best, dubious. Given their commitments to justice and the common good, most liberals have rejected David Hume's dictum that it is 'a just political maxim, that every man must be supposed a knave'.[32] To be sure, as James Madison observed, there is some truth in this:

> Ambition must be made to counter ambition. The interest of man must be connected with the constitutional rights of the place. It may be a reflection on human nature that such devices should be necessary to control the abuses of government. But what is government itself but the greatest of all reflections on human nature? If men were angels, no government would be necessary. If angels were to govern men, neither external nor internal controls on government would be necessary.[33]

Yet Madison also insists that:

As there is a degree of depravity in mankind which requires a certain degree of circumspection and distrust, so there are other qualities in human nature which justify a certain portion of esteem and confidence. Republican government presupposes the existence of these qualities in a higher degree than any other form. Were the pictures which some have drawn ... faithful likenesses of the human character, the inference would be that there is not sufficient virtue among men for self-government; and that nothing less than the chains of despotism can restrain them from destroying and devouring one another.[34]

Given the aims of uncovering the truth about justice and the common good, Madison seems quite right: voting cannot be based simply on each voter seeking his self-interest.

Those who maintain that the common good arises out of majority voting typically conflate the interests of the majority with the common good, as in the following passage from *The Economist*:

Taxes are imposed for what government believes to be the common good. Some people will condemn the ends the government decides on: pacifists may object to defense spending, or greens to spending on new roads. Most pay anyway. They have other ways of making their case: through the press, through the legislature and even, as a last resort, by sitting down in the streets. But at the end of the day government must govern, and tax, in the interests of the majority.[35]

Note that at the beginning of the passage the concern was with the common good; by the end it was simply the interests of the majority.

I do not wish to suggest that voting cannot be a reliable procedure to answer some questions. However it seems very difficult indeed to show that *in general* it is the most reliable way to discover the right answer, because it is difficult to conclusively show that the average citizen is an epistemic asset on most disputed questions for which there is a right answer; and although it does seem plausible that the average voter is an epistemic asset in determining what is in her interests, it seems doubtful that the voting mechanism is a reliable way of aggregating judgments of individual interests into a judgment about what law or policy best promotes the public interest. (Familiar worries about the tyranny of the majority under democracy attest to these doubts.)

Vox populi, vox dei versus liberal individualism

If the average citizen has a 51 percent chance of being correct, then in an electorate of 10,000 citizens, the majority is virtually infallible. It would thus seem that, once the votes have been counted, members of the minority should not only accept the verdict of the majority, but change their minds.[36] As Rousseau puts it, a member of the minority should each say 'If my particular opinion prevailed against the general will, I should have done something other than what I had willed, and I should not have been free'.[37] It seems as if the voice of the people is the voice of God: it is infallible.

It is hard not to think that this gives far too much weight to a democratic vote. It certainly appears illiberal, as it endorses a radical conformism: each is to *believe what the majority decrees to be right* (recall here the neo-Wittgensteinian view, section 4.4). Persisting in one's minority belief in the face of a majority vote seems simply stubborn – if the Condorcet theorem is applicable, and if the majority passes the competency threshold, it is virtually certain that the majority is correct. Something must be wrong about this. Suppose that a competent majority has voted, and decided that abortion is always wrong (hardly an impossibility, at least in the United States). And suppose that you voted against this law. You have thought long and hard about this issue, and firmly believe that a woman's right to control her own body outweighs any moral status a fetus might possess. You have considered all the arguments for the majority's opinion, and they strike you as bad arguments. You just cannot see, for example, how the fetus could have a right to life. Now, however, the majority has spoken: being a good democrat, and having understood the Condorcet jury theorem, you ask yourself – 'To be rational, must I believe as the majority believes?'

Immanuel Kant, for one, thinks not. He identifies three maxims of 'common human understanding ... (1) to think for oneself; (2) to think from the standpoint of everyone else; and (3) to think always consistently'.[38] This book has been exploring the second (and in doing so I have put great weight on the third). However, a devotion to what Kant calls 'the public use of reason' – thinking from the standpoint of others – should not lead us to abandon Kant's first maxim – to think for yourself. Indeed for the liberal, thinking for oneself is crucial to being a rational individual. In our abortion case, if you have rejected all the arguments in favor of the majority's views, then it seems impossible that you can rationally come to adopt their opposition to abortion simply on the basis of the dictum that '1,000,000 Americans (in the majority) cannot be wrong'. To rationally believe that abortion is wrong must be to believe it for good, relevant, reasons – *to see why it is wrong*.[39] But you do not see why it is wrong: thinking for yourself, the reasons that you accept as good reasons, lead you to reject their view. How can it then be rational – consistent with thinking for yourself – to abandon your view and accept theirs?

It might be thought that we often do this, as for example when we accept the authority of a doctor, and do what she tells us even if we are unable to think the matter through for ourselves. Most of us do not have the expertise to evaluate the doctor's diagnosis and prescription; even if she seeks to explain it to us in detail, few of us have the background in biology, physiology or the clinical experience to really make a judgment about what should be done. To a very large extent we follow the doctor's judgment. Of course, we may get a second opinion, but then we are following another doctor's opinion. To be sure, we do not totally surrender our judgment: if the doctor tells us that we need to stand on our head for a week to cure our headache, few will take that judgment seriously. But, within a wide range, we rely on the doctor's judgment because we believe it is superior to our own. As one scholar observes 'the basic purpose of this sort of authority is to substitute the knowledge of one person for the ignorance or lesser knowledge of another person, although what the person who defers thereby comes to possess as a surrogate for his ignorance is not knowledge, but "true belief" in the sense of belief that is indeed justified, though the believer knows not why'.[40]

But in this case we employ the expert's judgment because we believe that if we did take the time to study the problem, and were able to understand the relevant considerations, then we would agree with the expert. The expert's judgment is taken to be a proxy for what we would decide if we had the knowledge she has. But in our voting case, *we have thought things through and we have come to the opposite conclusion.* This seems more like the case where the doctor tells us to stand on our head: everything we know (except that everyone tells us that this is an expert) leads us to believe that this is a totally stupid thing to do. In this case, respect for Kant's maxim to think for yourself should lead us to reject the doctor's advice, and the majority's judgment, as incorrect.

The thoroughly conformist view of the world suggested by the application of Condorcet's jury theorem to democratic decisions – in which public reason displaces thinking for yourself – is anathema to liberalism. As John Stuart Mill observed:

> There is always need of persons not only to discover new truths, and point out when what were once truths are true no longer, but also to commence new practices, and set the example of more enlightened conduct, and better taste and sense in human life. This cannot well be gainsaid by anybody who does not believe that the world has already attained perfection in all its ways and practices. It is true that this benefit is not capable of being rendered by everybody alike: there are but few persons, in comparison with the whole of mankind, whose experiments, if adopted by others, would be likely to be any improvement on established practice. But these few are the salt of the earth; without them, human life would become a stagnant pool. Not only is it they who introduce good things which did not before exist; it is they who keep the life in those which already exist.[41]

6.4 Estlund's modest epistemic conception

David Estlund recognizes that a Rousseauean view based on the jury theorem can 'get out of hand' – 'epistemic conceptions of democracy are, in a certain sense, too epistemic'.[42] His version of epistemic democracy – *epistemic proceduralism* – seeks to avoid some of these difficulties with the jury theorem while still advancing a case for democracy that relies on its ability to get the correct answer. According to his epistemic proceduralism, democracy seeks to combine procedural fairness with epistemic competency: a properly constituted democracy is, firstly, an impartial procedure for adjudicating differences among individual opinions and, second, is suited to its cognitive task because its reliability is 'just-better-than randomness' but still is the 'best available'.[43] Estlund sees the latter, epistemic, claim as 'conservative' insofar as he is maintaining only that a properly constituted democracy gives a just-better-than-fifty/fifty probability of yielding the correct answer. He thus takes great care to distance himself from the ambitious followers of Rousseau who, employing Condorcet's jury theorem, seem to make the majority's judgment infallible. As he sees it, the epistemic virtues of democracy are modest, but it is the best procedure we have for arriving at legitimate decisions about what is just or morally right.

Moral expertise versus democratic procedures

At this point the reader might be wondering why, if our aim is to get the morally correct or just answer, we should rely on the democratic majority rather than the rule by the enlightened or the wise – what Estlund calls 'epistocracy'. If we could identify a subset of the adult population who are especially apt to give the correct answers to disputed questions about justice and the common good, it would seem manifestly more reliable to let them decide than to ask everyone (i.e., to ask the less competent as well). Mill advances a plausible case for a version of epistocracy, in which those who are more educated, and presumably have a better grasp of public affairs, receive more votes.[44] If our regulative concern is to track public morality, the common good, or justice, as well as possible, it is reasonable to suppose that we ought to seek out political wisdom and give it special weight. Mill believes that all reasonable people would acknowledge that the political judgment of some is superior to that of others. 'No one but a fool, and only a fool of a peculiar description, feels offended by the acknowledgment that there are others whose opinion ... is entitled to greater consideration than his'.[45] Mill, then, suggests that our common concern with instituting the most reliable procedure would lead us to reject democratic political equality – hence his plural voting scheme. Mill thus maintains that epistemic considerations eliminate democratic equality. To be sure, the reasoning underlying the jury theorem tells us that things may be more complicated than this: it matters how much more competent the experts are, and how many of them there are. Still, it does not seem unreasonable to suppose that some group significantly smaller than the entire adult population may be the most reliable source of correct moral judgments.

Estlund replies to epistocracy by invoking what we might call the Reasonable Objection Criterion of Political Legitimacy.[46] 'Sovereignty', he says, should not be 'distributed according to moral expertise unless the expertise would be beyond reasonable objections of individual citizens'.[47] His basic claim, I think, is that while there may well be moral experts, it is always open to doubt precisely who they are; consequently any procedure that selects a specific group of experts will be subject to reasonable objections from some citizens that the experts are not especially reliable. As Estlund asks, 'who will know the knowers?'[48] Mill proposes an educational standard, but it can reasonably be disputed that eggheads have little practical experience. After all, not even many philosophers believe that philosophers ought to be kings. But philosophers will have reasonable objections to the special claims of the world-wise, who will have plausible objections to the special claims of the religious, or the old, etc. If so, epistocracy fails to satisfy the Reasonable Objection Criterion of Political Legitimacy.

What is the best?

If Estlund is going to show that democracy is the best available method of resolving moral disputes (that meets the Reasonable Objection Criterion of Political Legitimacy), he needs to provide a pretty clear idea about what constitutes 'bestness'. He asks us to

> [a]ssume that for many choices faced by a political community, some alternatives are better than others by standards that are in some way objective. (For example, suppose that progressive income tax rates are more just than a flat rate, even after considering effects on efficiency.) If so, it must count in favor of a social decision procedure that it tends to produce the better decision.[49]

It seems that Estlund is attracted to a probabilistic interpretation of this property that counts in favor of the social decision procedure, let us call it *probabilistic reliablism*:

> Given two social decision procedures D_1 and D_2, that D_1, over a run of cases, yields a higher percentage of correct answers counts in favor of D_1 (over D_2).

If we adopt probabilistic reliablism as our sole criterion of the epistemic value of social decision procedures, then the claim that democracy is the best available method of resolving moral disputes (that meets the Reasonable Objection Criterion of Political Legitimacy) amounts to the claim that, over a run of cases, it yields a higher percentage of correct answers than any other decision procedure that passes the test of political legitimacy.

In endeavoring to show this, Estlund is tempted to draw on a modified version of the jury theorem (although in the end he is hesitant about relying on it):

It is possible to have majority rule perform better than .5 (random) even if voters are on the average worse than .5, *so long as individual competencies are arranged in a certain way.* For majority rule in a given society to be correct more often than not, all that is required is that, more often than not, voters have, for a particular instance of voting, an average competency only slightly better than .5. The group is almost certain to get it right in every such instance, and so more often than not.[50]

This weakened jury theorem does not endorse the extreme deference that seemed so implausible in the original version. That the majority is, over the long run, somewhat more apt to be correct than incorrect hardly makes them the voice of God, with whom it is an impertinence to disagree. We thus would seem to have an epistemic case for democracy – the majority tends to be correct – without going too far.

Suppose Estlund could offer a definitive proof that majoritarian procedures were selected by probabilistic reliablism. (As I said, he is reluctant to rely on this modified version of the jury theorem). Would that be sufficient to show that democracy is epistemically suited to its task? I think not. Estlund observes that '[g]ood performance should take into account more than just how likely it is to get the correct answer, but also *how far* it is likely to deviate from the best outcome'.[51] If we assume an issue space in which the correct answer is at point x, then a social decision procedure's virtue depends not only on how often it hits x but on its usual or maximum deviation from x. For example, if we consider simply probabilistic reliablism, we might select D_1 over D_2 if D_1 selects the correct answer 52 percent of the time while D_2 selects it 49 percent. But suppose that in the case when D_1 doesn't select the correct answer it deviates greatly – picking not just the wrong answer but one far away from it – while D_2 is always in the neighborhood of the correct answer, even if it more often fails to find the exact address. On the minimal deviation criterion of bestness, D_2 would be better than D_1.

The minimal deviation notion of bestness seems to help the majoritarian defeat an important rival, what Estlund calls 'Queen for a Day',[52] according to which a single voter is picked at random to make a decision. Queen for a Day is interesting because it seems procedurally fair (each person stands the same chance of being selected) and over the long run its average competency is the average competency of the population. So it is arguably just as fair and as competent as majoritarian democracy. But Queen for a Day seems to do badly indeed if we adopt a minimal deviation conception of bestness, for it will sometimes select crazy proposals that only one person supports, something a majoritarian system will never do. If we assume that the extreme tails of the distribution of voters in our issue space are apt to be far from the right answer, Queen for a Day will have a larger deviance over the long run from the right answer, and so not be best on this dimension.

> The existence of a small number of evil voters is literally no threat to a majoritarian procedure's performance, but they would occasionally, or at least with some chance, be Queen for a Day. This counts against that method. On the other hand, a small number of esoteric moral experts is no benefit to a majoritarian procedure, but they will have some chance of being Queen for a Day. These two considerations appear to balance out.[53]

Let us interpret this as saying that a few evil voters can make Queen for a Day not only give a wrong answer, but a very wrong one, thus hurting it on the minimal deviation dimension; on the other hand, there are times when, because the moral expert will be Queen, it may perhaps have an edge over majoritarianism in probabilistic reliability. So we might say their strengths and weakness offset each other: majoritarianism (say) wins on the minimal deviation dimension and may lose on probabilistic reliability, while Queen for a Day has the opposite result. But there is no reason why we should think, these balance out.[54] Some might insist that minimal deviation is much more important than probabilistic reliablism, while others may follow Estlund in essentially giving them equal importance. As soon as we introduce two dimensions the problem of determining what procedure is best becomes terribly complex, and it is hard to see how any firm conclusion can be reached that one procedure is unequivocally 'the best'. The point is not that, somehow majoritarianism and Queen for a Day tie, but that there is no clear way to say which is better, because it is not clear what constitutes being better.

It is not just that majoritarianism and Queen for a Day score differently on the two dimensions. Consider *median with a vengeance*:

> Given an issue space ranging from 0 to 10 on a metric scale, always choose the option at 5 regardless of the distribution of the voters.

Median with a vengeance can never diverge more than 5 from the correct answer; almost any other system of voting can diverge more than 5. If bestness is understood as minimizing the maximum divergence, median with a vengeance is hard to beat. If we assume that the correct answer is randomly distributed along the space, the average divergence of median with a vengeance will be less than 3. Yet if the correct answers are randomly distributed on the scale, it will get the correct answer only one time in eleven, not at all excelling on the probability of getting it right dimension. It is thus reasonable to conclude that majoritarianism will have a lower score on the minimal deviation dimension than median with a vengeance but will do better on probabilistic reliablism. On the face of it, one reasonable way of ordering these procedures on the two dimensions looks like:[55]

Probabilistic reliablism	Minimal deviation
Queen for a Day	Median with a vengeance
Majoritarianism	Majoritarianism
Median with a vengeance	Queen for a Day

Given this complexity about bestness, if Estlund bases his case for democracy on the claim that it is the best way to get at the truth, he has two options. One is to drop the minimal deviation criterion of bestness. But not only would that give Queen for a Day a big boost in its competition with majoritarianism, it seems wrong. It does, after all, matter not only how often a system is wrong, but how far it goes astray. A system that typically selects a just government but with periods of extreme oppression is not obviously epistemically better than one that chooses a slightly unjust government more often but is never oppressive. The other option, then, is to give up probabilistic reliablism, and restrict bestness to the minimal deviation criterion. But this leads to a problem that has been under the surface all along – just how we understand minimal deviation is itself a highly controversial issue. Do we minimize maximum deviation from the correct answer or average out all deviances over the long run? Do we ignore small departures from the right answer and only average out big mistakes? Do we, perhaps, just measure how likely a system is to make a big mistake? All these will lead to different conceptions of bestness, even if we restrict ourselves to simply the minimal deviation criterion.

Democracy and public justification

My point here is that, leaving aside all the doubts about the applicability of the jury theorem, any claim that democracy is epistemically the best available social decision procedure (that meets the test of political legitimacy) is inherently controversial, as the idea of 'bestness' is itself open to reasonable dispute. Estlund does not think that that this is a serious problem; even if we have some reasonable doubts about the idea of bestness, he replies, 'there might be no reasonable controversy about what is the *best* procedure'.[56] But, although he insists that the matter must be studied further, it certainly looks reasonable on epistemic grounds to dispute that democracy is the best procedure: indeed, many democratic theorists have been deeply skeptical of the claim that the best way to decide issues of justice is to take a vote. As we have seen, Mill, for example advanced cogent objections to mass democracy (on one person, one vote) as the best way to seek truth and justice.

Now Estlund is quite right to point out that, as a sort of 'epistocracy', Mill's own proposal cannot meet the Reasonable Objection Criterion of Political Legitimacy. But we see here that epistemic democracy too has difficulties meeting this criterion. If democracy is to be politically legitimate as a definitive way to resolve our disputes about justice and the common good, it should not rest on claims that citizens have good grounds for rejecting. Just as sovereignty should not be 'distributed according to moral expertise unless the expertise would be beyond reasonable objections of individual citizens',[57] neither should democracy claim authority over the lives of citizens if its core claims are open to reasonable doubt. Democracy offers us a procedure to resolve our conflicting moral judgments; if we have reasonably divergent beliefs about the soundness of democracy as a way to do this, it does not really resolve our problem of conflicting judgments. We should recall here Robert Nozick's warning: 'When sincere and good persons differ, we are prone to think they must accept some procedure to decide their differences, some procedure they both agree to be reliable and fair. Here we see the possibility that this disagreement may extend all the way up the ladder of procedures'.[58]

It appears, then, that Estlund's epistemic proceduralism fails to meet his own Reasonable Objection Criterion of Political Legitimacy: the claim that democracy is best is open to reasonable doubt. Even the claim that it is epistemically better than Queen for a Day is open to reasonable doubt, because it is open to doubt what is the best conception of bestness. Although Estlund sees his defense of democracy as resting on a modest epistemic claim, it is still too strong. We might try an even more modest claim:

> *Democracy's minimal epistemic claim:* No method for resolving moral disputes can be shown beyond a reasonable doubt to be epistemically better than democracy.

Democracy's minimal epistemic claim insists that no alternative social decision procedure can be shown beyond a reasonable doubt to be epistemically superior. On epistemic considerations alone, it is reasonable to doubt whether any alternative is better. For many this reasonable doubt may be based on Estlund's innovative and interesting weak version of the jury theorem: although it does not show beyond reasonable doubt that democracy is the best, it provides the grounds for reasonable doubt that other decision procedures are better. The strong version of the jury theorem also provides grounds for such reasonable doubts. And proposals such as epistocracy, while not unreasonable, are open to reasonable doubts that they can reliably identify the moral sages and that, once identified, these sages will effectively implement the correct policy.

Epistemic incommensurability, democracy and public justification

Estlund believes that democracy's minimal epistemic Claim is 'no use to an epistemic approach to democracy at all, since it is based on the assumption that no procedure can be legitimately compared on epistemic grounds with any other procedure'.[59] Now in one way he is right: the argument contends that from the perspective of public justification, democratic and non-democratic procedures are incomparable in the sense that it cannot be shown beyond a reasonable doubt that democracy is epistemically worse than, better than, or just equal to, its competitors. Recall our incompleteness analysis of incommensurability in section 2.3, according to which:

> Values V_1 and V_2 are incommensurable if there is no ordering of them according to which one (and only one) of the following holds: (a) V_1 is better than V_2, (b) V_2 is better than V_1, (c) V_1 is equal to V_2.

Now given our reasonable disagreements about the best way to weigh probabilistic reliability and minimum deviance, it does seem that we are unable to publicly justify the claims that democracy is epistemically better than Queen for a Day, Queen for a Day is epistemically better than democracy, or that democracy is epistemically equal to Queen for a Day. But given Estlund's commitment to public justification in the guise of the Reasonable Objection Criterion of Political Legitimacy, this incommensurability has the consequence that epistemological considerations do not eliminate democracy.[60] The distinctive feature of democracy – what separates it from all other procedures that cannot be eliminated on epistemic grounds – is its distinctive moral quality: it is a fair and impartial way to resolve disputes and treats all with equal respect (see sections 5.2 and 8.5). The claim, then, is that, pace Mill, democracy *cannot be shown* to be epistemically inferior to its competitors. If democracy is superior, it is not, I think, because it can be clearly shown to be epistemically better, but because it can be shown to be morally superior. It is morally superior insofar as it can be verified from the public perspective, and, as Cohen stresses, it accords to each the status of political equal (see section 5.2).

So what is wrong with random procedures? – back to deliberation

This, though, does not show what is wrong with a random procedure such as Queen for a Day, which also accords to each an equal voice (interpreted as an equal chance of being selected queen for a day) and cannot be shown to be epistemically inferior to democracy. It seems that Queen for a Day is warranted in making the same claims as democracy: (1) none can be shown beyond a reasonable doubt to be epistemically superior and (2) it is fair to everyone by according each an equal chance. I think we can see, however, that Queen for a Day-like procedures are deeply objectionable on both epistemological and moral grounds because they provide incentives to ignore public justification.

For the epistemic democrat, we require a social decision procedure because we differ about what is the morally best policy or candidate. This is a problem because we are committed to publicly justifying our political proposals. That others disagree with me is not simply a practical problem; even if I have sufficient power to impose my will, their dissent nevertheless poses a moral problem. As deliberative democrats rightly stress, unless I can justify my proposals *to them*, I am not warranted in imposing *on them* (see section 5.2). Because we face constant disagreement on these matters, we require a way to resolve our disagreements: democracy is justified because, from the epistemic view, no other system can be shown (beyond a reasonable doubt) to be more reliable, and it is uniquely fair.

We thus must keep in mind that our interest in democracy derives from our interest in publicly justified policies. Now random procedures do not induce one to justify one's views to others. Even if the random selection takes place after a period of deliberation, it remains the case that, once one is queen one's proposal can be enacted into policy even if it is manifestly unjustified and self-serving. Although one might insist that proposals under Queen for a Day must pass through a deliberative period, their selection is not at all tied to their deliberative success. Indeed, policies that did not withstand deliberative scrutiny stand an equal chance of success with policies that met the challenge of public justification. Such social decision making procedures induce citizens to ignore the very point of democracy: to arrive at publicly justified decisions.

As Estlund and deliberative democrats recognize, the property of being reason-recognizing is indeed fundamental to a social decision procedure. By divorcing – or under modified versions, 'distancing' – decision from deliberation in this way, Queen for a Day undermines the moral foundations of the democratic order. Deliberation is not simply that which comes before a decision – it must be the basis of it in a democratic order. The epistemic, procedural *and deliberative* aspects of democracy all must be synthesized by an adequate conception of the democratic ideal.

6.5 Summary

In this chapter I have examined several interpretations of the idea that a democratic vote can constitute or reveal the will of the people, the moral truth or public reason, and thus aggregative democracy shows how a notion of public reason can arise out of a diverse and conflicting set of individual judgments. In section 6.2 I examined two versions of this thesis: (1) that the act of voting itself aggregates individual judgments into an overall public judgment and (2) the act of voting is *evidence* of a public will which is formed through aggregating private wills. Riker is certainly right that the former is implausible: given the inability of any system of preference aggregation to meet both the uniqueness and Arrovian requirements, it is impossible to see voting as producing a public will.

Riker's criticisms also weaken the second, more sophisticated, popular will theory: if there is in principle no reasonable and unique way of combining individual wills into a social will, then there is no 'popular will' for voting to be evidence of.

Section 6.3 examined 'epistemic' theories of democracy, according to which voting is an indicator of 'political truth' or 'the correct answer'. We saw that reliance on Condorcet's jury theorem is worrying on at least two counts. (1) We have, in fact good reason to doubt that the average competency of the average voter is greater than 50 percent, given the complexity and multidimensionality of political issues. (2) If the jury theorem does hold, the voice of the people becomes the voice of God, instructing us what to believe, even if we cannot accept as compelling the reasons given to us for these beliefs. This, I suggested, would lead us to violate Kant's liberal maxim – 'think for yourself'.

Section 6.4 considered David Estlund's more complex epistemic view, which weakens the epistemic claims made for democracy. Even Estlund's modest epistemic case, I argued, seems unable to meet his own criterion of political legitimacy: if we are unsure of what constitutes the best – as well as unsure as to whether democracy gets us the best, whatever that is – some citizens will have reasonable objections to democratic procedures. At the close of section 6.4 I argued that a minimal epistemic claim can be made for democracy: no method for resolving moral disputes can be shown beyond a reasonable doubt to be epistemically better than democracy. Conjoined with the Reasonable Objection Criterion of Political Legitimacy, this does at least show that epistemic considerations do not lead us to reject democracy.

Notes

1 Jon Elster, 'The Market and the Forum' in James Bohman and William Rehg, eds, *Deliberative Democracy: Essays on Reason and Politics* (Cambridge, MA: MIT Press, 1997), pp. 3–33.
2 *Thomas Jefferson on Democracy*, Saul K. Padover, ed. (New York: Appleton-Century-Crofts, 1939), p. 15.
3 See my *Justificatory Liberalism: An Essay on Epistemology and Political Theory* (New York: Oxford University Press, 1996), pp. 269ff.

4   See Jean-Jacques Rousseau, *The Social Contract*, G.D.H. Cole, trans. (London: J.M. Dent & Sons, 1973), p. 185 (Book II, Ch. iii).

5   Rousseau's theory is perhaps uninteresting in this way. 'If we take the term in its strict sense', he writes, 'there never has been a real democracy, and there never will be ... how many conditions that are difficult to unite does such a government presuppose!'. *The Social Contract*, Book III, Ch. iv.

6   Ibid., p. 175 (Book I, Ch. vi.).

7   Ibid., pp. 183 (Book II, Ch. ii.), 213 (Book III, Ch. iii.).

8   Ibid., pp. 184–186 (Book II, Ch. iii.).

9   William Riker, *Liberalism Against Populism* (Prospect Heights: Waveland Press, 1988), p. 11.

10 Or ordering of options in terms of the person's best judgments about justice, the common good, etc. While I shall talk here of 'preferences' the same points could be made about 'judgments'.

11 In one version of this system, the candidate with the least first-place votes is eliminated, with its votes going to its voters' second choice. In Figure 6.1, z is thus eliminated, with its five votes going to x, the second-choice of z voters. The votes are then recalculated to see if any candidate has a majority; in this case, none does, so the weakest remaining candidate is eliminated (y), with its votes going to y voters' second-choice (or, if the second-choice already has been eliminated, their third-choice). In Figure 6.1, two y voters have a second choice of x, so x gets those votes; four y voters have a second choice of z, but since z has already been eliminated, these voters get their third choice, x. Candidate x now has a majority of voters: the six it has as a first choice of its own voters, the five it has from z voters and the six it receives from y voters, giving it nineteen votes. On this method see Riker, *Liberalism Against Populism*, pp. 48–51.

12 Jules Coleman and John Ferejohn, 'Democracy and Social Choice', *Ethics*, vol. 97 (October 1986): 6–25, at 15.

13 According to one psychiatrist, when talking to a schizophrenic it is 'as if one was talking to a series of complexes or mental processes, not to a single person; as if one was presented with all the parts of a body dissected from each other with no unity to bind them into a single body'. Anthony Storr, *The Integrity of the Personality* (Harmondsworth: Penguin, 1964), p. 68.

14 Riker, *Liberalism Against Populism*, p. 115.

15 These are rough definitions. I have tried to make them intuitively clear, if not formally rigorous.

16 Michael Argyle, *The Psychology of Interpersonal Behavior*, 3rd edn (Harmondsworth: Penguin, 1978), p. 211.

17 Riker, *Liberalism Against Populism*, p. 238. There has been considerable debate about several of these requirements, most famously the much-disputed independence condition, which has generated a large body of literature. I shall not consider these disputes here; however, the rejection of the Arrovian requirements does not greatly affect my main point, as the main points follow simply from the uniqueness requirement. Of course, if we do accept that a reasonable method for computing the popular will must meet all the Arrovian requirements, we are confronted with the impossibility of guaranteeing that any method does so.

18 Ibid., pp. 111ff.

19 See Arend Lijphart, 'The Political Consequences of Electoral Laws, 1945–85', *American Political Science Review*, vol. 85 (June 1990): 481–496.

20   Riker shows this in detail in *Liberalism Against Populism* and his *The Art of Political Manipulation* (New Haven, CT: Yale University Press, 1986).

21   Riker, *Liberalism Against Populism*, p. 3.

22   See Joshua Cohen, 'An Epistemic Conception of Democracy'. As I suggest at the close of this chapter, deliberative and aggregative democracy might be combined into a more adequate account of democracy. See also section 8.5.

23   Rousseau, *The Social Contract*, p. 182 (Book II, Ch. 1).

24   Bernard Grofman and Scott L. Feld, 'Rousseau's General Will: A Condorcetian Perspective', *The American Political Science Review*, vol. 82 (June 1988): 567–576.

25   For broadly epistemic accounts of democracy, see Rex Martin, *A System of Rights* (Oxford: Clarendon Press, 1993), Chs. 6 and 7; David Estlund, 'Making Truth Safe for Democracy' in David Copp, Jean Hampton and John E. Roemer, eds, *The Idea of Democracy* (Cambridge: Cambridge University Press, 1993), pp. 71–100; Susan Hurley, *Natural Reasons* (New York: Oxford University Press, 1989).

26   Rex Martin, *A System of Rights*, p. 142. See also Elaine Spitz, *Majority Rule* (Chatham, NJ: Chatham House, 1984), p. 206; Brian Barry, 'The Public Interest' in Anthony Quinton, ed., *Political Philosophy* (Oxford: Oxford University Press, 1967), pp. 112–126; Bernard Grofman and Scott L. Feld, 'Rousseau's General Will: A Condorcetian Perspective'. For discussions of Grofman and Feld, see the responses by David Estlund and Jeremy Waldron, as well as Grofman's and Feld's rejoinder in volume 83 of the *American Political Science Review*, pp. 1315–1335. For an extension of Condorcet's theorem to cases presenting more than two options, see Christian List and Robert E. Goodin, 'Epistemic Democracy: Generalizing the Condorcet Jury Theorem', *Journal of Political Philosophy*, vol. 9 (September 2001).

27   Arthur Kuflik, 'Majority Rule Procedure' in J. Roland Pennock and John W. Chapman eds, *NOMOS XVIII: Due Process* (New York: New York University Press, 1977), p. 306.

28   Rousseau, *The Social Contract*, Book II, Ch. iii.

29   See David Estlund, 'Making Truth Safe for Democracy', p. 93.

30   Martin, *A System of Rights*, p. 138.

31   Rousseau's comment that 'take away from these wills the pluses and minuses that cancel one another, and the general will remains as the sum of the differences' is sometimes interpreted as upholding such a view. *The Social Contract*, p. 195 (Book II, Ch. iii).

32   David Hume, 'Of the Independency of Parliament' in his *Essays Moral, Political and Literary* (Oxford: Oxford University Press, 1963), pp. 42–43.

33   James Madison, Alexander Hamilton and John Jay, *The Federalist Papers*, Clinton Rossiter, ed. (New York: New American Library, 1961), Madison, Federalist 51, p. 322.

34   Ibid., Madison, 55, p. 346.

35   *The Economist*, August 6, 1994, p. 20, col. 2.

36   In a similar vein Robert E. Goodin has recently shown that if one adopts a Bayesian account of rational belief, according to which one takes other people's judgments as a reason to revise your own judgment, then (over a very wide range of values), it will be rational to think what the majority thinks. See his 'The Paradox of Persisting Opposition', *Politics, Philosophy and Economics*, vol. 1 (February 2002): 109–46.

37   Rousseau, *The Social Contract*, p. 250 (Book 4, Ch. 2).

38   Immanuel Kant, *Critique of Judgment*, Werner S. Pluhar, trans. (Indianapolis: Hackett, 1987), p. 160 (section 40). See also Immanuel Kant, 'What is

Enlightenment?', in Hans Reiss, ed., *Kant's Political Writings*, H.B. Nisbett, trans. (Cambridge: Cambridge University Press, 1977), pp. 54–60.

39 See here David Estlund, 'Beyond Fairness and Deliberation', in James Bohman and William Rehg, eds, *Deliberative Democracy* (Cambridge, MA: MIT Press, 1997), pp. 186–187.

40 Richard B. Friedman, 'On the Concept of Authority in Political Philosophy', in Richard E. Flathman, ed. *Concepts in Social and Political Philosophy* (New York: Macmillan, 1973), pp. 142–143.

41 John Stuart Mill, *On Liberty* in John Gray, ed., *On Liberty and Other Essays* (Oxford: Oxford University Press, 1991), p. 71 (Ch. 3, para. 11).

42 David Estlund, 'The Epistemic Dimension of Democratic Authority', *The Modern Schoolman*, vol. 74 (May 1997): 264. This essay was published in an expanded and revised version as Estlund, 'Beyond Fairness and Deliberation', in James Bohman and William Rehg, eds, *Deliberative Democracy* (Cambridge, MA: MIT Press, 1997), pp. 173–204.

43 Estlund, 'The Epistemic Dimension of Democratic Authority', p. 272.

44 See Mill, *Considerations on Representative Government* in Gray, ed., *On Liberty and Other Essays*, pp. 334ff (Ch. VIII). At one point Mill provides the following scale of voting power: Unskilled laborers – 1 vote; Skilled laborers – 2 votes; Foremen – 3 votes; Farmers, manufacturers and traders – 3 or 4 votes; Professionals – 5 or 6 votes; University graduates – at least 5 or 6 votes. Mill, 'Thoughts on Parliamentary Reform', in *The Collected Works of John Stuart Mill*, J.M. Robson, ed. (Toronto: University of Toronto Press, 1977), vol. 19, pp. 324–325.

45 Mill, *Considerations on Representative Government*, p. 335 (Ch. VIII).

46 See Estlund, 'Making Truth Safe for Democracy'.

47 Estlund, 'Beyond Fairness and Deliberation', p. 183.

48 Estlund, 'Making Truth Safe for Democracy', p. 84.

49 Ibid., p. 174.

50 Ibid., p. 188. Emphasis added.

51 Ibid., p. 192. Emphasis in original.

52 See ibid., pp. 191ff.

53 Ibid., p. 192.

54 Ibid., Estlund acknowledges that 'we have no clear reason to assume that deviations in one direction would be balanced in the other'. Estlund, 'The Epistemic Dimension of Democratic Authority', p. 272. However, the point here is that about their overall strengths and weaknesses.

55 I tend to think that Queen for a Day would actually score low on probability of being correct, for reasons I suggest in section 6.3. This might seem to save Estlund's case for democracy, as majoritarianism is now best on both dimensions. Thus the importance of 'median with a vengeance': it still beats democracy on minimal deviation. The point, though, is a more general one: so long as there exists some dimension of bestness on which majoritarianism does not rank first, the problem discussed in the text is relevant.

56 Estlund, 'The Epistemic Dimension of Democratic Authority', p. 273. Emphasis in original.

57 Ibid., p. 265.

58 Robert Nozick, *Anarchy, State and Utopia* (New York: Basic Books, 1974), p. 98.

59 Estlund, 'The Epistemic Dimension of Democratic Authority', p. 274.

60 I have argued this more fully in 'Public Justification and Democratic Adjudication'. *Constitutional Political Economy*, vol. 2 (Fall 1991): 251–281.

7

Rawls's Political Liberalism: Public Reason as the Domain of the Political

7.1 Political liberalism: the basic idea

Rawls and the post-Enlightenment liberalism

John Rawls's *A Theory of Justice*, published in 1971, changed contemporary political theory. In that book Rawls presented a reformulation of the social contract theory of Locke, Rousseau and Kant, providing a justification of the liberal state. This theory, which he called 'justice as fairness', argued that parties to an original contract, situated without knowledge that might bias them, would accept two principles of justice to regulate the basic structure of society:

1. Each person is to have an equal right to the most extensive system of equal basic liberties compatible with a similar system of liberty for all.
2. Social and economic inequalities are to be arranged so that they are both

(a) to the greatest benefit of the least advantaged....
(b) attached to offices and positions open to all under conditions of
     fair equality of opportunity'.[1]

Rawls, however, came to believe that as presented in his *Theory of Justice*, justice as fairness was, like J.S. Mill's liberalism, a form of 'Enlightenment liberalism, that is a comprehensive liberal ... doctrine' that overlooked the problem of reasonable pluralism, the fact that the free exercise of human reason in modern democratic societies leads us to embrace a 'diversity of reasonable comprehensive doctrines'.[2] As with Mill's liberalism, Rawls now believes that justice as fairness, as presented in *A Theory of Justice*, pre-supposed the possibility of agreement on a liberal conception of value and goodness. Given reasonable pluralism, Rawls insists, any (successful) attempt to unite society on a shared comprehensive doctrine – which would include the doctrine of *A Theory of Justice* – requires the oppressive use of state power to suppress competing, reasonable, comprehensive doctrines. The aim of his political liberalism is to defend such a liberal political conception – a post-Enlightenment liberalism that takes seriously the problem of reasonable pluralism, and which all reasonable citizens can affirm regardless of what reasonable comprehensive doctrine they hold.

Rawls stresses that political liberalism searches for more than a *modus vivendi* (see section 3.1). His question is not whether people devoted to conflicting doctrines can manage to live with each other for essentially self-interested reasons, but how it is possible for those adhering to very differ-ent and conflicting comprehensive doctrines to be 'wholehearted members of a democratic society who endorse society's intrinsic political ideals and values and do not simply acquiesce in the balance of social forces'.[3]

The basic argument

Rawls, then, tells us that his motivation for writing *Political Liberalism* was the realization that, as presented in *A Theory of Justice*, justice as fairness was a 'comprehensive, or partially comprehensive' doctrine (*PL*: xviii).

> The serious problem is this. A modern democratic society is characterized not simply by a plurality of comprehensive religious, philosophical and moral doctrines but by a pluralism of incompatible yet reasonable comprehensive doctrines. No one of these doctrines is affirmed by citizens generally. Nor should one expect that in the foreseeable future one of them, or some other reasonable doctrine, will ever be affirmed by all, or nearly all, citizens. Political liberalism assumes that, for political purposes, a plurality of reason-able yet incompatible comprehensive doctrines is the normal result of the exercise of human reason within the framework of free institutions of a constitutional regime. (*PL*: xviii)

Elsewhere Rawls goes so far as to claim that there exists a plurality of 'perfectly reasonable' comprehensive doctrines (*PL*: 24n). This reasonable pluralism of *comprehensive views* renders them unacceptable as bases for the justification of political power: '[P]olitical power is always coercive power backed by the government's use of sanctions' (*PL*: 136). Now, says Rawls, according to the 'liberal principle of legitimacy':

> our exercise of political power is fully proper only when it is exercised in accordance with a constitution the essentials of which all citizens as free and equal may reasonably be expected to endorse in the light of principles and ideals acceptable to their common human reason. (*PL*: 137)

Thus it would seem that because there exists a reasonable plurality of comprehensive doctrines, basing the justification of political power on any single doctrine – or subset of comprehensive doctrines – would violate the liberal principle of legitimacy.

This leads Rawls to seek a political conception that 'all affirm' (*PL*: 38) and is 'shared by everyone' (*PL*: xxi). Such a conception would be supported by, or at least not conflict with, the diverse reasonable comprehensive doctrines that characterize our democratic societies. This political conception is a 'module' (*PL*: 12–13; 144–145)[4] that fits into our many reasonable, yet irreconcilable, comprehensive views. And because this political conception can be affirmed by all reasonable comprehensive doctrines, oppressive state power is not required to uphold it (*PL*: 37). Rawls now reinterprets justice as fairness, seeing it not as a comprehensive doctrine (as in *A Theory of Justice*) but as such a political conception: 'If justice as fairness were not expressly designed to gain the reasoned support of citizens who affirm reasonable although conflicting comprehensive doctrines . . . it would not be liberal' (*PL*: 143).

The interpretation of Rawls's texts is notoriously difficult; at different points Rawls appears to reinterpret his earlier statements, and at times apparently affirms competing interpretations of his views.[5] Is not difficult to find in Rawls's work passages that support widely different interpretations. Rather than, as it were, patching together passages from Rawls (which can be done to make quilts of many different patterns), I shall try to make his basic argument more precise. I do not claim that this captures everything Rawls says (I think it is doubtful than any consistent interpretation could do that). It will, though, give us an insight into the basic structure of Rawlsian political liberalism. I propose, then, that we reconstruct Rawls's argument along the following lines:

1 *The Principle of Liberal Legitimacy*: The exercise of political power is legitimate only if it accords with a constitution the essentials of which all free and equal citizens may reasonably be expected to endorse.
2 In our democratic societies, there exists a reasonable pluralism of comprehensive religious, philosophical and moral views.
3 If (i) free and equal citizen Alf holds a reasonable comprehensive view C_α, and (ii) if citizen Betty's reasonable comprehensive view C_β is

'irreconcilable' with C_α, then (iii) Alf cannot reasonably be expected to endorse C_β.

4   If Alf cannot reasonably be expected to endorse C_β, he cannot reasonably be expected to endorse a constitution whose justification requires endorsing C_β.

5   Therefore a constitution relying on C_β as in step 4 violates the Principle of Liberal Legitimacy (step 1).

6   Given step 2, for every reasonable comprehensive view C_x there exists another reasonable comprehensive view held by some free and equal citizen that is irreconcilable with it.

7   Therefore, there exists no constitution satisfying the Principle of Liberal Legitimacy that requires the endorsement of any specific comprehensive view.

8   However there exists a political conception P such that there exists no reasonable comprehensive view C_x, where it is the case that C_x is irreconcilable with P.

9   Given step 8, a constitution relying on P for the justification of political power does not violate the Principle of Liberal Legitimacy.

Step 3 is necessary. Fundamental to Rawls's political liberalism is the (uncontentious) claim that it is unreasonable to expect a person to endorse an otherwise reasonable comprehensive view that is irreconcilable with his own reasonable view. Step 8 also seems necessary; unless step 8 holds, a constitution depending on P is open to the same objection as a constitution depending on a comprehensive view. Interestingly, Rawls sometimes qualifies the claim in step 8. He tells us, for example, that consensus on the political conception should include 'all the reasonable opposing religious, philosophical, and moral doctrines *likely to persist over generations and to gain a sizable body of adherents*' (PL: 15).[6] This suggests an alternative to step 8:

> 8* However there exists a political conception P such that there exist *few* reasonable comprehensive views C_x, where it is the case that C_x is irreconcilable with P.

7.2 What is the political? Comprehensive conceptions distinguished from political values in terms of three features

What is a comprehensive conception?

Rawls's core argument – and so his entire political liberalism – apparently depends on the fundamental contrast between comprehensive views and the political conception. Indeed, the very contrast between 'Enlightenment liberalism' and 'political liberalism' turns on the basic distinction between a comprehensive view and a politic? What, then, is a 'comprehensive view', and how is it to be from the political conception?

Rawls repeatedly describes 'philosophical', 'moral' 'doctrines' (*PL*: xxvii, 4, 36, 38, 160) or 'beliefs' (*PL*: 63) as 'cc. Indeed, so often does Rawls characterize comprehensiveness in ιω moral, religious and philosophical doctrines or beliefs that a reader may be tempted to conclude that doctrine C is comprehensive if and only if it is a moral, religious or philosophical doctrine or belief. This would make sense of Rawls's insistence that 'political liberalism applies the principle of toleration to philosophy itself' (*PL*: 10). Philosophy is like religion – something about which politics should not take sides. Just as a traditional liberal political order tolerates a variety of religious views and does not invoke any in the justification of laws and policies, Rawls apparently seeks to tolerate all reasonable philosophical and moral doctrines while abjuring appeal to any in the justification of constitutional essentials. But though it is tempting to understand 'comprehensive conceptions' in this way, it would be wrong. Rawls is clear that:

> the distinction between the political conception and other moral conceptions is a matter of scope; that is, the range of subjects, to which a conception applies and the content a wider range requires. A moral conception is general if it applies to a wide range of subjects, and in the limit to all subjects universally. It is comprehensive when it includes conceptions of what is of value in human life, and ideals of personal character, as well as ideals of familial and associational relationships, and much else that is to inform our conduct, and in the limit to our life as a whole. A conception is fully comprehensive if it covers all recognized values and virtues within one rather precisely articulated system; whereas a conception is only partially comprehensive when it comprises a number of, but by no means all, nonpolitical values and virtues and is rather loosely articulated. Many religious and philosophical doctrines aspire to be both general and comprehensive. (*PL*: 13)

Comprehensive and general doctrines cover a wide range of topics, values and ideals applicable to various areas of life while, in contrast, the scope of the political is narrow.

However, Rawls tells us later on that '[m]ost people's religious, philosophical, and moral doctrines are not seen by them as fully general and comprehensive, and these aspects admit of variations and of degree' (*PL*: 160). It is not certain whether Rawls believes that most people are correct in this self-conception, but it seems clear that they must be. Few people have all-embracing philosophies of life that provide a single, coherent perspective on questions of value, human character and social life.[7] So most people do not actually possess, and so cannot rely on, (fully) comprehensive moral, religious and philosophical doctrines. This itself is a bit of a puzzle: why should the contrast between comprehensive views and the political be the point on which the entire doctrine rests when most people do not actually possess fully comprehensive doctrines?

ee features of political values

Rawls tells us that 'liberal political principles and values' 'fall under the category of the political', and that 'these political conceptions have three features:'[8]

> First, their principles apply to basic political and social institutions (the basic structure of society);
>
> Second, they can be presented independently from comprehensive doctrines of any kind (although they may, of course, be supported by a reasonable overlapping consensus of such doctrines); and
>
> Finally, they can be worked out from fundamental ideas as seen as implicit in the public culture political culture of a constitutional regime, such as the conceptions of citizens as free and equal persons, and of society as a fair system of cooperation.[9]

The second feature relates to Rawls's crucial claim that political liberalism 'aims for a political conception of justice as a freestanding view' (*PL*: 10). It is thus 'expounded apart from, or without reference to, any … wider background' (*PL*: 12). In particular, it must be the case that the justification for appeal to any specific political value makes no necessary reference to a comprehensive view. How, then, can a political conception be justified? This seems to lead to the third point: 'they can be worked out from fundamental ideas as seen as implicit in the public culture political culture of a constitutional regime'. Unlike non-political values, political values can be 'worked out' by drawing simply on the fundamental ideas implicit in the public political culture of a constitutional regime. It might seem that this characterization of the political values renders non-political the apparently political values of those who reject constitutional regimes (recall here the Nazi apologist Carl Schmitt, section 1.3); if their values are alien to the very idea of a constitutional regime it would seem that these values cannot be genuinely political. However, Rawls insists that this is not the case:[10] these non-liberal conceptions of the political are unreasonable political conceptions (because they fail to meet the third requirement), but are nevertheless genuinely political, because they meet the first condition. '[A] value is political only when the social form is itself political; when it is realized, say, in parts of the basic structure and its political and social institutions'.[11]

The first and third features of political values do not much help us in understanding the political: each of them itself refers to the idea of the political. A political value is one that applies to basic political and social institutions' (first feature) and a reasonable political value can be worked out from the public, political, culture of a constitutional regime. Neither of these help us identify the idea of the political, since both presuppose that we already know what a political institution is. But that is precisely what we want to know: what characterizes the political? To say that political values apply to political institutions, and can be worked out from our political culture, presupposes what we need to know: what is the mark of the political that distinguishes it from other values in our culture? That political values can be worked out independently of comprehensive doctrines does not tell us how to locate the political.

Can the core idea of 'freestandingness' do the job? No. As we see here, the claim that political values are freestanding is explained by saying that they can be worked out from the public political culture; but since we do not know what the political is, we cannot rely on it when explaining how the political is freestanding. It seems as if Rawls is saying that the political conception is freestanding because it relies only on political values; but that still leaves us in the dark about what a political value is.

What about the possibility that V is a political value if and only if it can be expounded apart from any comprehensive view? Given that a comprehensive view is a system of thought that is wide in scope and rich in content, ranging over many areas of life, a simple prohibition on appeal to comprehensive views (as in step 7 above) is unable to exclude moral, religious or philosophical *beliefs* – as opposed to comprehensive views or general theories – from serving as the basis for an exercise of political power that meets the criterion of Liberal Legitimacy. That a belief is moral, religious or philosophical does not itself show that it is comprehensive or general. Indeed, Rawls himself indicates that the political conception has moral, epistemological and metaphysical elements (PL: 10, 11, 13, 62). Moral, religious and philosophical beliefs need not be, and very often are not, comprehensive or general. They may cover a limited topic and stand alone. Consider, for example, the beliefs that:

(A) God exists;
(B) the external world is real, and a proposition is true if it describes the world accurately;
(C) children should respect their parents;
(D) stealing is wrong;
(E) people who work hard deserve more than those who do not.

Each of these beliefs may be narrow in scope, and is embraced by a wide variety of people with different comprehensive views and is the object of a wide, though certainly not complete, consensus in the United States. Together, these beliefs would seem good candidates for meeting the test of (8*) – which is supposed to be the distinctive feature of the political. Belief (B) is interesting; it is philosophical, and is debated by philosophers, but there is probably much more consensus on it than on any political claim that Rawls makes. Beliefs (C)–(E) are all very widely shared moral beliefs, though it seems that Rawls is one of the few who denies (E).[12]

It might be objected that, although (A)–(E) are simply beliefs and are not themselves comprehensive doctrines, they inherently are parts of comprehensive doctrines and so we might say are necessarily dependent on comprehensive doctrines. If so, the ban on appeal to comprehensive doctrines in step 7 would apply to them. It is hard, though, to see why we should accept this, unless we suppose, for example, that one cannot have religious intuitions without having a full-blown religious system. It seems manifest that a belief in a deity can be 'expounded apart from, or without reference to, any ... wider background' – at least no 'wider background' than is necessary to establish the political conception. People have moral, religious and philosophical intuitions ('there must be a design to the universe', 'there must be a creator') that do not rely on any wide-ranging or general philosophic or religious view of the world. Many people have abstract and isolated intuitions that there is a deity, that true statements in some way correspond to a real external world or that certain actions simply are morally right or wrong. Remember, 'the distinction between the political and other moral conceptions is a matter of scope'. A mere belief in a deity does not imply a general view that regulates many areas of one's life. Indeed, it may regulate no areas, insofar as this belief may have no consequence for one's actions or plans. (Even deism, which influenced American founders such as Franklin and Adams, and which goes beyond a simple belief in a deity to include a general philosophical conviction that there must be some sort of first cause or designer, hardly constitutes a comprehensive doctrine. In contrast to Christian theological religions, it need not advance a plan for life or provide values for a number of areas of life, but can and did serve as a general unpinning for scientific understanding of the universe.)

My point here is that intuitions (A)–(E) can well be freestanding in the sense that they are not *necessarily* imbedded in any comprehensive doctrine. They only seem intimately related to comprehensive doctrines if one supposes that 'comprehensive' means 'religious' or 'moral', but we have already rejected that interpretation of Rawls. But if this is so, then a ban on appeal to comprehensive doctrines will not imply a ban on appeal to a belief in a deity in political reasoning. A Rawlsian should want to exclude beliefs such as A, C and E, but this exclusion does not follow from the principle of Liberal Legitimacy as applied in steps 7 and 8*.

Two significant points follow from this. First, we cannot accept a simple understanding of the political in terms of freestandingness alone, while moral, religious and philosophical doctrines are inherently parts of comprehensive views. But Rawls's other two features of the political conception do not help, because each presupposes that we have already identified the political. We still are in search of the criteria that sets off the political and makes it distinctive. Second, I think that it is not *comprehensive doctrines* that Rawls must object to, but simply appeal (in the justification of constitutional essentials) to any *belief b* when it is the case that some citizen entertains a reasonable belief that is irreconcilable with *b*. The relevant distinction is not between the comprehensive and the political, but the reasonably disputed and the not reasonably disputed. Thus it would appear that we should reformulate step (3) as:

> If (i) free and equal citizen Alf holds a reasonable comprehensive view C_α, and (ii) if Betty's reasonable belief b is 'irreconcilable' with C_α, then (iii) Alf cannot be reasonably expected to endorse b.

But this is still not quite correct. As we have seen, Rawls himself apparently admits that most people do not possess fully comprehensive doctrines. Suppose Alf is one of these citizens whose views do not hang together into a highly coherent scheme; but suppose that, while he does not obtain the integration of a fully comprehensive view, he still has various reasonable beliefs, and b is inconsistent with them. His system of beliefs is 'partially comprehensive' insofar as it does form *some* sort of *system*, but it has no single or few leading idea(s), and a number of issues are not covered. It still would seem unreasonable to expect him to endorse b. Thus we have:

> (3*) If (i) free and equal citizen Alf holds a reasonable belief b_α and (ii) if reasonable belief b is 'irreconcilable' with b_α, then (iii) Alf cannot be reasonably expected to endorse b.

I suspect that some – perhaps Rawls, and certainly Joshua Cohen (see section 5.2) – would object that downgrading the source of Alf's objection to b (from that premised on a comprehensive view of life to a mere reasonable belief) undermines the conviction that it is wrong to expect Alf to endorse b. Recall that Cohen insists that it is *deeply held beliefs* that should be respected; thus while he may well respect an objection to a constitution based on a deep religious conviction, he is apt to dismiss one based on a merely 'reasonable belief'. We have already examined some worries about this 'depth' requirement (see section 5.2). More generally, the focus of political liberalism on reasons deriving from 'comprehensive views' indicates its prepossession with the political implications of theistic religious disagreement. In this respect political liberalism is a distinctively American political theory; understandably, it has less resonance with Europeans, whose political culture is characterized by more secular disputes. A more general political liberalism – one suited to the modern condition of reasonable pluralism rather than simply its American manifestation of religious pluralism – would concern itself with disagreement arising from the plurality of reasonable beliefs in general. After all, ignoring Alf's objection just because it is based on a reasonable belief and not a 'comprehensive' doctrine seems unjust. Alf is not a schizoid personality without an integrated belief structure; he has obtained sufficient integration such that, having considered his other beliefs and values, he has come to a reasonable belief that b_α. To disregard this still seems to ignore his status as a free and equal person. Recall, moreover, that Rawls does not think that most people possess fully comprehensive doctrines: to insist that only fully comprehensive doctrines are the grounds for genuine complaints based on the Principle of Liberal Legitimacy implies that most citizens are precluded from appealing to Liberal Legitimacy. Surely this would be an unwelcome result for a political liberal.

7.3 What is the political? The 'a priori' interpretation

The political as whatever concerns the basic structure

Rawls believes that political is focused on the justice of the basic structure (*PL*: Lecture VIII). He gives us a list of obviously political values:

> those mentioned in the preamble to the United States Constitution: a more perfect union, justice, domestic tranquility, the common defense, the general welfare, and the blessings of liberty for ourselves and our posterity. These include under them other values; so, for example, under justice we also have equal basic liberties, equality of opportunity, ideals concerning the distribution of income and taxation, and much else.[13]

Rawls says that 'other social forms' – non-political forms, such as clubs and teams – may share some of the political values, such as efficiency, but a value is only properly political when it applies to a social form that 'is itself political' such as the basic structure and its social and political institutions.[14] The upshot of this seems to be that a value becomes a political value when it applies to political matters, and political matters concern the basic structure of society and its corresponding social and political institutions. So the crucial contrast is between political values, which concern the political structure, and comprehensive doctrines, which appeal to other sorts of values.

As Habermas has pointed out, Rawls appears to be positing a conceptually basic (in Habermas's words, an 'a priori') distinction between the political and non-political spheres.[15] Rawls seems to suppose there are various fairly well-defined concepts – 'the moral', 'the philosophical', 'the religious', which combine into 'comprehensive views', and that these can be distinguished from 'the political', which applies to the basic structure, on which all reasonable people necessarily agree. For example, in the above quotation Rawls explains the difference in scope between comprehensive doctrines and the political conception by pointing out that '[a] conception is fully comprehensive if it covers all recognized values and virtues within one rather precisely articulated system; whereas a conception is only partially comprehensive when it comprises a number of, but by no means all, *non-political values and virtues* and is rather loosely articulated' (*PL*: 13)[16]. The italicized phrase indicates that the distinction between the political and the non-political is logically prior to the distinction between the comprehensive and the political: Rawls explicates a comprehensive doctrine as one that appeals to non-political values. If this is his view, then we need to know what is political before we can know what is a comprehensive doctrine, for the very idea of the comprehensive is defined in relation to the political. So the idea of the political is conceptually prior to the idea of a comprehensive doctrine. Notice that this is inconsistent with explicating the political in terms of freestandingness, for freestandingness presupposes that we already know what a comprehensive doctrine is, and then identify the political as one that does not appeal to such doctrines. Now we see that comprehensive doctrines are identified as ones that are not political, reversing the order of conceptual priority.

Habermas seems correct that Rawls's political liberalism relies on conceptually basic contrast between the concepts of the political and non-political (or social), one that on reflection seems dubious and contentious. Rawls (though he denies it[17]) seems to posit a basic distinction between the 'political' and the 'social', the latter being the realm of 'comprehensive doctrines of all kinds – religious, philosophical, moral'. (*PL*: 14). As Habermas observes in his own criticism of Rawls, 'the boundaries between public and private' [by which he means the political and non-political] are 'historically shifting' and 'in flux'[18] – indeed, they have been one of the main sources of dispute between different 'comprehensive' theories of theories of self and society – i.e., what we often call 'political theories'.[19] The concept of politics, it has been argued, is 'essentially contested', being composed of a number of dimensions that can be ordered differently, producing different conceptions, each of which is a reasonable interpretation of the concept.[20]

That the political is focused on the justice of the basic structure (*PL*: Lecture VIII) is a reasonable – perhaps the correct – view, but it is by no means an uncontentious conception of the political endorsed by all reasonable citizens. This is, I think, well illustrated by Rawls's own discussion of whether monogamy is a political value. Acknowledging that traditionally the state's interest in the family has been 'specified very broadly', he continues:

> But in a democratic regime the government's legitimate interest is that public law and policy should support and regulate, in an ordered way, the institutions needed to reproduce political society over time. These include the family (in a form that is just), arrangements for rearing and educating children and institutions of public health generally. This ordered support and regulation rest on political principles and values, since political society is regarded as existing in perpetuity and so maintaining itself and its institutions and culture over generations. Given this interest, the government would appear to have no interest in the particular form of family life, or the relations

between sexes, except insofar as that form or those relations in some way affect the orderly reproduction of society over time. Thus appeals to monogamy as such, or against same-sex marriages, as within the government's legitimate interest in the family, would reflect religious or comprehensive doctrines. Accordingly, that interest would appear improperly specified.[21]

Although Rawls's understanding of the appropriate sphere of politics is reasonable, it is hardly unreasonable to entertain different conceptions of the role of the state. Consider the view of Lord Devlin who, in the United Kingdom in the 1960s, argued against the Report of the Committee on Homosexual Offences and Prostitution which proposed, essentially, legalization of homosexuality. Devlin argued:

> Society is entitled by means of its laws to protect itself from dangers, whether from within or without .... Societies disintegrate from within more frequently than they are broken up by external pressures. There is a disintegration when no common morality is observed and history shows that the loosening of moral bonds is often the first stage of disintegration, so that society is justified in taking the same steps to preserve its moral code as it does to preserve its government and other essential institutions. The suppression of vice is as much the law's business as the suppression of subversive activities.[22]

Thus Devlin believed that societies disintegrate if 'vices' such as homosexuality are not suppressed. It might seem that Devlin actually embraces Rawls's conception of politics as the 'institutions needed to reproduce political society over time'; they just disagree about what is required to achieve that aim. But the disagreement is deeper: it concerns what is meant by a society, and what is required for its preservation. Devlin is arguing that a society is partially *constituted* by a code of morality, which includes public acknowledgment of conceptions of virtue and vice. This being so, it is the proper office of a government to protect this morality by legally punishing those who engage in vicious acts, such as homosexuality.

Rawls, of course, would insist that Devlin is improperly drawing on a comprehensive view. But Devlin's reply is that the enforcement of such social norms of good conduct is quintessentially political. If, as Rawls sometimes does, we define a comprehensive doctrine as that which draws on non-political values, then Devlin will insist that he does not draw on a comprehensive doctrine, since the enforcement of shared morality is the crux of the political. If, in contrast, Rawls appeals to the idea that a comprehensive morality is one that is wide in scope and rich in content, ranging over many areas of life, Devlin can dispute that his understanding of shared morality is comprehensive. It includes, to be sure, norms that prohibit some sexual acts, but there is no reason to think that the regulation of sexual activity is more comprehensive than in Rawls's own theory, which would regulate the family to ensure that it is consistent with justice.

Indeed, Rawls goes so far as to say that 'a liberal conception of justice *may* have to allow *for some* traditional gendered division of labor within families ... provided it is fully voluntary and does not result from *or lead to* injustice'.[23] Given that a mark of a comprehensive doctrine is that it includes 'ideals of familial ... relationships' (*PL*: 13), it is not at all obvious why this is not comprehensive. If we compare the areas of family life potentially subject to regulation by Rawls's and Devlin's political values, it is dubious indeed that Devlin's is more comprehensive. Which is more comprehensive: prohibiting homosexual acts or abolishing most gendered division of labor in the household?

The point here is that the boundaries of the political are themselves disputed. A Rawlsian, then, cannot rest content relying on a generally accepted understanding of the properly political. But if that is so, then we still have not yet identified what constitutes the political; and if we do not know that, we do not know what 'political liberalism' is, or how political liberalism is to be distinguished from Enlightenment or comprehensive liberalism.

7.4 What is the political? The political as a constructed realm of reasonable agreement

Rawls's discussion of whether autonomy is a political value suggests a more fruitful path to identifying the political. The value of autonomy, Rawls tells us, may take two forms: (1) political autonomy, the legal independence and assured integrity of citizens and their sharing equally with others in the exercise of political power and, (2) moral autonomy, which 'characterizes a certain way of life and reflection, critically examining our deepest ends and ideals, as in Mill's ideal of individuality'.[24] Now, says Rawls, '[w]hatever we may think of autonomy as a purely moral value, it fails to satisfy, given reasonable pluralism, the constraint of reciprocity, as many citizens, for example, those holding certain religious doctrines, may reject it'.[25] Rawls argues here that moral autonomy cannot be a reasonable political value because some citizens would reject it. A political value[26] is reasonable if it meets several conditions. First, it must affirm – or at least be consistent with – the importance of achieving a fair system of cooperation, and it must support abiding by the requirements of such a system. Second, it will not seek to repress competing reasonable doctrines. Third, it must recognize that the 'burdens of judgment' lead to conflicting judgments about questions of the good and the claims that others have on us (see section 1.3). Thus, maintains Rawls:

> Citizens are reasonable when, viewing one another as free and equal in a system of social cooperation over generations, they are prepared to offer one another fair terms of cooperation according to what they consider the most

reasonable conception of political justice.... The criterion of reciprocity requires that when those terms are proposed as the most reasonable terms of fair cooperation, those proposing them must also think it is at least reasonable for others to accept them, as free and rational citizens.[27]

So perhaps we should see the *politically reasonable* as *constructed out of* that on which we reasonably agree, or at least that which is not subject to reasonable veto. On this reading the non-political is, by definition, those matters on which our use of reason leads us to different, reasonable conclusions. It is, by its very nature, the realm of reasonable pluralism. In contrast, we can, at least in part, *define* the political as those matters on which human reason converges, and so necessarily generates constitutional principles that satisfy the Principle of Liberal Legitimacy.[28] As Rawls says, the 'spheres of the political and the public ... fall out from the content and application of the conception of justice and its principles'.[29] Once we reasonably agree on a conception of justice, this identifies a political perspective on which we all agree. So rather than seeing the idea of the political as one that is logically prior to the notion of a comprehensive doctrine, now the order of priority is reversed: we start out with people's comprehensive views, and construct out of them the notion of the political.

This interpretation links up with Rawls's description of the political as a module. In addition to describing the political as 'freestanding' (see section 7.2 above), Rawls says that, '[t]o use a current phrase, the political conception is a module, an essential constituent part, that fits into and can be supported by various reasonable comprehensive doctrines that endure in the society regulated by it' (*PL*: 12). On this interpretation of the political, the liberal political conception is a module that can form a part of every comprehensive doctrine because we have defined that politically reasonable in just that way: that which every comprehensive doctrine shares.

This approach to identifying the political avoids the problems I have thus far been canvassing. It does not rely on an a priori or uncontroversial (within the limits of reasonability) notions of what is inherently political, moral, philosophical or religious. To be sure, it implies that what prima facie appears to be a moral belief can end up part of the political (should it turn out to be shared), but Rawls expressly allows this: the political conception, he tells us, 'is a moral conception worked out for a specific kind of subject, namely, for political, social, and economic institutions' (*PL*: 11).[30]

Convergent and consensus justifications

Fred D'Agostino has identified two ways in which human reason can agree: *consensus and convergence*.[31] A consensus argument seeks to show that everyone has reason *R* to accept belief *X*. Such an argument seeks to show that we *share a reason for endorsing X*. In contrast, a convergence argument seeks to show that we have different reasons for endorsing X, though we all have some reason for endorsing it. Rawls employs both types of arguments in his case for agreement on the political.

As we have seen, Rawls argues that the political conception can be justified as freestanding (*PL*: 10): it is based on a conception of persons as reasonable and rational, free and equal – a conception that is said to be implicit in our democratic society, and so shared by all. Justice as fairness thus expresses 'shared reason' (*PL*: 9). Rawls argues that justice as fairness is a justified political conception because it articulates the requirements of the concepts of the person and society that all reasonable citizens in our democratic societies share. However, Rawls does not believe that this exhausts justification. In later stages of justification – what he refers to as 'full' and 'public' justification – citizens draw on their full range of beliefs and values and find further reasons for endorsing the political conception.[32] Thus 'overlapping consensus' constitutes a convergent public justification, drawing on our various 'comprehensive doctrines'.

Reasonable pluralism and political conceptions

The key idea, then, is that the political conception exemplifies a consensus and convergence of the powers of our reasoning. The content of this political conception is 'broadly liberal in character':

> By this I mean three things: first, it specifies certain basic rights, liberties, and opportunities (of the kind familiar from constitutional democratic regimes); second, it assigns a special priority to these rights, liberties and opportunities, especially with respect to claims of the general good and of perfectionist values; and third, it affirms measures assuring all citizens adequate all-purpose means to make effective use of their basic liberties and opportunities. (*PL*: 223)

Justice as fairness, as Rawls now interprets it, is simply *one* such liberal conception; because 'each of these elements can be seen in many different ways, so there are many liberalisms' (*PL*: 223). This is significant: Rawls acknowledges that there are diverse interpretations of the basic concept of a liberal political order. Indeed, he insists that '*it is inevitable and often desirable that citizens have different views as to the most appropriate political conception*; for the public culture is bound to contain different fundamental ideas that can be developed in different ways' (*PL*: 227).[33] Rawls also accepts that citizens arguing in good faith and employing public reason will not accept 'the very same principles of justice' (*PL*: 214).

This is puzzling. If citizens entertain 'different views as to the most appropriate political conception' a society cannot be what Rawls calls 'well-ordered'. In a well-ordered society 'everyone accepts, and knows everyone accepts, the very same principles of justice' (*PL*: 35). Now in *A*

con risoluto

Theory of Justice, achieving a well-ordered society was necessary for us to adjudicate our disputes while treating each other as free and equal moral persons. If we possess a public conception of justice to resolve our disputes, and we all know that we all accept this conception of justice, then despite a great diversity in personal ideals – in personal notions of what makes life worth living and how it is best lived – we possess a common standard by which to peacefully resolve our disputes without any resolutions simply being imposed on some by others. However, Rawls now seems to think that reasoning together will not itself lead us to a well-ordered society; the reasoning of free and equal citizens may lead them to all accept the liberal concept of justice, but will not lead them to all embrace justice as fairness, the 'very same principles of justice', or the same views of constitutional essentials. And no evidence indicates that Rawls believes disputes about the favored political conception and the principles of justice are a sign that some citizens are either irrational or unreasonable. Indeed, it seems an instance of the 'burdens of judgment', which was originally introduced to show why we disagree about moral, philosophical and religious matters (see section 1.2). In his account of the burdens of judgment, Rawls stresses the complexity of value disputes, and the different way of ordering and weighing values (*PL*: 54–58). It seems that it is precisely this complexity in ordering and weighing 'political values', and the complexity of developing democratic ideals, that leads to competing reasonable political conceptions. *Reasonable pluralism does, after all, apply to political conceptions.* At only the most abstract level – the level of the very concept of a liberal order – does Rawls indicate that the exercise of the powers of human reason produces agreement. At more specific levels – and by 'specific' here, I mean something as abstract as justice as fairness (see section 7.1) – our use of reason leads to reasonable disagreement.

Some passages in *Political Liberalism* indicate that Rawls's argument is that: (1) justice as fairness is a reasonable liberal political conception of justice and (2) citizens living under it will tend to develop allegiance to it, and thus (3) a society ruled by justice as fairness will move toward being well-ordered as citizens come to see that it coheres with their moral, religious and philosophical views. Thus, we might interpret Rawls as saying that, while reason alone does not *now* produce consensus on his favored liberal political conception of justice, the long-run tendency of a society living under justice as fairness is to converge on it. As Rawls stresses, there is a path to an overlapping consensus on justice as fairness that, through a series of steps, leads to a well-ordered society (*PL*: 158–168).

However, before a society converges on justice as fairness, there will be some period in which free and equal citizens exercising their reason will disagree whether justice as fairness is the favored political conception. (Indeed, it is very difficult to believe that this period will not extend indefinitely. That the reasoning of free and equal people will some day lead everyone to accept justice as fairness seems, at best, a controversial prediction.) During this period – however long it lasts – the exercise of political power on the basis of a constitution justified by appeal to justice as fairness violates the criterion of Liberal Legitimacy (see sections 7.1 and 7.2). Recall:

> The exercise of political power is legitimate only if it accords with a constitution the essentials of which all free and equal citizens may reasonably be expected to endorse.

and

> (3*) If (i) free and equal citizen Alf holds a reasonable belief b_α and (ii) if reasonable belief b is 'irreconcilable' with b_α, then (iii) Alf cannot be reasonably expected to endorse b.

Now suppose citizen Alf believes that the most reasonable liberal political conception of justice enshrines private property, allows for a social provision of a minimum income (with no further provision of equality), and seeks to award people differentially on the grounds of economic desert. We can assume that this reasonable articulation of the liberal concept of justice – which is in fact a popular one[34] – departs in important ways from justice as fairness. Assume further that the majority accepts justice as fairness as the favored political conception; on that basis, they adopt a constitution that allows socialism, and the legislature proceeds to institute a market socialist regime. Citizen Alf, however, has a reasonable political doctrine that includes a reasonable belief that private property ought to be protected by a just constitution; it is thus unreasonable to expect him to endorse a constitution that allows socialism. Consequently, if we demand allegiance to the Principle of Liberal Legitimacy, a society cannot start on the path to being well-ordered under justice as fairness.

It might be replied in Rawls's defense that, while there may be reasonable disagreement as to whether justice as fairness is the favored political conception, rational and reasonable citizens can reach consensus on what he calls 'constitutional essentials'. As Rawls notes, Kurt Baier suggests that Americans already have broad consensus on these matters (*PL*: 149).[35] The Principle of Liberal Legitimacy does not require consensus on a *conception of justice*, but only on *constitutional essentials*. Moreover, in Rawls's steps to a well-ordered society based on justice as fairness, a constitutional consensus is prior to an overlapping consensus based on justice as fairness. So, as long as rational and reasonable free and equal citizens endorse the same constitutional essentials, the Principle of Liberal Legitimacy is satisfied.

Rawls, however, explicitly tells us that reasonable and rational free and equal citizens disagree about constitutional essentials. 'A vote can be held on a fundamental [constitutional] question as on any other; and if the question is debated by appeal to political values and citizens vote their sincere opinion, the ideal is sustained' (*PL*: 241). Public reason, Rawls tells us, rarely leads to close agreement, even on matters of constitutional essentials and basic justice (*PL*: 241). And, again, this is essentially because of what we might call the 'burdens of (political) judgment' (see section 1.2). The political values relevant to constitutional essentials are multiple and complex, and so free and equal citizens exercising their powers of practical rationality and reasonability come to good-faith different answers about their proper weighing, leading to diverging views of justified constitutional essentials. Even in the political – in this case, constitutional – sphere reasonable pluralism manifests itself. If citizen Alf has a reasonable belief that clause X is essential to a just constitution, then employing political power under a constitution that contains Y, where Y is irreconcilable with X, violates the Principle of Liberal Legitimacy. And, as a matter of fact, such debates occur in constitutional deliberations in the United States. Some American liberals insist that constitutional clauses upholding freedom of contract and preventing the taking of private property are constitutional essentials (that have been ignored); others follow Rawls in insisting that the protection of extensive private property rights is not a constitutional essential.[36]

To be sure, here too Rawls believes that a series of steps can lead to a constitutional consensus (*PL*: 158–164). But, as we saw above, it must be true that before there is such a consensus the exercise of political power is illegitimate. As long as the Principle of Liberal Legitimacy is honored, the process cannot get under way. If we view Liberal Legitimacy as a constraint on the exercise of political power, it not only blocks a constitution premised on 'comprehensive' doctrines, it blocks justice as fairness – and indeed any specific liberal conception – as well. Of course, if Rawls could distinguish political from non-political values, then he would have a ground for distinguishing reasonable disagreement about political values from reasonable disagreement about non-political values; but we are now trying to explicate the political/non-political distinction in terms of reasonable disagreement, so it cannot be employed to resolve the problem.

So what? Recall that we began section 7.4 by exploring the idea that, for Rawls, the liberal conception of the political might be constructed out of that on which all reasonable persons agree. But we have seen that on Rawls's own estimation, there is hardly any such area at all. No specific liberal conception of the political is vindicated.

The weakened principle of liberal legitimacy

Rawls is aware of these problems; his response is to implicitly weaken the Principle of Liberal Legitimacy to allow for such reasonable political pluralism.

Rawls seems to exploit an ambiguity between strong and weak senses of what it is 'reasonable' to endorse. He often tells us that the 'political conception is a reasonable expression of the political values of public reason and justice between citizens seen as free and equal' (*PL*: 247; see also, 243, 246, 253) or gives 'reasonable' answers to questions about how to weigh political values and constitutional essentials (*PL*: 225). We are also told that citizens may 'reasonably accept' the terms of cooperation specified by the political conception (*PL*: 16). Now this is much less than Rawls required proposals based on 'comprehensive doctrines'. Recall step (3):

> If (i) free and equal citizen Alf holds a reasonable comprehensive view C_α, and (ii) if citizen Betty's reasonable comprehensive view C_β is 'irreconcilable' with C_α, then (iii) Alf cannot reasonably be expected to endorse C_β.

The political parallel would be:

> If (i) free and equal citizen Alf holds a reasonable political view of constitutional essentials, P_α, and (ii) if citizen Betty's reasonable political view P_β is 'irreconcilable' with P_α, then (iii) Alf cannot reasonably be expected to endorse P_β.

If we accept this, the claim that P_β is 'reasonable' or gives 'reasonable answers' is in no way sufficient to show that it passes the test of Liberal Legitimacy; simply put, on this stronger criterion, *it is not reasonable to expect a citizen to endorse a doctrine just because it is a reasonable doctrine.* Indeed the whole problem of reasonable pluralism is that there are numerous reasonable views that are irreconcilable with other reasonable views; political liberalism's search for consensus in the domain of the political was intended as a response to this very problem: to 'resolve the impasse in our recent political history . . . that there is no agreement on the way basic social institutions should be arranged if they are to conform to the freedom and equality of citizens as persons' (*PL*: 300). Yet Rawls often seems content to rely on the claim that his favored political conception is simply *a* reasonable political view. But that would imply the following *Principle of Weak Liberal Legitimacy*:

> The exercise of political power is legitimate if it accords with a constitution the essentials of which all free and equal citizens can see as reasonable.

Weak Liberal Legitimacy suggests that it is reasonable to expect a citizen to endorse a political view just because it is a reasonable political view. In another place, however, Rawls seems to insist on a stronger requirement:

> we honor public reason and its principle of legitimacy when three conditions are satisfied: a) we give very great and normally overriding weight to the idea

it prescribes; b) we believe public reason is suitably complete, that is, for at least the great majority of fundamental questions, possibly for all, some combination and balance of political values *alone* reasonably shows the best answer; and finally, c) we believe that the particular view we propose, and the law or policy based thereon, expresses a reasonable combination and balance of those values. (*PL*: 241)[37]

Clause (b) is more demanding than the test implied in Weak Liberal Legitimacy. It requires us to assume that there is a *uniquely* reasonable *best* answer to the political question. Surprisingly, however, clause (c) does not require a person to believe that the answer she is proposing is the best answer supposed in (b), only that it is *a* reasonable answer (thus reverting to the view I considered in 1 above). It is not clear that this is simply an oversight.[38] Rawls tells us that the answer provided by public reason 'must at least be reasonable, if not the most reasonable' (*PL*: 246). Again, this suggests that any reasonable answer is sufficient. However, even supposing that one interprets (c) to require a good-faith belief that one's reasonable answer is the uniquely most reasonable answer, if we apply this criterion to 'comprehensive doctrines', it would allow, say, one to advocate a constitution upholding Millian 'comprehensive' liberalism. For the Millian could claim: (1) that he believes that there is a uniquely best answer to this question (the Millian one), though of course there are other reasonable views too, and (2) he is advocating the doctrine which, in good faith, he believes is the uniquely most reasonable one. If we reduce the demands of Liberal Legitimacy to requiring simply a good-faith belief that one's reasonable view is the best or most reasonable one, constitutions relying on 'comprehensive' doctrines are legitimate.

Rawls, however, insists that the 'answer provided by public reason must at least be reasonable, if not the most reasonable, *as judged by public reason alone*' (*PL*: 246).[39] Thus Rawls can insist that in the case of a Millian constitution, its reasonability is not judged by public reason alone, but in reference to the Millian comprehensive view. This reply brings us full circle, for it supposes a basic (what Habermas called an 'a priori') contrast between the political (or public) and the non-political (see section 7.3). If we could distinguish in an uncontentious manner the properly political from the non-political or social, then we would be in a position to distinguish what is inconclusive on political grounds from what is non-politically inconclusive. However, having given up that attempt, we have been seeking to construct the notion of the political out of the reasons we can share. If both Millian liberalism and justice as fairness are reasonable views, that their adherents believe to be correct but which cannot be shown to be uniquely reasonable to others, we do not have the conceptual resources to say that one appeals to the properly political while the other does not. Each has its own reasonably acceptable, but alas, also reasonably rejectable, conception of the political.

The dilemma of political liberalism

We now can see the dilemma of political liberalism. If Rawls could identify a uniquely reasonable conception of the political – one which manifestly excluded Millian and other 'comprehensive' liberalisms as reasonable political doctrines – he could identify a realm of reasonable though conflicting political opinions that was restricted to a small family of political conceptions, one of which would be justice as fairness. Thus the idea of a basic contrast between 'comprehensive' and 'political' doctrines. We have seen, though, that this basic contrast cannot be maintained. We have reasonable differences about what is properly political, while many beliefs associated with comprehensive doctrines are widely shared. The alternative, then, is to abandon any logically basic contrast between the political and the social, and to instead construct the notion of the political out of the reasons we share. But since the use of human reason leads us to reasonable disagreement about conceptions of justice and constitutional essentials, the political qua shared is limited to the abstract concept of a liberal political order.

7.5 Political liberalism and deliberative democracy

Rawls on public deliberation, normal politics and fundamental politics

In many ways political liberalism and deliberative democracy (see Chapter 5) are distinct doctrines. Political liberalism stresses justification of basic political principles that can be the focus of an overlapping consensus among irreconcilable comprehensive doctrines, while deliberative democrats stress an open-ended discourse that validates political claims. Rawls, however, describes himself as a deliberative democrat.[40] And Cohen, our example of a liberal deliberative democrat, is in many ways a follower of Rawls's political liberalism.

While there is clearly overlap between them, Rawls's idea of the public use of reason significantly departs from deliberative democracy. Most important, for Rawls the clear exemplar of public reason is the supreme court of a constitutional regime (*PL*: 231). 'The idea of public reason applies more strictly to judges than others'.[41] Now on the face of it, this accords ill with deliberative democracy. In the United States – which is, manifestly, Rawls's model – the Supreme Court is made up of a handful of lawyers, hardly representative of the citizenry at large. If we understand the point of deliberation as an actual discourse that validates norms among those to whom they apply (see section 5.1), it is impossible to understand how the discourse among these nine lawyers can validate norms. So the idea must be a counterfactual test of validity: the court's reasoning is the best evidence of what the citizenry at large *would* agree to *if* they brought to a successful conclusion the right sort of discourse. We thus again encounter the worry that a highly elitist procedure may be best for discovering what the people *would* agree to (see section 5.1). Despite its difficulties, the argument for deliberative democracy based on the need for actual discourse among those to whom the norms apply provides a firmer link between public reason and *democratic* deliberation.

It is important to note that the principle of Weak Liberal Legitimacy applies only to matters of basic justice and constitutional essentials. In *Political Liberalism* Rawls thus allowed that 'citizens and legislators may properly vote their more comprehensive views when constitutional essentials and basic justice are not at stake' (*PL*: 235, but cf. 252).[42] Suppose, then, a matter is before us that does not involve a constitutional essential, say, whether we should have a government-provided education system or one which is government funded but which is provided by private schools (e.g., through vouchers). Now suppose that the main argument given by those supporting government provision is that a single, government-run, system will be better able to ensure that citizens are raised to endorse certain controversial views: overall, the system will be more favorable to, say, multiculturalism and environmentalism. It will not go so far as to repress competing views, for it will be careful to remain within the bounds of the basic liberal constitution; but within those bounds the majority explicitly advocates the use of state power to uphold its own comprehensive views.

It is hard not to conclude that this is an illiberal and oppressive policy. Some citizens are to be subjected to coercive state enactments that are designed to further (reasonable) doctrines that are irreconcilable with their own reasonable views. It is hard to see why any citizen should reasonably be expected to accept a coercively-imposed law when this law has been justified by appeal to comprehensive doctrines that the citizen reasonably opposes. To be sure, a Rawlsian state will not be grossly oppressive, as it must respect the publicly justified essentials; it does, though, allow many small coercive impositions that are explicitly justified on what seem manifestly non-public grounds. In its day-to-day operations, political liberalism sanctions the majority's use of state power to advance its 'comprehensive doctrines'.

We can understand why Rawls is driven to this conception of politics. If the political is the realm of respect for the freedom and equality of our fellow citizens because it manifests our agreement, the political obviously cannot be instantiated in day-to-day politics, which is, first and foremost, about the ways in which we differ. Hence Rawls must accept a dualistic conception of politics, sharply distinguishing the constitutional (which, at least at times) Rawls depicts as a matter of shared reasoning, and the normal business of politics, which is about the ways in which we differ and which constitutes a hostile arena for the use of public reason.

The proviso

In his later 'The Idea of Public Reason Revisited' Rawls seems to bring legislators and citizens closer to the reasoning of the courts. He tells us that the idea of public reason is 'realized, or satisfied, whenever judges, legislators, chief executives, and other government officials, as well as candidates for public office, act from and follow the idea of public reason and explain to other citizens their reasons for supporting fundamental political positions in terms of the political conception of justice they consider most reasonable'.[43] It would seem that any public official expresses the ideal when she articulates her 'fundamental' political position in terms of what she understands as the most reasonable conception of justice. Rawls now also extends this to citizens at large: 'From the point of view of public reason, citizens must vote for the ordering of political values they sincerely think is the most reasonable'.[44] It seems that Rawls still has in mind, however, only matters of basic justice and constitutional essentials.

Is it, then, a violation of the ideal of public reason to give reasons based on comprehensive doctrines in political debates about basic justice and constitutional essentials? Surprisingly, it seems that advancing such reasons is, after all, consistent with the ideal of public reason:

> reasonable comprehensive doctrines, religious or nonreligious, may be introduced in public political discussion *at any time*, provided that *in due course* proper political reasons – and not reasons given solely by comprehensive doctrines – are presented that are sufficient to support whatever the comprehensive doctrines are said to support. This injunction to present proper political reasons I refer to as the proviso.[45]

The proviso is at odds with deliberative democracy. According to the proviso, a reason based on a comprehensive doctrine (call it R_C) justifying policy P legitimately can be introduced into public discourse if 'in due course' a political reason R_P, which also justifies P, is presented. But surely R_C cannot function in a public discourse aimed at reasoned agreement; it is not a reason that others (who do not share the comprehensive view) can accept, and so R_C cannot provide reasons to them. To advance 'reasons' that are in principle not considerations that can appeal to others is not to engage in public deliberation with them. Since, ex hypothesi, we do not expect reasoned convergence on comprehensive doctrines, then we cannot expect reasoned convergence on the case for P based on R_C. As Rawls himself stresses, 'public justification is not simply valid reasoning, but argument addressed to others'.[46]

The proviso does this much: if one knew that the case from R_C to P satisfied the proviso, then a citizen who advocated P would know that her position was publicly justified, because she knew that (in addition to this non-public argument, which does not justify) there is another, public justificatory, argument – that R_p supports P. And so her support for P, after all, meets the test of public justification (see section 5.3). However, if she already knows that her argument for P from R_C satisfies the proviso because there is a public argument for P from R_p, it is mysterious why she does not advance the good (public) argument to her fellow citizens. Why give an argument that will not appeal to reasonable others when one has an argument that will? If, on the other hand, she does not know that the proviso is met because she does not know of the argument for P on the basis of R_p, then it seems she has no business advancing R_C. The only case in which the proviso makes (some sort of) sense is when a person knows that there is a good public argument for P but does not know what it is, so instead she advances an argument based on her comprehensive doctrine, which she knows does not provide public reasons. But it really is hard to see how one can be confident that there is a good public argument without knowing what it is, and why, faced with that knowledge, one's response is to provide an argument that one knows is *not* a good public argument.

Although Rawls, like Cohen (see section 5.4) wishes to insist that his conception of the reasonable is political and minimal, introducing the proviso adds a clear logical-epistemic element. For according to the proviso, the argument from R_C to P is allowable in public discourse only if there exists another argument, for P from R_p. But then we need to have a good grasp of whether R_p really (logically and factually) supports P. To decide those issues, though, we need to deal with matters of justified belief, good inference, and so on.

7.6 Conclusion and summary

Five leading ideas

I have been critical of Rawls's political liberalism. It is important to stress, though, that its problems are important, as they stem from five compelling ideas.

1 Respect for the freedom and equality of our fellow citizens requires that the state's exercise of coercive authority must be justified to each and every citizen. This, of course, is the core idea of the Principle of Liberal Legitimacy. Difficulties arise when we add the second compelling idea:

2 The free exercise of human reason leads us to disagree on a wide variety of issues concerning value, goods, ideals of the good life and so on. One citizen's reasonable views are often reasonably rejected by others. This, of course, is our Post-Enlightenment quandary. Consequently:

3 Many of the beliefs we hold most dear are not available to us in our efforts to satisfy the Principle of Liberal Legitimacy, as they are the subject of reasonable disagreement.
4 If we are to meet the Principle of Liberal Legitimacy we must thus restrict the beliefs or considerations to which we appeal, restricting ourselves somehow to those reasons which we all share.
5 However, as we have seen, even in politics our reason leads us to disagree. We cannot go very far by understanding the political as characterized by the absence of reasonable disagreement.

To accommodate all five of these ideas we need to better grasp the idea of reasonable disagreement, and how it leads to problems in satisfying the Principle of Liberal Legitimacy. We shall turn to this problem in the next chapter.

Summary

In this chapter I examined John Rawls's 'political liberalism'. A shared liberal political conception of justice, he argues, is 'freestanding', or a 'module' in all reasonable comprehensive views, and thus can form the basis of a well-ordered society under conditions of modern pluralism.

In section 7.1 I tried to tease out of Rawls's complex writings a more specific and formal argument for his political liberalism. We saw that the argument apparently hinges on the fundamental distinction between comprehensive doctrines – about which there is reasonable disagreement – and the political conception, on which reasonable people can agree. Section 7.2 then turned to the crucial ideas of the political as the freestanding, and its contrast to comprehensive doctrines. I questioned this distinction: numerous apparently non-political beliefs are freestanding and are neither comprehensive nor necessarily parts of comprehensive doctrines. Overall, I expressed skepticism about the pivotal role Rawls assigns to the idea of a comprehensive doctrine: I suggested that the idea of objections to constitutional essentials based on reasonable beliefs was the really crucial notion.

Whereas section 7.2 focused on the characterization of the political in terms of the idea of freestandingness, sections 7.3 and 7.4 examined the metaphor of the political as a 'module'. Rawls might be interpreted as saying that the distinctive features of our notion of the political renders it inherently modular (section 7.3) or that we can construct a shared module out of our comprehensive views (section 7.4). I tried to show how, under Rawls's political liberalism, the domain of the political is a response to the reasonable pluralism of comprehensive doctrines: Rawls wishes for a common point of view that allows the Principle of Liberal Legitimacy to be satisfied. However, I have argued that (1) the domain of the political is itself characterized by reasonable pluralism and (2) Rawls does not, and I believe cannot, show how this reasonable pluralism is a distinctive political sort of pluralism that does not run afoul of the Principle of Liberal Legitimacy, and so is not a worry for political liberalism. There is no way to understand the political – either as an inherently distinct sphere or as a construction of shared human reasons – that insulates it from the problems of reasonable pluralism. Although Rawls plausibly argues that there is a convergence on the very basic idea of a liberal order that respects individuals as free and equal beings, it does not seem that this agreement extends further into constitutional essentials or understand-ings of basic justice. Whereas deliberative democrats (see Chapter 5) and Rawlsian political liberals would have us see politics as a realm of agree-ment, it seems first and foremost a sphere of disagreement.

Section 7.5 then briefly analyzed the nature of public deliberation under Rawlsian political liberalism, and whether it constitutes a form of deliber-ative democracy. We saw that for Rawls the exemplar of public reasoning is not democratic deliberation but the Supreme Court: an elite group of constitutional experts. I argued that this focus on the reasoning of the Court does not accord well with an actual discourse view of public justifi-cation, but is consistent with a counterfactual view of public justification – what the people *would* agree to under the right circumstances. Finally, we considered the way in which Rawls allows citizens to appeal to non-public reasons in political discourse and, in particular, his 'proviso'. To a surprising extent, non-public reasons would be an entirely legitimate part of political discourse under Rawlsian liberalism.

Notes

1   Rawls, *A Theory of Justice* (Cambridge, MA: Harvard University Press, 1971), pp. 490–491. I provide an overview of Rawls's argument of *A Theory of Justice* in my *Social Philosophy* (Armonk, NY: M.E. Sharpe, 1999), Ch. 6.
2   John Rawls, *Political Liberalism*, paperback edn (New York: Columbia University Press, 1996), pp. xl, 36. I refer to this book as *PL* in the text.
3   John Rawls, 'The Idea of Public Reason Revisited', *University of Chicago Law Review*, vol. 64 (Summer 1997): 764–807, p. 781. Reprinted in John Rawls, *The Law of Peoples* (Cambridge, MA: Harvard University Press, 1999) and in John Rawls, *Collected Papers*, Samuel Freeman, ed. (Cambridge, MA: Harvard University Press, 1999), Ch. 26.
4   See also Rawls's 'Reply to Habermas', *Journal of Philosophy*, vol. 92 (March 1995): 132–180, p. 143. Reprinted as Lecture 11 of the paperback edition of *Political Liberalism*.

5   This has long been a problem in understanding Rawls. See for example Robert Paul Wolff, *Understanding Rawls* (Princeton: Princeton University Press, 1977).
6   My emphasis.
7   I do not mean to bemoan this fact. It is difficult not to be a bit frightened by those who embrace fully comprehensive and general views of life. They remind one of Isaiah Berlin's 'hedgehog' who sees only one truth, as opposed to the 'fox' who grasps the plurality of considerations. Isaiah Berlin, *The Hedgehog and the Fox* (London: Weidenfeld and Nicholson, 1953).
8   Rawls, 'Public Reason Revisited', p. 776.
9   Ibid.
10 Ibid., p. 777.
11 Ibid.
12 For a discussion, see my *Social Philosophy*, Chs 6, 9.
13 Rawls, 'Public Reason Revisited', p. 776.
14 Ibid., p. 777.
15 See Jürgen Habermas, 'Reconciliation through Public Reason: Remarks on John Rawls's Political Liberalism', *Journal of Philosophy*, vol. 92 (March 1995): 109–131, p. 129. See also S.I. Benn and G.F. Gaus, 'The Liberal Conception of the Public and Private' in Benn and Gaus eds, *Public and Private in Social Life* (New York: St Martin's Press, 1983), pp. 31, 65.
16 My emphasis.
17 John Rawls, *Justice as Fairness: A Restatement*, Erwin Kelly, ed. (Cambridge, MA: Harvard University Press, 2001) pp. 166, 190. I consider Rawls's alternative way of conceptualising the political in section 7.4 below.
18 Habermas, 'Reconciliation through Public Reason', p. 129.
19 See here my *Political Concepts and Political Theories* (Boulder, CO: Westview Press, 2000).
20 See William E. Connolly, *The Terms of Political Discourse*, 2nd edn (Princeton: Princeton University Press, 1983), Ch. 1. See also W.B. Gallie, 'Essentially Contested Concepts' in his *Philosophy and the Historical Understanding* (New York: Skocken, 1968), Ch. 8.
21 Rawls, 'Public Reason Revisited', p. 779.
22 Patrick Devlin, *The Enforcement of Morals* (London: Oxford University Press, 1968), pp. 12–14.
23 Rawls, 'Public Reason Revisited', p. 792. Emphasis added.
24 Ibid., p. 778.
25 Ibid.
26 Rawls characterizes reasonableness in terms of the virtues of persons (*PL*: 48), which leads us back to what I called public justification among reasonable people (see section 5.3).
27 Rawls, 'Public Reason Revisited', p. 770.
28 Rawls's notion of 'political constructivism' (*PL*: Lecture III) suggests this interpretation, but even there Rawls supposes an a priori understanding of what is political. Only by assuming an a priori conception of the political can we make sense of the claim that 'political constructivism is limited to the political' (*PL*: 89).
29 Rawls, 'Public Reason Revisited', p. 791.
30 Once again, Rawls suggests here that some topics are inherently (and within the bounds of reasonability) uncontroversially, political.

31 Fred D'Agostino, *Free Public Reason: Making It up As We Go* (New York: Oxford University Press, 1996), pp. 30–31.
32 See Rawls's 'Reply to Habermas', pp. 142–143.
33 My emphasis.
34 For a basic exposition, see my *Social Philosophy*, Ch. 9.
35 See Kurt Baier, 'Justice as the Aims of Political Philosophy', *Ethics*, vol. 99 (July 1989): 771–790, pp. 775ff.
36 The now-classic work on this matter is Richard A. Epstein, *Takings: Private Property and the Power of Eminent Domain* (Cambridge, MA: Harvard University Press, 1985). Cf. Bruce Ackerman, *We The People*, vol. I: *The Foundations* (Cambridge, MA: Harvard University Press, 1991), Ch. 5 and *PL*: 262–265.
37 My emphasis.
38 See, however, 'Public Reason Revisited' (p. 797) where Rawls holds that citizens must sincerely think that their view is the most reasonable.
39 My emphasis. Note that I omitted the italicized phrase when I quoted this sentence in the previous paragraph.
40 Rawls, 'Public Reason Revisited', p. 772.
41 Ibid., p. 768.
42 This 'dualist' conception of democracy has been more fully articulated by Ackerman, *We The People*.
43 Rawls, 'Public Reason Revisited', p. 765.
44 Ibid., p. 798.
45 Ibid., pp. 783–784. Emphasis added.
46 Ibid., p. 786.

8

Justificatory Liberalism and Adjudicative Democracy: Public Reason and Umpiring

8.1 Why reason publicly?

Five good reasons

Our analysis of theories of public reason has, thus far, uncovered five reasons that each of us has to reason publicly.

(1) As Hobbesian accounts (Chapter 3) rightly stress, the clash of private judgments – especially about matters relating to politics – leads to conflict. If we are to have a peaceful cooperative social life, we at least require public reasons about what we shall all *do*, even if we do not have to adopt these reasons as guiding our beliefs.

(2) We often need to act in concert. The coordinative analysis of reason and politics reminds us that social life holds out the possibility of coordinated action that benefits everyone, but for that we cannot each be guided by our own understandings of what is best (Chapter 4).

(3) As deliberative democrats (Chapter 5) maintain, public deliberation can lead us to what is the true or best judgment. Epistemic democrats

(sections 6.3–6.4), we have seen, also search for what is true through consulting the public, and aggregating their opinions into a social decision.

(4) Cohen (section 5.2) and Rawls (Chapter 7) remind us that if we are to treat others as free and equal persons we must respect the principle of liberal legitimacy: 'our exercise of political power is fully proper only when it is exercised in accordance with a constitution the essentials of which all citizens as free and equal may reasonably be expected to endorse in the light of principles and ideals acceptable to their common human reason'.[1] Only if our claims on others can be justified to them, do we respect them.

(5) Habermas's analysis of 'reactive attitudes' (section 5.1) reveals that our basic view of others presupposes that norms of justice are justified to them. We are indignant when we are attacked or treated without due consideration. In this sense we view ourselves as moral persons who have claims on others that they restrain themselves in certain ways, and we view others as capable of acting on these claims. But we can only expect others to act on these constraints if they have adequate reason to do so. Thus we suppose that our norms of justice – our public morality regulating our social life – can be justified to others.

Another reason: the liberal principle and justification

Let us consider more carefully the sort of constraints we suppose apply to others, and how this shows our commitment to public justification. Consider Stanley Benn's story of Alan the pebble splitter:

> Imagine Alan sitting on a public beach, a pebble in each hand, splitting one pebble by striking it with another. Betty, a casual observer, asks him what he is doing. She can see, of course, that he is splitting pebbles; what she is asking him to do is to explain it, to redescribe it as an activity with an intelligible point, something he could have a reason for doing. There is nothing untoward about her question, but Alan is not bound to answer it unless he likes. Suppose, however, that Betty had asked Alan to justify what he was doing or to give an excuse for doing it. Unlike explanations, justifications and excuses presume at least prima facie fault, a charge to be rebutted, and what can be wrong with splitting pebbles on a public beach? Besides, so far as we can tell, Alan is not obliged to account to Betty for his actions. ...
>
> Suppose Betty were to prevent Alan from splitting pebbles by handcuffing him or removing all the pebbles within reach. Alan could now quite properly demand a justification from Betty, and a *tu quoque* reply from her that he, on his side, had not offered her a justification for splitting pebbles, would not meet the case, for Alan's pebble splitting had done nothing to interfere with Betty's actions. The burden of justification falls on the interferer, not on the person interfered with. So while Alan might properly resent Betty's interference, Betty has no ground for complaint against Alan.[2]

Benn's claim – and I think it is the quintessential liberal claim – is that there is a basic asymmetry between you acting and another interfering with your actions. Alan does not have to justify his pebble splitting to Betty: he is under no standing requirement to show Betty that he has good reasons for what he is doing. On the other hand, it is required of Betty that she justify to Alan interfering with his actions, or stopping him from what he is doing.

Benn's point is not simply that Alan and Betty may see the world this way, but it is almost impossible for them (and us) not to see social relations as being governed by this principle of non-interference. Suppose Alan did not accept the principle. It follows that he cannot reasonably experience resentment or indignation when, for no good reason, Betty stops him from doing what he intends to do. Admittedly, in some cases Alan might be able to claim the protection of special rights, such as the right to free speech or privacy. However, the interest in Benn's pebble-splitting case is that Alan is performing an inconsequential act on a public beach, so it is not protected by any of the famous 'rights of man'. Nevertheless, Alan must claim a right to freedom to perform such inconsequential activities. Unless he claims a general right to non-interference, it would be perfectly permissible for Betty to follow him around all day long, gently pushing him aside or snatching up every object he is about to reach for (as long as she does not violate, say, any of his basic rights as specified by the United States Constitution's Bill of Rights). I venture that Alan would be indignant. Betty is setting about thwarting his agency without being able to give him any good reason; she is trying to undermine Alan's ability to decide what *he* will do. In effect, she is seeking to supplant *him* as the decision maker about what *he* will do. As do we, Alan sees an important asymmetry between himself and others in deciding what he will do: unless good reason can be provided to the contrary, *he* is the one who makes decisions about what *he* will do. It takes a special case for Betty to interfere. As John Stuart Mill said, '[o]ver himself, over his own body and mind, the individual is sovereign'.[3]

The liberal tradition in political philosophy maintains that each person is free to do as he wishes until some justification is offered for limiting his liberty. All men, said John Locke, are naturally in 'a State of perfect Freedom to order their actions...as they see fit...without asking leave, or depending upon the Will of any other Man'.[4] As liberals see it, we necessarily claim liberty to act as we see fit unless reason can be provided for interfering. I shall call this the *Liberal Principle*:

(1)   A person is under no standing obligation to justify his actions;

(2)   Interference with another's action requires justification; unjustified interference is unjust.

The Liberal Principle proclaims a presumption in favor of liberty. It places the onus of moral justification on one party rather than another; liberty is the moral status quo in the sense that it requires no justification while departures from it do. What Benn calls the 'principle of non-interference' and what Locke called the 'right to natural liberty' are alike in insisting that liberty determines the point of departure for all subsequent ethical and political justification.

Benn's argument provides the basis for an extended version of Rawls's Principle of Liberal Legitimacy. It will be recalled that Rawls applies the Principle of Liberal Legitimacy only to political institutions (see Chapter 7); Benn's argument shows that its scope should not be so restricted. Just as a governmental use of power that cannot be justified to reasonable citizens manifests disrespect for their freedom and equality, an interference by Alf against Betty, interfering with her freedom, manifests the same disrespect. The Principle of Liberal Legitimacy is a constraint on individuals as well as states. Liberals are thus committed to what we might call the *Individualized Principle of Liberal Legitimacy*:

> Alf's interference with Betty is legitimate only if there exists a justification for it that Betty may reasonably be expected to endorse.

Supposing then, that all liberal individuals are committed to The Individualized Principle of Liberal Legitimacy, they have but two options: (1) to abjure interference with others or (2) arrive at publicly justified principles that allow some impositions. As the Hobbesians have taught us, the first is not a real option. To opt for (1) would be to unilaterally renounce what Hobbes called 'the right of nature' – to defend ourselves.[5] Rational liberal citizens are thus committed to option (2); arriving at justified principles that sanction interference. It is because we all have a moral interest in arriving at such a justification that, as Rawls puts it, we all have reason to seek a mutual accommodation[6] and meeting others half-way is a virtue of civility.

8.2 Public justification

Personal and public reasons

Alf could easily satisfy the Principle of Individualized Liberal Legitimacy if his perspective was universally valid, in the sense that whatever was a reason for Alf to act was also a reason for every agent to act. His standpoint and the public standpoint would then be identical. But once again the problem of modern pluralism arises. Because there is reasonable disagreement about values, in particular how they are to be ordered and traded-off against each other (see sections 1.2 and 2.3), my appeal to what I value (or, we might say, my preference ordering) is not apt to provide others with good reason to refrain from acting in ways they desire, based on their own value orderings.

As a liberal citizen seeking to justify a moral demand on Betty, then, Alf must be able to distinguish between his personal or private reasons from public reasons – considerations that are reasons for others as well as for him. The former are reasons that flow from his values, ends and plans; though they may well be central to Alf's way of living and his character, he must acknowledge that no matter how important they are to him, they are not in themselves reasons for Betty. Public reasons, in contrast, are considerations that are not only verified from Alf's perspective, but from Betty's as well.

Justifications and challenges

What is required, then, is that we be able to consider matters impartially, and understand that many considerations that are crucial to us may not matter to reasonable others. And we must refrain from appealing to the personal in our public justifications, despite the fact that the private or personal reasons may, in our own lives, be far more salient. Now in his discussion of the place of religious convictions in politics, Kent Greenawalt maintains that such compartmentalization is as unattractive as it is impossible:

> To demand that many devout Catholics, Protestants, and Jews pluck out their religious convictions is to ask them how they would think about a critical moral problem if they had to start from scratch, disregarding what they presently take as basic premises of moral thought. Asking that people perform this exercise is not only unrealistic in the sense of the impossible; the implicit demand that people try to compartmentalize beliefs that constitute some kind of unity in their approach to life is positively objectionable.[7]

Greenawalt concludes 'that the threads of publicly accessible reasons cannot be disentangled from religious convictions and personal bases of judgment, and that strenuous efforts to make the separation would carry psychological costs and impair people's sense of individual unity'.[8]

Our examination of Rawls's political liberalism shows the element of truth in Greenawalt's view. The attempt to show that the political conception of justice is a module, that fits into any comprehensive doctrine without being modified by the doctrine in which it is embedded, fails (see section 7.3). One's beliefs are interconnected. But to deny that political justice is an autonomous module is not to say that people are incapable of impartiality, and cannot see the difference between reasons that matter to them and reasons that matter to others. Considerable evidence indicates that what Jean Piaget called 'decentering' is a normal human cognitive achievement.[9] Whereas the child is egocentric and so 'mixes up subjective and objective facts', equating his perspective with a universally valid one (and develops universalistic proposals based on it), as a person develops through adolescence, he comes to appreciate the difference between his perspective and others', and so develops objectivity.[10] Again, while this says nothing specifically about religious beliefs, it does indicate that distinguishing personal and important beliefs from those that can be validated from the perspectives of others is within the grasp of normal adults.

Suppose, then, that as a normal adult Alf develops the ability to distinguish what matters to him and what matters to others – he develops an understanding of impartiality. On the basis of this understanding, Alf offers a reason R_α to Betty that he claims justifies proposal P, that she must redistribute some of her holdings to Charlie. As is fairly likely, suppose that Betty resists; she believes that Alf has erred. To support her claim she might advance several different challenges.

(1) She may, firstly, contest Alf's notion of impartiality: what he calls a public reason, she charges, actually stems from his private concerns. The line between personal and public reasons is not clear and bright for all to see; we can and do disagree. Some claim that this shows impartiality cannot be achieved,[11] but this seems wrong. As we have seen, a valid claim that R_α is a public reason may be controversial. Indeed, perhaps the greatest problem with deliberative democracy was its failure to appreciate this (see section 5.3); the search for public justification and the search for actual consensus are distinct. That we all accept that R is an impartial reason is neither necessary nor sufficient for its impartiality. We all can be mistaken in thinking a consideration to be a public reason (since any person can be mistaken about what reasons he has); and so too I may be entirely correct that R is a public reason despite your dissent. To be sure, disputes about the correct account of impartiality pose difficulties for liberal theory (and resolving such disputes will occupy us presently), but disputes about the demands of impartiality do not show that impartiality is a chimera.

(2) Secondly, Betty may argue that Alf's purported reason just isn't a reason at all, as it is based on false beliefs, a misinterpretation of her values, etc.

(3) Lastly, Betty may acknowledge that Alf has advanced a genuine public reason in support of redistribution, but she may advance a counter-reason (R_β), which she insists is stronger, against redistribution.[12]

Responses to challenges

What is Alf to do in the face of these challenges? As I have said, the easy and automatic response – that Betty's dissent ipso facto shows that his public justification is not valid – won't do, for we have seen in this book that consensus is neither necessary nor sufficient for a valid public justification. As a citizen committed to advancing public justifications, Alf ultimately has no choice but to evaluate the cogency of Betty's challenges (see section 5.3). Even if he seeks to rely on the judgment of a third party whom he believes has superior wisdom, this still could be justified only if Alf has grounds for believing that the third party was better able to evaluate the cogency of Betty's challenges; and that means that Alf's response to Betty would ultimately be based on his conclusion about the merits of her challenge. In the end, Alf cannot help but rely on his own reasoning in deciding what constitutes a valid public justification. After all, what *other* resources *could* he rely on to make a judgment? Ultimately, he must think for himself (see sections 4.4 and 6.3).

One judgment Alf might make is that Betty has *defeated* his proposed justification. Let us say that, characteristically, Alf's justification R_α is defeated by Betty's response R_β if:

> (a) R_α and R_β are directly competing; R_α and R_β are directly competing for Alf if, given Alf's other beliefs, Alf's accepting R_β rationally undermines his belief that R_α.[13]
> (b) Given Alf's beliefs, Betty's shows (i) that he has adequate reason to accept R_β and (ii) he has better reason to accept R_β than he has to accept R_α.

A word of explanation about this second clause: it does not require that Betty is correct.[14] The point, rather, is that the R_β is such that, given his system of beliefs, Alf has adequate reason to accept it, better reason to accept it than he does R_α, and that acceptance rationally undermines his acceptance of R_α. To better see this, consider a case in which Betty's response does not meet condition (b):

> *Betty Gets Lucky*: Alf argues that justice demands that the highest marginal tax rate should be 65 percent; that, he claims, would result in a political-economic order that works to the benefit of all citizens. Betty responds that this rate is far too high; after a top marginal rate of 25 percent, economic growth slows, unemployment increases, and the least well off are disadvantaged. Rawls told her so in a dream. It just so happens that Betty is right about the relation of marginal tax rates, growth and the advantages to the least well off.

Even though she turns out to be correct, it is not more reasonable for Alf to embrace R_β than R_α, as her case relies on a non-public consideration. Recall here that, according to Public Justification as Agreement in Reasonable Belief, Principle/policy P is publicly justified if and only if everyone has reasonable grounds for accepting it (or no one has reasonable grounds for rejecting it) (see section 5.3). Thus it is not enough for Betty to be lucky, or to have a mysterious ability to guess how tax rates will affect economic growth[15] – Alf must have reasonable grounds for accepting her response.

The requirement that Betty 'show' that it is more reasonable for Alf to embrace R_β than R_α is also meant to indicate that Betty's position is strongly justified. It seems manifest that our moral and political beliefs can be justified to varying degrees;[16] we can distinguish arguments that provide some evidence for a belief from those that are conclusive. This is not a matter of the simple probability that the belief is true;[17] it is better described in terms of the metaphor of the strength of the reasons for accepting it. The intuitive idea here is that to claim soundly to have rationally defeated a competing proposal we must provide a strong case that the other has reason to adopt our view and abandon his challenge. 'We must be able to *show* that the other person is mistaken if he persists in his earlier decision about how to act. For that, we must be able to show that the principle invoked is somehow valid beyond reasonable doubt'.[18]

The second possibility, of course, is that Alf may conclude that his justification is *victorious* over Betty's challenge. Let us call a justification victorious if it has been open to public challenges for a considerable period[19] and has defeated all of them. Surely deliberative democrats are correct that actual, widespread public discussion and debate, is crucial to achieve justification of our beliefs and norms (see Chapter 5). That is, R_α is a victorious justification if, each time it has been confronted with a challenge, someone has replied in such a way as to defeat the challenging claim – i.e., all challengers have been shown that it is more reasonable for them to embrace R_α than their competing position. Of course, the status of the claim that R_α is a victorious justification is provisional; it may be defeated by future challenges. Recall here Mill's insistence on both free debate and his stress on our fallibility (see section 1.1).

Undefeated justifications and minimal rationality

Some philosophers have described this justification game as a trial by combat, one that 'is usually terminated by an admission of defeat or a proclamation of victory or both'.[20] Indeed, philosophers who adopt this general approach to justification typically maintain that defeat or victory are the only two options. If one does not meet (i.e., defeat) every challenge, it is often said, one must abandon one's claim.[21] It should be clear, however, that defeat and victory do not exhaust the possibilities; claims can be *undefeated but not victorious*. Alf's justification R_α is undefeated if no challengers have shown that it is more reasonable for Alf to accept their challenge than to continue believing R_α; but for this to occur does not imply that Alf has shown any of them, much less all of them, that it is more reasonable for them to accept R_α than continue holding to their challenges. As we saw in our examination of Rawls's Weak Principle of Liberal

Legitimacy (see section 7.4), showing your own beliefs to be reasonable is not equivalent to showing competing beliefs to be unreasonable.[22]

The widespread resistance to this idea stems, I think, from what may be called the ideal of the comprehensively rational agent. According to this ideal, Alf's belief that R_α is a fully rational belief only if it is based on full consideration of all the relevant evidence and all his well-grounded beliefs, all his premises are true and his deliberations leading to R_α are logically impeccable.[23] To be sure, it is acknowledged that actual agents usually can only approximate this ideal, but that is only to say that actual agents can seldom be fully rational (see again section 5.3). However, insofar as one has done one's best, and so has concluded that R_α is the best reason, one then (on this idealized view) must conclude that belief not-R_α is less reasonable. This does not imply that one believes one's own deliberations to be infallible, but insofar as one has concluded that R_α is the soundest reason, one has also ipso facto concluded that others manifest a defect of reason if they embrace not-R_α even after one has defended the virtues of R_α. If all this is so, then as long as one is convinced that R_α is the soundest reason, one must believe that all competing positions are less reasonable. Victory or defeat then seem the only possible outcomes of justificatory combat.

The ideal of comprehensive rationality understands information gathering and computational costs as excuses for falling short of the ideal, but not as the basic conditions of human cognition. Employing computational complexity considerations from computer science, Christopher Cherniak nicely demonstrates that ideal rationality is *so ideal* 'that it cannot apply in an interesting way to actual human beings'.[24] In place of the comprehensive ideal, Cherniak proposes a conception of the minimally rational agent; a minimally rational agent makes some, not all, sound inferences from his belief set and he responds to some, not all, inconsistencies.[25] Indeed, that is all any human can do, as searching a belief set for all possible inferences or checking it for all possible inconsistencies is hopelessly beyond the capacity of human cognitive resources. On the other hand, checking inferences and inconsistencies that are actually brought before us (into our active memory) is much less costly; and so responding to actual challenges rather than all possible ones is fundamental to justification, given the limits of our reasoning resources.[26]

We can now perhaps better understand why Rawls is driven to the Weak Principle of Liberal Legitimacy: our beliefs, including our beliefs about basic justice, politics and common good, are often reasonable, but hardly conclusively correct. Indeed, different people will reasonably disagree on the justification of policies and programs. We are so far from perfectly rational agents (see section 5.3), that our normal condition is one of reasonable disagreement, even about the political (see sections 7.3–7.4). And that being the case, the confrontation between our beliefs may result in neither defeat nor victory but an epistemological standoff.

We thus have good grounds to embrace a version of what I earlier (see section 5.3) called *Public Justification as Agreement in Reasonable Belief*:

> Principle/policy P is publicly justified if and only if everyone has reasonable grounds for accepting it over all challengers to it.

In terms of victory and defeat, a principle or policy P is only publicly justified if it is victorious – it defeats all challenges and competing reasons. For then it has been shown not only that each person has a good reason to embrace it, but all reasons not to embrace it have been defeated, and so not embracing P is unreasonable.

8.3 When public reasoning is inconclusive

Inconclusiveness distinguished from indeterminacy

This, of course, is a demanding requirement. Because our belief systems are so complex, and so many considerations are relevant to disputes about what is publicly justified, it is often impossible to defeat another's proposed justification and proclaim victory. To be sure, it is not always impossible to do so; we must be careful not to press the point too far. There is good reason to think that liberal theory has had some important victories; free speech and other civil rights, some rights of private property and some redistributive (i.e., welfare) rights are, I think, elements of a publicly justified conception of justice.[27] Yet even these important victories point to the limits of public reason; as John Gray emphasizes, as soon as we move beyond these abstract principles to their application in specific cases, 'indeterminacy' arises.[28] However, talk of 'indeterminacy' can easily lead us astray (see section 4.4). Because two roots of inconclusiveness are the complexity of our belief systems and our limited ability to process all the information at our disposal, it seems to me quite misguided to claim, as do some, that in such cases public reasons 'run out', and so must be supplemented by private reasons.[29] The problem is not that public reasoning is indeterminate in the sense that there are not enough reasons to yield a conclusion; the difficulty is that there are so many relevant reasons that all cannot be adequately canvassed and weighed. (We again see that, there are solid grounds for adopting the weaker rather than the stronger analysis of incommensurability (see section 2.3)).

It is because our moral disputes are not typically indeterminate that it makes sense to form opinions and keep arguing about them. If the totality of reasons is really insufficient to form a conclusion, forming *any* opinion is unreasonable. If the only way to get enough reasons to form an opinion is to rely on essentially private reasons, arguing with others is generally pointless, for we know that many others, though reasonable, simply do not share these private reasons. And even if we do form our opinions on such private reasons, to impose a morality based on them is to abandon the liberal commitment to public justification. Moral debate among liberal citizens makes sense because we can and do form opinions on the basis of public reasons; it is so inconclusive because so many considerations are relevant either directly, or because problems about which of two reasons is 'weightier' can only be discussed by appealing to yet other, background, considerations, thus reintroducing problems of complexity.

Consider, for instance, disputes about the protection of animals. Some, such as Greenawalt, claim that publicly accessible reasons simply are not enough to tell us what to do;[30] it is as if one who restricted herself to public reasons would be, quite literally, speechless on this issue. Greenawalt leads us to this conclusion, though, by examining the differing, but very definite and not at all uncertain, views of such philosophers as Peter Singer and Tom Regan. Now assuming that neither has achieved victory on this issue, there are two possibilities: (1) since the relevant public reasons are not sufficient to ground a conclusion, Singer and Regan can only come to their conclusions by relying on essentially private considerations or (2) they arrive at their conclusions by relying on publicly accessible reasons, but because questions of the nature of agency, consciousness and moral rights are so complex, they defend different positions neither of which defeats the other. Our account of reasonable belief points to the latter. Differences of opinion on such matters are apt to result from the abundance of relevant public reasons and our inability to process all of them rather than the paucity of such reasons. Moreover, the latter has the advantage over the former of making sense of the ongoing public debate on such problems.

Epistemological standoff, the state of nature and adjudication

Philosophers can keep arguing and publishing about these unresolved issues – indeed, *these* are just the issues that philosophers typically *do* argue and write about. However, as citizens we are in a different position. Whether animals are to be protected or income redistributed are pressing matters of practice, not just material for philosophical reflection. If, as seems likely, most of our moral disputes result in epistemological standoffs, what are liberal citizens committed to public justification to do right here and now?[31] If Alf has an undefeated, reasonable, belief that Betty's wealth should be redistributed to Charlie, but he acknowledges that he has not defeated her challenges, what should he do? They seem to have two options: wait for victory or make moral demands based on his (merely) reasonable belief.

Waiting for victory (or defeat) On the face of it, there is much to be said for waiting until his view is victorious (or has been defeated). It is, I think, at the heart of deliberative democracy: until discourse has vindicated a proposal to everyone, no norm has been validated (see section 5.1). And after all, if Alf is really committed to public justification, in a fairly obvious sense he has yet to justify his view to Betty; he has not yet shown that she has reason to adopt his view and abandon her competing position. So imposition of his view on her would seem unjustified. Moreover, we have seen that according to the Liberal Principle (section 8.1), there is a presumption in favor of liberty: the burden of proof, we have said, is on those who would limit the liberty of others. If so, then, the burden of proof would appear to lay squarely on Alf, as his moral demands aim to restrict Betty's liberty. Until his public justification of restraints is shown to be victorious, it would seem that he is committed to non-interference. Supposing that outright victory is rare, the upshot would be a regime of minimal restraints, or perhaps even some version of anarchism in which we simply 'agree to differ'.[32]

We need, however, to distinguish two cases of inconclusive justification:

(A) *Merely Inconclusive Justification.* Alf favors policy P, but he cannot defeat reasonable objections to it.

(B) *Inconclusive Interpretations of Justified Principles.* Principle P has been publicly justified; everyone has been shown to have good reasons to accept it, and no one has good reasons to reject it. But P is open to interpretations P_1, P_2 and P_3, none of which can be conclusively justified as the correct interpretation.

In the case of (A), a merely inconclusive justification, the wait for victory option really does seem appropriate: the proposal has not been adequately justified. Here Alf is seeking to override other people's reasonable objections but has not been able to show that they are committed to P. It seems quite right that the Liberal Principle is a barrier to such proposals: it insists that others should be free to go about their business unless interference is justified *to them*, and this is precisely what Alf has not been able to do. Case (B) is more complicated. Here, we suppose, a principle P has been victoriously justified, so others such as Betty have conclusive reason to embrace it, and to act in accordance with it (other things equal). The problem, however, is that it remains an open question just what action P requires: Alf has an undefeated, unvictorious case that P requires, say, P_1, but Betty offers a competing inconclusive case that P_2 is the best interpretation.

This is not a mere possibility: it seems a standard condition. And it is the problem at the heart of Rawls's political liberalism: although the basic idea of a liberal order can be justified, there are competing reasonable interpretations of what that requires. As the legal scholar Alexander Bickel remarked about 'majestic concepts' such as freedom of speech, 'men may in full and equal reason and good faith hold differing views about … [their] proper meaning and specific application'.[33] It seems that the actual consequence of waiting for victorious justifications would be a social life in which few specific moral demands could be made, and in which our publicly justified principles could never be applied. Indeed, for Alf and Betty to do nothing at all in case (B) would, for practical purposes at any rate, to embrace the *defeated* option that P is not justified or is irrelevant to practice. For if Alf waits until his specific proposal is victorious, and Betty waits until her specific proposal is victorious, then no specific course of action will be justified – P will be of no consequence.

The distinction between merely inconclusive and inconclusive interpretations of justified principles, I believe, allows us to unite two aspects of public reason. Rawls understands public reason as reasoning based on justified principles: '[o]nly a political conception of justice that all citizens might reasonably be expected to endorse can serve as *a basis* of public reason and justification'.[34] On the face of it, this is puzzling: it would seem that the justified political conception is an *outcome* of public reason, not the *basis* of it. We can now see, though, that both are true. First, public reason is the basis of the public conception of justice insofar as the conception is victoriously justified. But, once articulated in this manner, the public conception becomes itself the basis of further public reasoning. Although victorious justifications are no longer forthcoming, proposals based on the public conception nevertheless are exercises in public reason. In contrast, inconclusive demands on others that cannot be expressed in terms of the public conception must be dismissed.[35]

Imposition of one's judgment Waiting for victorious justification, then, would commit us to an essentially de-moralized social life in which our justified principles would have no practical import. Because of that even deliberative democrats admit that we must cut-off deliberation and take a vote (see section 5.3). In the end the deliberative democrats, as well as Rawls (see section 7.4) embrace another alternative: one must rely on one's best judgment about what is publicly justified, and take that as determining what moral demands one can make on others. We impose our reasonably rejectable policies on others. To Immanuel Kant, though, relying on one's individual judgment characterizes the state of nature:

> Although experience teaches us that men live in violence and are prone to fight one another before the advent of external compulsive legislation, it is not experience that makes public lawful coercion necessary. The necessity of public lawful coercion does not rest on a fact, but on an a priori Idea of reason, for, even if men were to be ever so good natured and righteous before a public lawful state of society is established, individual men, nations and states can never be certain they are secure against violence from one another because each will have the right to do what *seems just and good to him*, entirely independently of the opinion of others.[36]

Kant goes on to insist that justice is absent in the state of nature because each relies on his own judgment, and thus 'when there is a controversy concerning rights (*jus controversum*), no competent judge can be found to render a decision having the force of law'.[37] Indeed, Hobbes, Locke and Kant all maintain that the chief inconveniences of the state of nature arise from individuals relying on their individual, controversial, judgments about natural rights and natural law. The chief inconveniences are two, one moral and one practical.

The moral flaw of the state of nature ruled by individual judgment is that we act without justification. As I have already argued, to impose an undefeated but unvictorious public justification on another fails to meet the demands of public justification. To have satisfied yourself that your demands are justified is far short of showing others that your demands are justified. If public justification is the 'moral lodestar of liberalism',[38] and reflects a commitment to respect for persons, relying on one's individual judgment in this way manifests disrespect and is unjust. Jeffrey Reiman persuasively argues that imposing such inadequately justified principles on another is an act of *subjection*: one is supplanting the other's own judgment about what the other should do, and replacing it with your (merely personal) judgment about what the other should do.[39]

Leaving aside its moral shortcomings, as Hobbesians have taught us (Chapters 3 and 4), a state of nature (i.e., a regime in which people all relied on their undefeated but unvictorious judgments) would be characterized by uncertainty and conflict, undermining the basis for cooperation. Inconsistent interpretations of each other's rights and responsibilities would lead to conflict and thwart the development of settled expectations. This, of course, is a familiar theme in liberal, and especially contractualist, political philosophy: Hobbes's, Locke's and Kant's accounts of the state of nature all aim to establish variations of it. Although on some matters we can agree to differ, disputes engendered by competing judgments will block common action and, as R.E. Ewin points out, this includes 'common recognition of the limitations on individual or private action'.[40]

8.4 The liberal umpire

Locke versus Hobbes

Alf appears trapped in a dilemma. The option of waiting for victorious judgments is consistent with the Liberal Principle, but seems to doom him to an amoral life in which even justified principles have no effect, since they cannot be interpreted. On the other hand to simply impose a reasonable, but not conclusively justified belief, seems inconsistent with the demand for public justification and the principle of Individualized Liberal Legitimacy. I have stressed that, in the end, the deliberative democrats and Rawls take this second route. Although they begin by embracing a strong conception of the requirements of public justification, in the end the demands of practice require that a much weaker test be applied.

It is here, I think, that our examination of Hobbesian-inspired liberalism is illuminating. We saw in Chapter 3 that Hobbes was sensitive to the problems caused by conflicts of private judgment, and provides a case to adopt a public reason as defined by the sovereign:

> And because, though men be never [sic] so willing to observe these laws [of nature], there may nevertheless arise questions concerning a man's actions; first, whether it were done, or not done; secondly, if done, whether against the law or not against the law; the former whereof, is called a question *of fact*; the latter a question of *right*, therefore unless the parties to the question, covenant mutually to stand to the sentence of another, they are as far from peace as ever. This other to whose sentence they submit is called an ARBITRATOR. And therefore it is of the law of nature, *that they that are at controversy, submit their right to the judgment of an arbitrator.*[41]

Hobbes, we saw (section 3.2), would have our private reason supplanted by the sovereign's, but sincere reasoners cannot accept that: as I argued, we cannot accept something as true just because it benefits us, or helps secure social peace (section 3.2). Locke provides a better model for adjudicating the requirements of public reason among private reasoners who arrive at conflicting judgments – a model of arbitration that avoids Hobbes's more extreme claims. Locke argued that in order to escape the inconveniences of each relying on his own moral judgment, we appoint an 'Umpire'[42] to adjudicate our disagreements. Consider an umpire in a game, such as baseball. The umpire is needed, first and foremost, because when players have disputes, they need to get on with the game. They require some interpretation of the facts and/or the rules, so that play can proceed. Thus the key role of the umpire, as the voice of public reason, is not to tell us what to believe, but what to do: once the umpire has spoken, the players will accept his judgment as guiding action, if not necessarily belief.

Yet, although the first function of the umpire is to give practical resolutions of our disagreements, its decisions are not mere Hobbesian acts of will, proclaiming that its reason is definitive. Rather, its authority is partially based on his claim to be at least competent – to be good at getting the answers right. The umpire does his best to track the best arguments. In baseball, for example, the umpire seeks to provide the correct ruling based on shared rules and concepts.[43] Thus umpiring has an epistemic element – it is truth-seeking, but its claims to have authority do not suppose that it always reaches the correct answer. Even when we believe that the umpire gets it wrong, we still have reason to accept his judgment, for generally we need some practical resolution of our dispute.

what is taken for granted here?
first question of politics?

Umpiring, then, is based on the supposition that (1) there is intractable difference of opinion; (2) to proceed with practice, there must be a practical resolution of the dispute; (3) that this practical resolution need not be accepted by all the parties as the correct solution but (4) the authority of the umpire's decision requires that it seeks to arrive at the best answer. Sincere reasoners committed to public justification who also wish to get on with their lives require precisely this sort of umpiring of their disputes. *It honors their commitment to sincerity and thinking for themselves* (see sections 3.2, 5.3 and 6.3) since it never requires anyone to abandon what she thinks is the best reason. It also *honors their commitment to public justification* because no one simply imposes her will, or even her reasoning, on another: each accepts the action directives of the umpire, who seeks an impartial resolution of the dispute. Lastly, the umpire *honors the commitment to deliberation*, for the umpire always seeks to act on the basis of the best possible reasons, and considers the merits of the opposing views.

Liberal politics, reasonable disagreement and umpiring

Citizens committed to the Individualized Principle of Liberal Legitimacy in a pluralistic world require precisely this sort of umpiring of their disputes. They do not act coercively against another simply on the basis of their own controversial reasoning: all have conclusive reason to submit their dispute to the umpire, who provides an impartial practical resolution of the dispute.

The umpire's legitimate decision is, then, simply *a* reasonable judgment. Umpires are not sages who we suppose always give the best answer. It is not at all inconsistent with accepting the authority of an umpire to insist that your opinion is more reasonable. Rather, umpires are unique in that they alone have the authority to use coercion to support a reasonable, though contentious, interpretation of liberal principles. Note, then, that justificatory liberalism provides a coherent account supporting Rawls's observation that the judgment of public reason – the umpire – 'must at least be reasonable, if not the most reasonable'.[44] Because of their intractable disputes about what is the most reasonable interpretation of publicly justified liberal principles, free and equal individuals would embrace an umpire who is empowered to act on its reasonable, but by no means conclusively correct, judgment about these matters.

This is important. Liberal legitimacy, Rawls and I have agreed, requires that coercion must be justified in a way that is not subject to reasonable objection; because of that the justification must be *conclusive* – not subject to reasonable dissent or objection. But because of political pluralism, normal politics can, at its best, only claim to result in *reasonable* conclusions; in Rawls's words, they are 'reasonable, if not the most reasonable' (section 7.4). Citizens can reasonably dissent from reasonable laws and policies. The idea of liberal adjudication explains why the government can satisfy the

Individualized Principle of Liberal Legitimacy even though it can only be shown that its judgments are reasonable, not conclusively justified. Because (1) we require a common answer on questions of justice, (2) we have *conclusive reason to embrace an umpire*, (3) we thus have a good reason to follow the directives of the umpire even though they are only reasonable. *In short, there is a conclusive justification to follow the reasonable but not conclusive decisions of the umpire.*

Status quo affirming

Is the liberal state too limited?

It has been objected that this view too greatly limits the scope of state action.[45] On this view, a specific action P undertaken in some area of social life by the liberal umpire is justified only if there is a conclusive reason for the government undertaking some sort of action in that area, of which P is a reasonable option. Thus, for example, a specific national health care scheme could only pass the test of liberal legitimacy if there is a conclusive justification – a justification that no citizen has sound reasons for rejecting – that there be some sort of national health care (or that there be some sort of distributive justice arrangement, of which the health care scheme is a case). If there is no conclusive justification for a principle or a type of policy, then the 'wait and see' stance seems dictated by the Liberal Principle: if thus far no conclusive justification has been given, then thus far no government action is justified. Only when government action can be justified as a reasonable interpretation of a conclusively justified requirement will it pass the test of the Individualized Principle of Liberal Legitimacy.

This is a demanding requirement; it has been pointed out that many social policies may fail to pass this test.[46] A small minority that has reasonable objections to such policies could block them if they cannot be brought under more general publicly justified requirements. This, of course, is a consequence of applying the test of public justification not simply, as Rawls would have it, to constitutional essentials and matters of basic justice, but to all interferences with individual liberty. The extent of legitimate political action is bound to shrink. There can be no good justification for the majority simply legislating pursuit of its own goals or concerns in the face of reasonable objections by the minority, even a small minority. In contrast to political liberalism, this seems a more genuinely liberal conception of politics. Liberals traditionally have been wary of government action, and have demanded that coercive legislation meet demanding requirements.

We might contrast two views of liberal political principles: the limiting and the empowering.[47] On one model, liberalism advances fundamental moral principles that government may not violate. A government is unjust if it enacts legislation that oversteps these bounds by, say, seeking to establish a religion or severely curtailing freedom of speech. However, in the eyes of some, as long as a government respects these constraints, its legislation is just. This view is advanced by Robert Bork, who argues that

> [t]he United States was founded as a Madisonian system, which means that it contains two opposing principles that must be continually reconciled. The first principle is self-government, which means that in wide areas of life majorities are entitled to rule, if they wish, simply because they are majorities. The second is that there are nonetheless some things majorities must not do to minorities, some areas of life in which the individual must be free of majority rule.[48]

I believe that this inadequately articulates the liberal ideal of limited government. Bork's underlying idea is that a majority may properly legislate its preferences except when it runs afoul of constitutional restraints.[49] To be sure, this is a limited government of sorts – the majority is not allowed to do some things. But, given the Liberal Principle, every legislative act by the majority, because it constitutes an imposition on the minority, stands in need of justification (see section 8.1). Unlike individuals, who can often act without imposing on others, all legislative acts of the majority are impositions, and so every such act stands in need of justification. 'Justice', said Madison, 'is the end of government'[50] and justificatory liberalism concurs. The basic problem that requires political society, according to traditional social contract theory and justificatory liberalism, is that our opinions about the demands of justice are inconclusive. Because of this, and because of our commitment to justify our demands to others, we are led to embrace an umpire, judge or arbitrator. The authority of the umpire, then, is based on its claim to adjudicate disputes about what can be publicly justified. The umpire only is empowered to speak on these matters.

To some, this is disconcerting as it limits the scope of politics and the state. But if action in some area is subject to reasonable objection by some, by what right does the majority coerce the unwilling minority to follow their lead? As the deliberative democrats rightly emphasize, only laws that pass the test of public justification treat all citizens as free and equal (see section 5.2). If it is indeed the case that many current government policies cannot be publicly justified, then a radical reevaluation of the proper scope of politics is in order. It is not clear that we should take a conservative attitude by assuming that what we now do in the political sphere must be justified.

What does that mean for policy?

8.5 Adjudicative democracy: deliberative, procedural and weakly epistemic

The virtues of an umpire: competency and fairness

All this has been assuming that a certain umpire, or method of umpiring reasonable disagreements, could be conclusively justified among reasonable citizens who disagree about what laws and policies pass the test of liberal legitimacy. Citizens require an umpire: what is required to be an excellent umpire?

Umpires must be competent. They must be competent because they are seeking to give the best judgments they can on the merits of the dispute. Umpires in sports must know the rules, be able to observe the players, and so on. In politics, the umpire must be able to give judgments that track what is publicly justified. It is here that the arguments of the advocates of deliberative democracy (Chapter 5) and aggregative democracy (Chapter 6) can teach us much. If our aim is to arrive at laws that pass the test of public justification then deliberative democrats have provided a strong case that a good way to do this is to ensure widespread deliberation and discussion. In a public arena in which arguments are advanced and criticized the most unreasonable proposals are unlikely to find favor. This is not to say that we should expect anything remotely approaching actual political consensus (see section 5.3). Disagreement is not an accidental or a transitory characteristic of politics: it is the crux of politics under conditions of reasonable pluralism. Here the case for epistemic democracy comes into play (see sections 6.3 and 6.4). Having deliberated, and done our best to eliminate unreasonable proposals, we have some reason to think that voting may provide a competent way to aggregate individual judgments into a social decision.

It may be thought that this backtracks on my criticisms of both deliberative and epistemic democracy. With respect to deliberative democracy, I argued that elitist procedures – such as a supreme court – may do just as well as the actual deliberations of the citizenry at large in deciding what *would* be agreed to by reasonable citizens deliberating in good faith (see sections 4.5, 5.1 and 7.5). And I was critical of Estlund's epistemic defense of democracy – the claim that it tends to give the best results (section 6.4). Reasonable pluralism, I argued, also extends to disagreements about what is the best. However, all that the advocate of deliberative-political democracy requires is what I called Democracy's Minimal Epistemic Claim: no method for resolving moral disputes can be conclusively shown to be epistemically better than democracy (section 6.4). It cannot be shown that rule by experts, for example, is better at tracking public justification than is political democracy.

Democracy's Minimal Epistemic Claim is enough because democratic procedures have a decisive advantage over all the others that cannot be shown to be epistemically inferior to democracy: democracy is fair, insofar as it gives each person an equal say in the outcome. We want a competent umpire, because we want the umpire to give us the best answer. But because we know that the umpire will often side against us, and so we will have reasonable disagreements with the umpire, we need to ensure that the umpire is fair. It is one thing for the decision to go against you, quite another when it goes against you because the umpire is biased against you. One has reasonable objections to an umpire that is biased against you and your views. Thus even if political democracy cannot show that it is superior to Mill's plural voting scheme (see section 6.4), those who are given less votes in Mill's scheme have a reasonable objection: their reasonable views will be disadvantaged – not because of their content, but just because they are held by them rather than members of the 'epistocracy'.

One might query, however, whether Democracy's Minimal Epistemic Claim really is enough. If all procedures were terrible, then democracy may not be worse than any, but it would not be competent. If all the umpires are blind, we would still not wish to submit our disputes to the fair blind umpire. But reflecting on the general arguments in favor of deliberative and political democracy, we have strong reason to think that democracy is not a terrible way to decide disputes. It may be too strong to say that it is the best, but a procedure that depends on extensive discussion and consulting a wide number of people is, given everything we know, not a terrible way to protect liberal rights. As J.S. Mill emphasized, 'the rights and interests of every or any person are only secure from being disregarded, when the interested person is himself able, and habitually disposed, to stand up for them'. He went on to insist that '[H]uman beings are only secure from evil at the hands of others in proportion as they have the power of being, and are, self-*protecting*'.[51] Following Mill, modern democrats have insisted that the chief benefit of democratic government is that the rights of citizens are more likely to be protected against incursion by those holding power. Such responsive government, it is claimed, is more apt to avoid injustice than are those that vest political power in an 'enlightened few'.[52]

This case for democracy as widely responsive institutions is particularly strong insofar as it supposes that justice and interest typically coincide when one's basic rights are at stake. A government enacting legislation that attacks one's basic rights and civil interests does one an injustice. Consequently, even a citizenry without a strong commitment to upholding justified principles is apt to disagree with such policies. This familiar point is so important it has a strong claim to be deemed the first theorem of liberal democracy: *political procedures that are widely responsive to the judgments of the citizenry have been shown to be reliable protectors of basic individual rights.*

The case for political democracy as an umpiring mechanism would be inconclusive if, while political democracy was fair, some other umpiring procedure was more competent. For then the two virtues of an umpire would point to different procedures, and reasonable people may disagree about how to weigh them. Some may prefer a slightly biased but much more competent umpire to a fair but considerably less competent one. But given (1) Democracy's Minimal Epistemic Claim and (2) its manifest fairness, it is the uniquely best method for umpiring our political disputes.

Democracy, then, is a conclusively justified umpiring mechanism. In his or her deliberations each citizen presents what he or she believes is the best public justification; the voting mechanism constitutes a fair way to adjudicate our deep disagreements about what is publicly justified. It does not seek political consensus, but reasoned debate about what is best justified, and procedures that do a tolerable job in tracking justification. Adjudicative democracy recognizes that our commitment to sincere public justification is precisely what produces principled disagreement; *democracy is required just because even rough consensus is not a plausible political ideal.* Thus the everyday institutions of democratic rule such as voting are, on the adjudicative conception, the heart of democracy, for they define how the umpire operates.

ideal theory!

Three types of disagreements

In contrast to deliberative democracy, on the adjudicative conception actual consensus is not even a regulative ideal. The normal condition of politics is that we disagree. We need, though, to distinguish three types of political disagreement.

Reasonable disagreement about justified policies and laws The adjudicative theory of democracy focuses on reasonable disagreement, i.e., where Alf and Betty disagree about what principle or policy is publicly justified, but understand the position of the other as reasonable (though erroneous). The adjudicative conception supposes that most of the disagreements between most of the people most of the time are this sort: people have different political views, but do not dismiss the views of most other citizens as unreasonable. This, I have argued, is just the sort of case in which our commitment to public justification leads us to submit to the democratic umpire:[53] I believe my proposal is correct, but I also see your objection as reasonable. If we are to arrive at a common policy, we need some way to adjudicate our dispute.

Unreasonable disagreement The second sort of disagreement is more troubling: one party sees the competing position of the other as unreasonable. Suppose Alf believes that *P* is publicly justified, and is entirely convinced that Betty's support of *not-P* is unreasonable. It is hard to see why Alf should submit the disputes to an umpire. Why submit to arbitration when the other's position is, in your view, manifestly unreasonable? It may thus seem that the adjudicative view has the same fatal flaw as the deliberative conception and political liberalism: we do not have consensus on the reasonable. Two considerations, however, indicate that the adjudicative conception can admit this lack of consensus without undermining the justification of the democratic order.

First, in complex communities we do not have simply dyadic disagreements. Alf may believe Betty's opposition to *P* is unreasonable, but there is also Charlie's and Doris's objections to consider. If Alf believes that their objections to P are reasonable, then he will still have reason to submit the justifiability of P to the umpire.

Second, indeed, assuming Alf has faith in the reliability of the umpire, he may even agree, for purely pragmatic reasons, to adjudicate his dispute with Betty. To revert to the baseball example, suppose that Betty claims a right to a fourth strike. If we understand umpiring simply as a way to resolve reasonable disputes, Alf has no reason to submit the dispute to adjudication as it is manifest that she has no case, and it would be outrageous for the umpire to rule in her favor. It is not a question open to reasonable dispute. Nevertheless, Alf may indeed refer the claim to the umpire for purely pragmatic reasons. If Betty also has faith in the umpire, it will be a quick way to resolve the conflict and get on with the game. *If he has faith in the reasonability of the umpire*, then he has good reason to appeal to the umpire even in the face of what he sees as an unreasonable proposal. Now, interestingly, both parties may be in the same position. Alf may believe that Betty's position is unreasonable, while she may view his as beyond the bounds of plausibility, yet each may view the umpire as a reasonable way to decide their disputes. They may do so because they may believe it is impartial, and that it is generally reasonable. What is of interest here is that political life is possible even in the face of mutual conviction of the unreasonability of others if each party has grounds for accepting the reasonability of the umpiring mechanism.

replication problem ?

Disagreement about the justifiability of the umpire   It may seem that all this at least supposes a basic consensus on the justifiability of the umpire. What if citizens disagree about *that*? It is here that philosophical questions of justification must be distinguished from questions of efficacy. The justification of the umpire does not depend on widespread actual consensus on its justifiability. Perhaps a large group of anti-democratic citizens wish to overturn democracy. This certainly does not show that democracy is unjustified. If, given all his cognitive resources, Alf concludes that there are no reasonable objections to the democratic method of resolving disputes – reasonable given his own epistemic standards – then he will conclude that democracy is justified, even in the face of its rejection by many. However if, for whatever reasons, many citizens reject the democratic method, it will no longer serve its practical function of actually resolving disagreements. Alf may well conclude that, however justified the democratic state, his fellow citizens are so irrational or immoral that it cannot perform its task of actually resolving disputes, and so appeals to it are pragmatically pointless.

Of course if his fellow citizens are thoroughly irrational or immoral, Alf himself may reject democracy on deeper grounds: when placed in the hands of his fellow citizens it yields consistently unreasonable results. In this case the dark side of jury theorem – demonstrating the incredible incompetence of some majorities – would come into play (see section 6.3). As I argued in section 8.4, an umpire has an epistemological task at which it must be competent. One's commitment to the umpire is thus contingent on one's evaluation that it does a reasonable job tracking the merits of the disputes. If Alf concludes that the umpire is incompetent, he will not see it as furthering the Ideals of Reason and Public Justification, and so will conclude that it is not justified. If many believe this, democracy will, again, not be efficacious. But whether or not democracy is a justified way to adjudicate disputes does not depend on how many people think it is justified, but whether it does indeed conform to the Ideals of Reason and Public Justification (see section 5.3).

Conflicts of personal reasoning

In my examination of Hobbesian-inspired liberalism in Chapter 3, I made much of Hobbes's dilemma. He wished to free subjects from relying on their personal reasoning. To make out his case he showed that following the reasoning of the sovereign would benefit them; to show that, however, requires appealing to the subjects' personal reasoning about what benefits them. And, since the point of following the sovereign's reason is to attain benefits, one does not have reason to follow it when one no longer benefits. This, though, drives subjects to constantly employ their private reasoning to see if they should follow the public reasoning of the sovereign, just what Hobbesians wish to avoid. Doesn't the same problem plague the Lockean umpire?

I think not. If a citizen judges that the umpire is making calls contrary to victorious justifications, the citizen must conclude that the umpire is seeking to enforce an unreasonable view, and is acting outside the bounds of the rule of law. It is here that the Lockean and Hobbesian accounts of the umpire differ. Hobbes insists on the inappropriateness of citizens making obedience contingent on their judgment of the substantive merits of the decision. The Hobbesian case has a certain plausibility so long as we suppose that we submit to an umpire solely because of practical problems that result from brute disagreement; in that case, *any* disagreement may be thought to be a matter for adjudication, for then we would always prefer 'action in concert' to any way of going it alone. We have seen, though, that this is not an especially plausible view of politics (section 4.2). On the more Lockean account I have defended here, our commitment to adjudication follows from our fundamental commitment to public justification. It is when Alf is unable to victoriously publicly justify his reasonable views about justice that he is led to arbitration; but he has no moral reason to submit his publicly justified principles to the umpire. He has (he believes) publicly justified them, so he cannot see how *his commitment to public justification* could give him a reason to submit them to an umpire; he has no conceptual resources that could allow him to recognize such a reason (though, as I have pointed out, he still may have pragmatic reasons for referring the dispute to the umpire). Certainly the mere fact that others disagree cannot show that he has failed to justify his claims, any more than the dissents of creationists show that evolutionary biologists have failed to justify their views. Citizens must, then, constantly employ their personal reasoning to ensure that the umpire only adjudicates within the bounds of reasonable disagreement.

Although it leads to a much messier account, Locke, not Hobbes, is right: whether we have reason to obey the law depends on its substantive merits. A citizen has no obligation to obey a law if the umpire is enacting defeated proposals. Now no doubt many readers, whose patience have been taxed for a number of pages, will wish to insist that this overlooks Hobbes's fundamental insight: a citizen at best *thinks* that a principle has been victoriously justified, while the umpire and other citizens obviously *think differently*. If Alf has judged that P has been victoriously justified while Betty thinks that it is within the bounds of reasonable disagreement, doesn't this dispute need adjudication too? Aren't we back where we began? Not from Alf's perspective, or from the perspective of any other liberal citizen. From any particular perspective, a citizen's commitment to public justification can lead him to submit to an umpire, but this very same reason will lead him to resist an umpire who, in his judgment, is seeking to impose defeated – publicly *un*justified – proposals on him. Any citizen can and will distinguish what is fundamental and justified from what is reasonably disputed; that he will submit the latter question to arbitration will not lead him also to submit the former issue to the umpire. Indeed, for liberals to submit all moral disputes to the umpire is to allow that, if challenged by an illiberal citizen such as Carl Schmitt (see section 1.3), fundamental liberal principles themselves might legitimately be overturned by the umpire.

The problem arises when Alf's judgments about what has been victoriously justified differs from Betty's. When that happens Alf and Betty disagree not simply on what is the correct outcome of political dispute, they disagree on what should be on the political agenda. The domain of the political, we have seen, can be contentious. Liberal politics will be, at best, imperfect in a community so divided, for one or the other section will refuse to admit that a political resolution of some issue is morally legitimate. If the division is restricted to a small number of issues, perhaps devices such as gag rules will allow liberal politics to function by insulating it from those conflicts that cannot, from a practical point of view, be successfully adjudicated.[54] However, if the community is deeply divided in this way on a wide range of issues, the practical resolution of moral disputes by the umpire will be precarious, for whatever the umpire decrees, some will declare that it is a violation of a conclusively justified rule or principle. In such a society the umpire might still typically be obeyed for pragmatic, Hobbesian reasons, but a gnawing cynicism seems inevitable.

It would be happy indeed if we had access to a God's-eye perspective, which would once and for all tell us what is really and truly verified by public reason and what we merely think is so verified. But no such perspective is to be had; each can only employ his own moral and cognitive resources to arrive at his own best judgments. We can, though, avoid the Scyllia of supposing that it is moral to impose any reasonable conviction on others and the Charybdis of fleeing from ever standing up for our fundamental principles, compromising on every issue or adjudicating every disagreement.

8.6 Summary and conclusion

Summary

In this chapter I have sketched a justificatory theory of liberalism, and have compared it to our other theories of liberal public reason. Section 8.1 began with a comparison of different post-Enlightenment liberalisms' answers to perhaps their most basic question: why engage in public reason? Hobbes's followers stress the need to abandon private judgment to attain peace and order; advocates of collective reason also stress the need for a public reason to guide us towards cooperation. Deliberative democrats maintain that the pursuit of validity requires actual public reasoning and, apparently, actual consensus. Rawlsian-inspired liberalism stresses that only public reasoning that accords with the principle of Liberal Legitimacy respects each as free and equal, and Habermas suggests that our reflective understanding of our norms presupposes that they are validated by public reasoning. All these are insights; justificatory liberalism – which draws on them all – adds that public reasoning is required given the basic liberal principle of not interfering with people unless good reasons can be provided *to them* for the interference.

Section 8.2 presented an analysis of public justification that stressed how difficult it is to meet a version of Public Justification as Agreement in Reasonable Belief (see section 5.3). Although there are undoubtedly some general moral principles, pointing to basic rights, to which there is no reasonable objection, most principles and interpretations of general principles are open to reasonable dispute. Section 8.3 then considered what reasonable moral persons would do in the face of our typically inconclusive public justifications. The option of waiting for a conclusive public justification seems inappropriate when our disagreements are about the best interpretations of conclusively justified principles: if we always wait and see on what interpretation to employ, we will never employ our justified moral and political principles. Even deliberative democrats admit that the requirements of practical life require that the discourse be cut off and a vote be taken. But simply imposing one's own reasonable, but also reasonably rejected, judgment fails to treat others with respect, and violates the Individualized Principle of Liberal Legitimacy. Unlike Rawls, I have resisted weakening the principle of

Liberal Legitimacy to allow merely reasonable policies to be imposed on those who reject them (see section 7.4).

Section 8.4 explored a way out of this dilemma: submit to an umpire. I argued that the liberal state can be understood as a way to umpire our disputes about the application of basic moral principles. I also explored whether this leads to a radical reconceptualizing of the scope of state activities. Lastly, section 8.5 argued that political democracy is the conclusively justified umpiring procedure. Although I rejected the more extreme claims of deliberative and political democracy, it does seem that they establish that democratic procedures are a reasonably reliable way to adjudicate our disputes, and they have the decisive virtue of being fair to everyone.

Conclusion: post-Enlightenment liberalisms

This brings to a close our examination of post-Enlightenment liberalism's quest for public reason. Although I believe that justificatory liberalism has decisive advantages over its competitors, drawing on many of their strengths while avoiding their weaknesses, we can see that most of the theories examined here share a common conviction: reasoning together about justice and the common good is not precluded by deep disagreements that characterize our societies. This is especially so with deliberative democracy, which is based on a conviction that reasonable pluralism does not lead us to a society ordered on a mere *modus vivendi* or the will of the sovereign. The pursuit of truth, justice and mutual respect can still structure such societies. Deliberative democrats, perhaps, do not sufficiently appreciate how intractable are our differences: Berlin, Gray, Hobbes, and the political democrats are more alive to these differences, though they tend to inadequately articulate just what public reasoning really is. The trick for post-Enlightenment liberals is to explicate a robust conception of public reasoning – citizens reasoning together – while avoiding making too much a matter of consensus, or looking for agreement where none is to be found. Rawls's political liberalism is so attractive because it recognizes both plurality while endeavoring to develop substantive theory of public reason. I have been critical of his proposal – I believe it cannot adequately distinguish, much less isolate, the political from our reasonable disputes about non-political values. And even if it could, its identification of the political with the realm of reasonable agreement leads it to abandon too much of normal politics to a contest between comprehensive conceptions. It is, though, a powerful conception of post-Enlightenment liberalism.

Our concerns in this book have been theoretical, and my approach philosophical. Political philosophy, however, is a rigorous and careful treatment of actual political problems. *Is an ordered politics based on mutual respect, and aiming at justice, still possible in the modern world of deep reasonable disagreement about values and the ends of life?* To post-Enlightenment liberals, this is *the* political problem of the modern era. Hopefully, my analysis has given the reader an appreciation of its importance, complexity, and the great sophistication with which post-Enlightenment liberals have approached the question. And, perhaps most importantly, I hope I have encouraged the reader to publicly reason about it, as I have tried to do in this book.

Notes

1   John Rawls, *Political Liberalism*, paperback edn (New York: Columbia University Press, 1996), p. 137.
2   S.I. Benn, *A Theory of Freedom* (Cambridge: Cambridge University Press, 1988), p. 87.
3   John Stuart Mill, *On Liberty*, in John Gray, ed., *'On Liberty' and Other Essays* (New York: Oxford University Press, 1991), p. 14 (Ch. I, para. 9).
4   John Locke, *Second Treatise of Government*, in Peter Laslett, ed., *Two Treatises of Government* (Cambridge: Cambridge University Press, 1960), p. 287 (section 4).
5   Thomas Hobbes, *Leviathan*, Michael Oakeshott, ed. (Oxford: Basil Blackwell, 1946), p. 85 (Ch. 14).
6   Rawls, *Political Liberalism*, p. 253.
7   Kent Greenawalt, *Religious Convictions and Political Choice* (New York: Oxford University Press, 1988), p. 155.
8   Ibid., p. 176.
9   For a survey, see Lawrence A. Kurdek, 'Perspective Taking as the Cognitive Basis of Children's Moral Development: A Review of the Literature', *Merrill-Palmer Quarterly*, vol. 24 (January 1978): 3–28. See also Dennis Krebs and Janet Gillmore, 'The Relationship among the First Stages of Cognitive Development, Role Taking Abilities, and Moral Development', *Child Development*, vol. 53 (1982): 877–886; Lawrence Kohlberg argues that only those at the highest stage of moral development fully assume the viewpoint of others. See his 'Justice as Reversibility: the Claim to Moral Adequacy of a Highest Stage of Moral Judgment', in his edited collection, *Essays on Moral Development*, vol. 1: *The Philosophy of Moral Development* (New York: Harper & Row, 1981), Ch. 5.
10   Bärbel Inhelder and Jean Piaget, 'The Growth of Logical Thinking from Childhood to Adolescence', in Howard E. Gruber and J. Jacques Vonéche, eds, *The Essential Piaget* (London: Routledge & Kegan Paul, 1977), pp. 403–444, at 440–441.
11   See Eric Mack, 'Liberalism, Neutralism and Rights', in J. Roland Pennock and John W. Chapman, eds, *NOMOS XXX: Religion, Morality and the Law* (New York: New York University Press, 1988), pp. 46–70, at 55–56. See also

Marilyn Friedman, 'The Impracticality of Impartiality', *Journal of Philosophy*, vol. 86 (1989): 645–656.

12 See Carl Wellman, *Challenge and Response: Justification in Ethics* (Carbondale and Edwardsville: Southern Illinois University Press, 1971), Ch. 3.

13 On the idea of defeat see John L. Pollock, *Contemporary Theories of Knowledge* (Totowa, NJ: Rowman & Littlefield, 1986), p. 38.

14 That R_B is correct is neither necessary nor sufficient for it to be justified. See George S. Pappas and Marshall Swain, 'Introduction' to their edited collection, *Essays on Knowledge and Justification* (Ithaca, NY: Cornell University Press, 1978), pp. 11–40, at 13ff.

15 See here Keith Lehrer, *Theory of Knowledge* (Boulder, CO: Westview, 1990), pp. 162ff.

16 See David O. Brink, *Moral Realism and the Foundations of Ethics* (Cambridge: Cambridge University Press, 1989), pp. 94–95. See also Douglas Odegard, 'Can Justified Belief Be False?', *Canadian Journal of Philosophy*, vol. 6 (1976): 561–568.

17 See Lehrer, *Theory of Knowledge*, pp. 127ff.

18 Jeffrey Reiman, *Justice and Modern Moral Philosophy* (New Haven, CT: Yale University Press, 1990), p. 1. Emphasis added.

19 I shall not seek to expand on this condition here. The intuitive idea is that claims become increasingly justified as they turn back actual challenges; consequently, only claims that have been open to challenges (i.e. publicly formulated) can achieve a high level of justification. Cf. here Mill's comments on justified action in *On Liberty*, pp. 24–26 (Ch. II).

20 Wellman, *Challenge and Response*, p. 98.

21 Ibid., 130–131. For rather different reasons, Lehrer also indicates that there are but two possibilities. *Theory of Knowledge*, pp. 151ff.

22 See Bernard Williams, *Ethics and the Limits of Philosophy* (London: Fontana Press/Collins, 1985), p. 85.

23 See here Kurt Baier, 'Rationality, Reason and the Good', in David Copp and David Zimmerman, eds, *Morality, Reason and Truth: New Essays on the Foundations of Ethics* (Totowa, NJ: Rowman & Allenheld, 1984), pp. 193–211.

24 Christopher Cherniak, *Minimal Rationality* (Cambridge, MA: MIT Press, 1986), Ch. 5. See also Stephen Stich's *The Fragmentation of Reason* (Cambridge, MA: MIT Press, 1990). My view, however, departs from Stich's; in the end, I am, alas, an 'epistemological chauvinist'.

25 This is a simplification.

26 See Cherniak, *Minimal Rationality*, Chs 3, 5.

27 See my *Social Philosophy* (Armonk, NY: M.E. Sharpe, 1999), Chs 7–11 for a sketch of the justified elements of a public morality.

28 John Gray, 'Contractarian Method, Private Property and the Market Economy' in his *Liberalisms* (London: Routledge, 1989), pp. 161–198, at 169ff, 186ff.

29 Greenawalt, *Religious Convictions and Political Choice*, pp. 39ff, Chs 6–8.

30 Ibid., Ch. 6.

31 Cf. Jeffrey Reiman's argument that substantive and determinate principles can be justified beyond a reasonable doubt. *Justice and Modern Moral Philosophy*. My argument supposes that Reiman's project fails, though obviously I cannot *show* that here.

32 Jeremy Shearmur, 'Epistemological Limits of the State: Reflections on Popper's *Open Society*', *Political Studies*, vol. 38 (1990): 116–125, at 124.

33 Alexander Bickel, *The Least Dangerous Branch: the Supreme Court at the Bar of Politics*, 2nd edn (New Haven, CT: Yale University Press, 1986), pp. 36–37. As Stephen Macedo observes, 'The contours of every one of our most basic liberties remains a matter of lively disagreement'. *Liberal Virtues: Citizenship, Virtue and Community in Liberal Constitutionalism* (Oxford: Oxford University Press, 1991), p. 57.

34 Rawls, *Political Liberalism*, p. 137. Emphasis added.

35 Rawls sometimes seems willing to insist on this. See ibid., p. 215.

36 Immanuel Kant, *Metaphysical Elements of Justice*, John Ladd (trans.) (Indianapolis: Bobbs-Merrill, 1965), section 44 (p. 76). Emphasis in original.

37 Ibid.

38 Macedo, *Liberal Virtues: Citizenship, Virtue and Community in Liberal Constitutionalism*, p. 78.

39 Reiman, *Justice and Modern Moral Philosophy*, Ch. 1. '[S]ubjection is a general evil against which everyone is to be protected'. Ibid., p. 71. Cf. R.E. Ewin, *Liberty, Community and Justice* (Totowa, NJ: Rowman & Littlefield, 1987), pp. 39, 108.

40 Ewin, *Virtues and Rights*, p. 32. The main theme of Ewin's work is the necessity of abandoning reliance on 'private' judgment to achieve cooperation. See also his *Liberty, Community and Justice*. See note 33, Ch. 3.

41 Thomas Hobbes, *Leviathan*, Michael Oakeshott, ed. (Oxford: Basil Blackwell, 1946), p. 102 (Ch. 15). Emphasis in original. See Ewin, *Virtues and Rights*, p. 34.

42 John Locke, *Second Treatise of Government*, section 7. See my *Justificatory Liberalism: An Essay on Epistemology and Political Theory* (New York: Oxford University Press, 1996), pp. 184ff.

43 It is worth pointing out that an umpire in baseball does not merely apply clear rules or make judgments of fact; the calling of balls and strikes is an exercise in the application of an abstract concept – the strike zone.

44 Rawls, *Political Liberalism*, p. 246.

45 See Christopher Bertram, 'Public Reason', *Imprints: A Journal of Analytical Socialism*, vol. 2 (June 1997): 72–85, at 83–84.

46 Ibid.

47 This distinction is recognized by Randall G. Holcombe, 'Constitutions as Constraints', *Constitutional Political Economy*, vol. 2 (Fall 1991): 303–328, at 303.

48 Robert H. Bork, *The Tempting of America* (New York: Simon and Shuster, 1990), p. 139. Compare Justice Holmes's assertion of 'the right of the majority to embody their opinions in law'. *Lochner v. New York*, 189 US 45 (1905).

49 'Conservative strict constructionists, like Bork, argue in effect that judges should enforce only explicit rights, rights plainly stated in the Constitution's text or very clearly implied in it. Legislators on the other hand, may do anything that is not plainly forbidden by the Constitution's text and its clear implications'. Stephen Macedo, *The New Right v. The Constitution* (Washington, DC: The Cato Institute, 1987), p. 27.

50 James Madison, Alexander Hamilton and John Jay, *The Federalist Papers*, Clinton Rossiter, ed. (New York: New American Library, 1961), *Federalist 51*, p. 324.

51 J.S. Mill, *Considerations on Representative Government*, in John Gray, ed., *'On Liberty' and Other Essays*, p. 245 (Ch. III).

52 On responsiveness, see J. Roland Pennock, *Democratic Political Theory* (Princeton: Princeton University Press, 1979), Ch. VII.

53 See ibid.

54 For a fascinating analysis of gag rules, see Stephen Holmes, 'Gag Rules or the Politics of Omission' in Jon Elster and Rune Slagstad, eds, *Constitutionalism and Democracy* (Cambridge: Cambridge University Press, 1988), pp. 19–58.

Index

Gray, John, *cont.*
  modus vivendi, 20, 57, 60–1, 62–3,
    64, 65–7, 79
Greenawalt, Kent, 209, 215
Grofman, Bernard, 158
group membership, 102, 104

Habermas, Jürgen, 20, 128, 143,
    186, 187, 206
  consensus, 123, 132
  discourse and democracy, 119–26
  validity, 121–3, 126, 132, 143
Hobbes, Thomas, 20, 92–3
  modus vivendi, 57, 59–65
  private reason, 63–5, 68, 69–70,
    71–4, 84, 219, 227
  public reason, 67–74, 79–80
homosexuality, 188
human rights, 65–6, 67, 122–3
Hume, David, 88, 161
Hurley, Susan, 104, 105, 107

Ideal of Public Justification, 131,
    134, 140
Ideal of Real Political Consensus,
    131–2, 134–5, 136–7
Ideal of Reason, 131, 133–4, 140
impartiality, 209–10
impure coordination games, 91–2
incommensurability of values, 31–42,
    50–1, 66, 79
  and diversity, 48
  epistemic, 171
incompleteness, 32, 33–7
inconclusiveness, 214–18
indeterminacy, 107–8, 214–15
indignation, 120–1, 207
individual judgments, 16, 217, 218, 219
individual maximization, 87–8, 114
individualism, 110, 111, 208
interference, *see* non-interference
interpretations, 74–7, 106–8
intersubjective agreement, 106,
    108, 119–20, 121

Jefferson, Thomas, 149
jury theorem, 159–64, 165, 167,
    170, 173
justice, universal, 122, 125
justice as fairness, 177–80, 191–4

justification, 17, 21, 67, 121–2, 128,
    129, 134
  see also public justification
justificatory liberalism, 205–22

Kahneman, Daniel, 135
Kant, Immanuel, 4–5, 16, 17, 163,
    217–18
Kuhn, Thomas, 11–12

law, 77, 78
  and cooperation games, 89–90, 94–9
  morality and, 125–6
law of the excluded middle, 9
laws of logic, 9
laws of nature, *see* natural law
legal positivism, 125
legitimacy, 66, 67, 79
  see also political legitimacy;
    principle of liberal legitimacy
Lewis, David, 91
liberal imperialism, 6
liberal politics, 228–9
liberal principle, 207–8, 216, 221
  see also principle of liberal
    legitimacy
liberal rationalism, 50
liberal state, 60–1, 221–2
liberal toleration, 56–7
liberalism, 15–16
  challenges to, 16–19
  pluralism and, 42–50, 56–7, 83,
    197–200, 202
  post-Enlightenment, 19–21
  see also political liberalism,
    justificatory liberalism
liberty, *see* freedom
Locke, John, 15, 93, 219, 227, 228
  liberal principle, 207, 208
Lucas, J.R., 120

Machiavelli, Niccolo, 42, 46
MacIntyre, Alasdair, 8–9
McMahon, Christopher, 86–7, 88–9,
    109, 113
Madison, James, 161–2, 222
majority, 123, 149, 159–60, 162, 163,
    165, 167–8, 169
Martin, Rex, 159, 161
Median with a Vengeance, 168–9